POLITICS OF DECOLONIZATION

AFRICAN STUDIES SERIES

The African Studies Series is a collection of monographs and
general studies which reflect the interdisciplinary interests of
the African Studies Centre at Cambridge. Volumes to date have
combined historical, anthropological, economic, political and
other perspectives. Each contribution has assumed that such broad
approaches can contribute much to our understanding of Africa,
and that this may in turn be of advantage to specific disciplines.

BOOKS IN THIS SERIES

1 *City Politics: A Study of Léopoldville, 1962–63*
   J. S. La Fontaine

2 *Studies in Rural Capitalism in West Africa*
   Polly Hill

3 *Land Policy in Buganda*
   Henry W. West

4 *The Nigerian Military: A Sociological Analysis of Authority
   and Revolt, 1960–67*
   Robin Luckham

5 *The Ghanaian Factory Worker: Industrial Man in Africa*
   Margaret Peil

6 *Labour in the South African Gold Mines, 1911–1969*
   Francis Wilson

7 *The Price of Liberty: Personality and Politics in Colonial
   Nigeria*
   Kenneth W. J. Post and George D. Jenkins

8 *Subsistence to Commercial Farming in Present Day Buganda: An
   Economic and Anthropological Survey*
   Audrey I. Richards, Ford Sturrock and Jean M. Fortt (eds.)

9 *Dependence and Opportunity: Political Chance in Ahafo*
   John Dunn and A. F. Robertson

10 *African Railwaymen: Solidarity and Opposition in an East
   African Labour Force*
   R. D. Ghillo

11 *Islam and Tribal Art in West Africa*
   Rene A. Bravmann

12 *Modern and Traditional Elites in the Politics of Lagos*
   P. D. Cole

13 *Asante in the Nineteenth Century: The Structure and Evolution
   of a Political Order*
   Ivor Wilks

14 *Culture: Tradition and Society in the West African Novel*
   Emmanuel Obiechina

15 *Saints and Politicians: Essays in the Organisation of a Senegalese
   Peasant Society*
   Donal B. Cruise O'Brien

16 *The Lions of Dagbon: Political Change in Northern Ghana*
   Martin Staniland

POLITICS OF DECOLONIZATION

KENYA EUROPEANS AND THE LAND ISSUE 1960–1965

GARY WASSERMAN

Medgar Evers College, City University of New York

CAMBRIDGE UNIVERSITY PRESS

CAMBRIDGE

LONDON · NEW YORK · MELBOURNE

Published by the Syndics of the Cambridge University Press
The Pitt Building, Trumpington Street, Cambridge CB2 1RP
Bentley House, 200 Euston Road, London NW1 2DB
32 East 57th Street, New York, NY 10022, USA
296 Beaconsfield Parade, Middle Park, Melbourne 3206, Australia

First published 1976

Printed in the United States of America
Typeset by Fuller Organization, Philadelphia,
Pennsylvania. Printed and bound by
Halliday Lithograph Corporation, West
Hanover, Massachusetts

Library of Congress Cataloguing in Publication Data
Wasserman, Gary, 1944–
Politics of decolonization.

(African studies series; 17)
Bibliography: p.
Includes index.
1. Land tenure–Kenya. 2. Kenya–Politics and
government. I. Title. II. Series.
HD990.K42W37   333.1'09676'2   75–2735
ISBN 0 521 20838 6

Burg.
HD
990
.K42
W37

CONTENTS

Acknowledgments viii

Introduction: Kenya as a case study 1

1 Consensual decolonization: conditions, process, and the salient aspects of the Kenyan case 4

2 Background to decolonization: trends and groups in the European community 19

3 1960, initiating the bargain: the lobbying on the land issue and the dividing of the European community 46

4 1961, negotiating the bargain: accelerating the bargaining, deepening the divisions 75

5 1962, making the bargain: the resolution of the land issue and the dissolution of the European groups 105

6 1960–1970, sealing the bargain: the implementation of the Kenya land transfer schemes 135

7 Conclusion: Europeans, land and decolonization 164

Notes 176

Selected bibliography 209

Index 219

To my parents

ACKNOWLEDGMENTS

This is a rather old-fashioned study. It represents a blend of historical narrative and political intuition researched and written by the author. But this book does not represent merely the efforts of one person. It owes a debt to a number of individuals and institutions.

The late Professor Wayne Wilcox guided me through the shoals of graduate school at Columbia and lent me support in this research. Professor Colin Leys of Sheffield University was my advisor in Kenya, and his own writings stand as a model to which the author's work would do well to aspire. I am grateful to both of them.

Three universities on three continents provided sanctuary for the author during the months of writing. The Government Department of the University of Nairobi, St Antony's College, Oxford University, and the Political Science Department and the African Institute at Columbia University provided people who were most kind and helpful. The funding for the first year of this study was provided by a Fulbright–Hays Fellowship. After turning down my initial project (on transnational politics between Britain and Kenya) as too politically sensitive, the Fulbright people respected the academic integrity of the research, and let the author get on with the work unhindered.

No research work can be better than the material on which it is based. The author was extremely fortunate in the cooperation shown him by the European community in Kenya. Invariably the Kenya Europeans were found to be interested in the research and hospitable to the researcher. Special thanks are due Sir Michael Blundell, N. S. Carey Jones, Peter Marrian, C. O. Oates, Jo Feingold, Sir Wilfred Havelock and Mrs Dorothy Hughes for the use of their papers and, in the first four instances, for their reading of early drafts and for the corrections they offered for the author's misperceptions.

Among the scholars who generously contributed their time to read this manuscript and to provide valuable insights are Gordon Adams, Henry Bienen, L. Gray Gowan, Graham Irwin, John Lonsdale, Jim Mittelman and Howard Wriggins.

Though this study was funded for one year it required almost three for completion. During the rather lean months of writing the author was supported by a number of friends and colleagues (the terms happily not mutually exclusive) with warmth and hospitality. The author especially wishes to thank Carohn Cornell, Rich and Marsha Hiller, John and Pat Rea, Joan Stephenson, Stan and Bea Trapido, and Rob and Kathy Whittier for their kindness. Mary Heston helped turn illegible drafts into a finished product, quickly and expertly. To his parents for their non-rational confidence in their son, and to his brother Ed, for his perceptive comments and help, a debt of gratitude is owed.

In spite of this assistance, errors undoubtedly remain. They are unintentional, and solely the responsibility of the author.

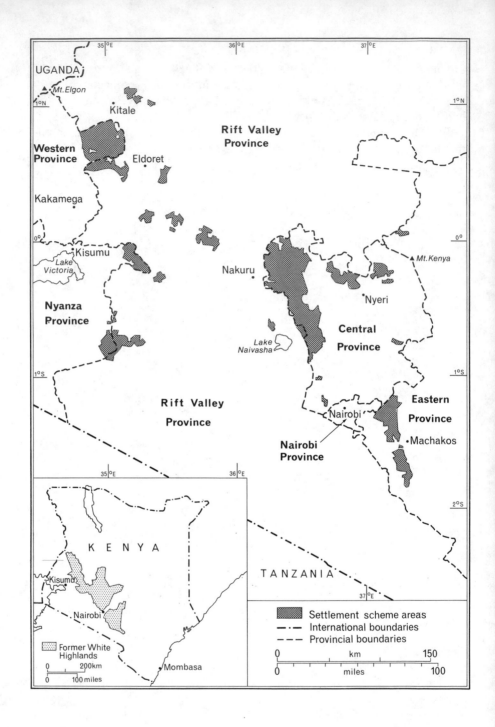

UGANDA

▲ Mt.Elgon

1°N

Kitale

Western Province

Eldoret

Rift Valley Province

1°N

Kakamega

0°

Kisumu

Lake Victoria

Nakuru

Mt.Kenya ▲

0°

Nyanza Province

Nyeri

Central Province

Lake Naivasha

1°S

1°S

Rift Valley Province

Nairobi

Eastern Province

Machakos

Nairobi Province

2°S

35°E

36°E

K E N Y A

Kisumu

Nairobi

Former White Highlands

0   200km

0   100 miles

Mombasa

T A N Z A N I A

37°E

Settlement scheme areas
·–·–· International boundaries
– – – Provincial boundaries

0   km   150

0   miles   100

Kenya: Settlement schemes, 1965.

INTRODUCTION: KENYA
AS A CASE STUDY

Although the rise of nationalist movements in Africa was certainly a contributing factor in the dismantling of the colonial empires, one cannot
wholly attribute the 'demise of colonialism' to the rise of nationalism. Decolonization occurred rapidly and along similar lines in territories where
nationalist movements were in very different stages of development. In the
Ivory Coast, for example, nationalist leaders were reluctant and tardy advocates of independence; in Kenya, the nationalist movement was not yet well
organized. This strongly suggests that an understanding of decolonization
requires special attention to the 'other side': the colonial interests involved.

This, then, is a study of the 'other side.' Central to the study is the idea
that the decolonization process was shaped by an adaptive reaction of colonial political and economic interests to the political ascendency of a nationalist elite and to the threat of disruption by the masses. An analysis of the
colonial elite's composition, alignments and bargaining activities is essential
to an understanding of the terms of the bargain called independence. In the
Kenyan case, the fate of the 'White Highlands' was the critical issue for the
European farming community, and was of major importance to the other
expatriate interests dominating the colonial political economy. The resolution of the land issue marked a decisive stage in the pre-emption of mass
unrest and the cooptation of the nationalist elite into their role as guardians
of this political economy.

The study focuses on three aspects of decolonization in Kenya. The first,
the actual process of moving from colony to independent state, delimits the
political arena. The second is European adaptation to this decolonization
process. The third is the bargaining over the land issue: the central conflict.
Decolonization, then, is the major process of which European adaptation is
a key feature and the land question the critical issue.

For a number of reasons Kenya provides a focal point for analyzing
decolonization and elite adaptation in Africa. In the first place, the period
of colonial transition was condensed and clearly demarcated.[1] The First
Lancaster House Conference, in January 1960, established African majority rule and reversed the expectations of African and European leaders that
Kenya Colony was set for a European-dominated multi-racial government.
Not only did the Conference surprise both sides, it also initiated the period
of colonial transition in which Kenya was headed for independence under
an African government. What this change would mean for the economy, the
expatriate communities and the political structure was subject to intense

1

debate. December 12, 1963, Independence Day, marked the end of colonial transition, although bargaining continued beyond that date.

Not only did the period of colonial transition have discrete boundaries but the issues and participants were also clear. Kenya's history as an 'abortive' colony had resulted in the polarization of the country both politically and economically. On one side was the European farming community, perched at the top of the political-economic hierarchy they had largely established. Though less than one per cent of the population, they owned twenty per cent of the arable land, produced eighty-five per cent of the agricultural exports and generated most of the taxable income in the colony. Politically, a Royal Commission in 1955 described them as still largely holding the reins of power in their hands. As a wealthy, expatriate, white landowning elite they were a conspicuously dominating presence over the African societies among whom they dwelled.

As such, they may be said to have spawned their antithesis: the conscious rural African masses aware of their disadvantaged position in the society. The direct nature of the colonial domination of Kenya, visible through the large European presence, created conditions of conflict which in other colonies, such as those under indirect administration, could have been more easily obscured. The need for cheap labor on European farms, the discouragement until late in the colonial period of African cash cropping, and the obtrusive racial discrimination in all areas of Kenyan life were daily reminders to Africans of their subservience. The widespread organized uprising in the early 1950s among Kikuyu peasants (the tribe perhaps most affected by the European presence) can be interpreted as a reaction to the blatancy of Kenyan colonial rule and the failure of the settled elite to fully consolidate its dominance.[2]

The conflict between the masses and the landowners brought to the forefront the central economic issue between them: the alienation and appropriation of 7.5 million acres of the Kenya Highlands for exclusively European use. The 'land issue' centered on the traditional claims to the land by sundry African groups opposing the essentially economic-functional arguments of the colonialists. The fate of the 'White Highlands,' was the linchpin determining the future of the European farming community and the colonial political economy. The European farmer holding non-liquid assets in a threatening environment had to adapt in some way to his surroundings – if only by leaving. With the general recognition of impending African political authority, the search for new political supports for their assets, economy and life style received the focus of European attention.

This, however, is not to make a case for the uniqueness of Kenya in colonial Africa. Certainly every colony had its own special features. However, one could argue that on a spectrum of imperial involvement in Africa Kenya falls close to the center. On one end of this series would be a Uganda with a pattern of peasant agriculture operating through a small colonial administration utilizing indirect rule. On the other is a Rhodesia where domination was direct and where the white expatriate community was able to squeeze out both African and metropolitan political influence. In Kenya both the colonial-settler and indigenous-peasant structures paralleled and intermeshed with each other. The nature of the joining of the conflict between these two forces in Kenya hopefully will highlight processes present in other decolonizations.

A final, if rather mundane, justification for the study of Kenyan decolonization lies in the availability of information. Perhaps because of their fetish for the written word, Europeans are eternally condemned to reappear in their own histories. Kenya Europeans are no exception. They took notes, kept records, and by making their papers available allow a history of the period earlier than if official documents alone were depended upon. Beside this secretarial function, the presence of a settled expatriate community, possessing considerable influence in the metropole, forced the decolonizing power to publicly assuage them as well as allow them access to at least parts of the 'official mind.'

The events that follow, then, are viewed through a European looking glass. While no apologies need to be made, the reader should be consistently conscious of the subjectivity involved. The numerous and economically important Asians of Kenya appear to play almost no role as a community in decolonization. Individual Asians were financial supporters of a number of groups, mainly the European liberals and moderate nationalists, and exerted influence through their standing in the commercial sector. African leaders and groups may often appear as ill-formed figures, from the European perspective. The nationalists were frequently objects of manipulation, divided and uncertain of the direction their rule would take. But centering on the months prior to independence should not cause us to neglect the years of struggle, imprisonment and violence which the nationalists endured in order to enter the political arena where they confronted their opponents in the colonial twilight.

CHAPTER 1

CONSENSUAL DECOLONIZATION: CONDITIONS, PROCESS, AND THE SALIENT ASPECTS OF THE KENYAN CASE

Their purpose is to capture the vanguard, to turn the movement of liberation towards the right and to disarm the people: quick, quick, let's decolonize. Decolonize the Congo, before it turns into another Algeria. Vote the constitutional framework for all Africa, create the *Communaute*, renovate that same *Communaute*, but for God's sake let's decolonize quick.'

Frantz Fanon, *The Wretched of the Earth*

Decolonization was 'the logical result indeed the triumph' of Imperial policies and tradition.

Harold Macmillan

This initial chapter will set the stage. By making explicit the conditions and process of consensual decolonization it will establish a context, within which the study will focus on two aspects of Kenya decolonization. While the study will not 'prove' this prefiguration of a decolonization model, these initial generalizations will aid in establishing the importance and relevance of the processes of adaptation and bargaining to be studied. Toward this objective, the chapter will define the relevant terms, discuss the conditions and process of consensual decolonization, and introduce the salient feature and issue of the Kenyan case – elite adaptation, and the bargaining and resolution of the land question.

SOME DEFINITIONS

Decolonization, as generally understood, means the transfer of political authority from a colonial state to indigenous leaders within the framework of state sovereignty. This definition deals only with the formal transfer of 'authority,' referring to the capacity to legitimate political decisions, and not with political 'power,' which may be taken to mean the ability to influence those decisions. Certainly the characteristics of authority and power overlap. Those with authority may be expected to have some power; those without authority may or may not be politically powerful. At one pole a state possessing authority without power is a 'satellite' to some other country; a state with relatively autonomous power is 'independent.' Decolonization or the 'attainment of independence' as such do not necessarily say anything about what is an empirical question of influence. Similarly, no inference can be drawn from the use of the phrase 'indigenous leaders' that decolonization necessarily implies the evolution toward a people's full social control over the instruments of government. Whether decolonization does in fact lead to greater popular participation and control remains a seldom debated issue.[3]

Within this context, the focus will be upon consensual decolonization – the process of transferring colonial political authority in which there is a large measure of agreement among the participants that the outcome of the process is to be independence. Although 'consensual decolonization' is often used synonymously with 'decolonization' in this study, cases where decolonization directly resulted from military conflicts (Algeria), or from sudden uncontrolled shifts of nationalist strength (Guinea) are excluded. In both Algeria and Guinea, there was a sufficient measure of opposition (from colonial interests) to exclude these from our definition. At the same time similarities of process can be expected in all types of decolonization.

But consensual decolonization is not merely the transfer of formal political authority to indigenous rulers. It is also a bargaining process surrounding this transfer, oriented to integrating a potentially disruptive nationalist movement into the structures and requisites of the colonial political-economic system.[4] 'Process' as used here is simply the actions and inter-relationships of groups of people as they struggle for, and use, power to achieve their purposes.[5] Hence, process is *not* a plan. In this analysis the decolonization process is an accumulation of, and abstraction from a series of policies, which may appear quite disjunctive to the participants. In that the metropole state is the initiator, authority, and participant with the greatest political resources in the decolonization process, it may be expected to have the greatest influence over that process.

Bargaining is a process of combining divergent interests and viewpoints to produce a common agreement. Implied in this definition is a situation '. . . in which the ability of one participant to gain his ends is dependent to an important degree on the choices or decisions that the other participant will make.'[6] Given this interdependency, there is likely a thrust toward consensus among all the participants in the bargaining. What this consensus will consist of is not a question to be answered in the abstract. It will depend on the skill, resources and objectives of the participants, as well as on the context of decolonization within which the negotiations proceed.[7]

Within the process of decolonization, we can distinguish three major themes. These themes are both conditions for the attainment of independence and aspects of the decolonization process leading to that attainment. The first is the *adaptation* of the colonial elites to the removal of colonial authority. The second is the *cooptation* of the nationalist elites into the colonial system. The third is the *pre-emption* or control of mass discontent, ensuring the acquiescence of the masses to the process of consensual decolonization.

By *adaptation* is meant the changes in a social group aiding the survival,

5

functioning, maintenance or achievement of purpose, of the group. It is a reaction to threats both external and internal. There are two aspects to this definition. One, taken from the narrower use of the word in biology, refers to changes necessary for survival. This is the type of adaptive behavior which the more precarious European farming groups pursued during decolonization. The second aspect of adaptation refers to modifications which aid in the functioning or maintenance of a system or group, or to the achievement of their purposes. The behavior of the European liberals and the metropole government are closer to this end of the spectrum of adaptive behavior. The one implies a gradual yielding to an inevitable alteration caused by a weakening bargaining position; the other is a more creative adjustment to new relationships and institutions considered not only as threats, but as opportunities as well.[8]

The process of decolonization is adaptive then insofar as it reflects the adjustment in political behavior of the colonial political and economic elites to the removal of metropole authority. Implied by this is that these elites will seek to preserve their values and positions by altering their methods of influence, modifying their own structures and institutions, and identifying with the new rulers as well as seeking to affect their composition and behavior. This adaptation is thus not only adaptive to decolonization, but is also an influence upon it.

Decolonization is *cooptive* insofar as it is the process of absorbing new or opposing elements into the leadership or policy-determining structure of the colonial system as a means of averting threats to its stability or existence. Philip Selznick describes formal cooptation by an organization as resulting when the organization's legitimacy is called into question, and when there is a need of greater administrative accessibility to the relevant public. Cooptation is needed 'when the requirements of ordering the activities of a large organization or state make it advisable to establish the forms of self-government.' Selznick further asserts that the locus of significant decisions is preserved in the initiating group.[9]

Cooptation in the context of decolonization also involves the political socialization of the nationalist party. An important aspect of this socialization is the learning directly linked to recruitment into, and performance of, specialized political roles in the bureaucracy and leadership positions. Another aspect is the ostensibly non-political learning which nevertheless ultimately affects political behavior. This would include the learning of politically relevant social attitudes and personality characteristics. That political socialization has an essentially conservative character with regard to existing political arrangements is a conclusion shared by a number of scholars.[10]

Finally, decolonization is *pre-emptive* in its attempts to anticipate and prevent in advance the formation and mobilization of a mass nationalist movement. The political quiescence and subordination of the masses is a necessary condition for the attainment of independence as well as a goal of the decolonization process. Conflict encourages mobility, and the fear of widespread violence and mass uprisings is both a cause of, and a threat to, decolonization in the sense adopted here. This fear of mass mobilization is also the catalyst encouraging the consensual resolution of the bargaining process.

The process of decolonization occurs during the period of colonial transition, although it is certainly not limited to this period. This is the span of time preceding independence in which the major participants in the decolonization process accept independence as the inevitable outcome of the bargaining, while continuing to accept colonial officialdom as authoritative. The major actors regard colonial transition as a time of 'preparation' for independence in the near future. Independence is to be marked by the predominance of representatives of the majority African racial groups in the formal instruments of government, i.e., offices and votes. Aside from this anticipation of a formal changeover, substantive changes in the patterns of political and economic relationships both within the colony and those linking the colony to the metropole remain obscure. The acceptance of the metropole officialdom as authoritative is an expression of the obedience that the participants still believe the colonial structure deserves. Despite the questionable neutrality of various colonial officials, the accepted means of modifying their unfavorable decisions generally involves influence upon other parts of the metropole governing structure. The legitimacy of the authority itself remains unchallenged.[11]

Colonial transition, then, is characterized both by its authority structure and its goal. These two 'ordering principles' serve to orient the process of decolonization toward the ritualized conclusion of independence and to limit the acceptable degree of conflict among the participants.[12]

CONSENSUAL DECOLONIZATION

Conditions

There were two sets of conditions generally applicable to the process of decolonization in Africa in the 1960s. The first were general historical conditions serving as permissive incentives encouraging the colonial divestment. These have been widely discussed and included the international political environment, the rise of Third World nationalism, and the changing intellectual climate toward colonialism. The second set of conditions were specific situational ones within the colony and metropole. These provided the strong likelihood of a successful process of consensual decolonization occurring. They included the orientation and capacities of the nationalist elite, the political quiescence of the masses, and the adaptive potential of the metropole power.

Historical conditions. The essential function of the historical conditions was to raise the colonial calculation of costs over benefits for the metropole. At some point metropole government leaders came to view the formal political link with the colony as more expense than it was worth, or soon to become so. As one student of British colonial policy wrote: 'A point had been reached beyond which the prolongation of the old tempo and style of colonial policy would simply incur greater political, social and economic costs than Britain could hope to meet.'[13] In the period of the late 1950s and early 1960s the calculation likely contained a number of factors.

The East–West conflict made the Third World a battleground and a prize for the competing powers. The presence of communist and neutralist countries in international forums gave the 'other side' an opportunity to exploit the widespread distaste for colonial holdings. In his famous 'Winds of Change' speech in December 1959, Prime Minister Harold Macmillan stressed: 'As I see it, the great issue in this second half of the Twentieth Century is whether the uncommitted peoples of Asia and Africa will swing to the East or to the West . . .' To drive nationalism back, he asserted, would be to drive it to communism.[14] Beyond this, nationalist forces were seen as a potential ally in the Cold War struggle. In his important book, *British Policy in Changing Africa*, the former head of the Africa Division of the Colonial Office, Sir Andrew Cohen, asserted that 'successful cooperation with nationalism is our greatest bulwark against communism in Africa.'[15] American assistance was expected in stabilizing the post-colonial areas, both by maintaining traditional interests and by inhibiting foreign rivals' inroads in the contested Third World.[16]

The rise of articulate, western-educated nationalist leaders threatening to raise the cost of maintaining colonial possessions undoubtedly accelerated the process of decolonization. The attainment of independence by colonies in Asia and Northern Africa had set a 'demonstration effect.'Independence for non-white states such as India and Ghana gave an impetus to nationalist arguments in other colonial territories. Examples of the costly (and unsuccessful) conflicts in Algeria, Indochina and Indonesia stood as precedents few colonial officials wished to emulate. As Peter Worsley wrote:

. . . if, in both colonisation and decolonisation, force has always been the ultimate sanction, it has not always been used. A few decisive military-political actions have established new balances of power for whole regions. The repercussions of the most decisive revolutions, too, established more than a local or even a regional change; they altered the whole field of forces on the world level.[17]

The international climate had cooled toward the rectitude of the imperial mission. Colonization itself appeared to be an anachronism, an affront to universally proclaimed truths of the United Nations Charter and the Atlantic Charter. The benefits of colonies for the metropole were widely disputed both from the Left and the Right. The European powers were turning inward to meet domestic priorities and hopes for European unity. The

Second World War had diminished the colonial powers' resources and its stature in the Third World. Crises like Suez in 1956 appeared to underline the new limits on the power of the European colonial countries. Third World nationalism, self-determination and independence seemed to be historical forces whose inevitable time had come.

Situational conditions. There was no inevitable connection between these conditions and decolonization. All the colonial powers at some time or place stood resolutely against the 'winds of change.' The French in Vietnam, Madagascar and Algeria, the Dutch in Indonesia, the British in pre-War India and Kenya – all chose to use force to suppress indigenous movements with which they were unwilling or unable to come to terms. In these cases the previous conditions were all to a greater or lesser degree present. The question then becomes: what situational conditions explain the probability of a relatively consensual, decolonization process occurring?

The first condition present in the colony was that the political elite of the colony be able to rule consensually among themselves and functionally in terms of a mastery of the inherited political framework. The functional aspect not only implied that they be well-educated in the metropole mold but that they had 'maturity' or 'responsibility.' These vague though catchy phrases referred both to some competency by the indigenous elite in managing metropolitan political procedures and to the absence of (as well as the elite's ability to prevent) upheaval in colonial-metropolitan relations.[18] The need for elite consensus did not prohibit attempts to divide and isolate potential nationalist threats during the period of transition. This divide-and-rule strategy, however, gave way to a desire for political consensus or quiescence as independence neared and as the undesirable segments of the elite were eliminated.[19]

The reason for this stress on consensus lay in a second political requirement of a colony for a successful consensual decolonization: the prevention of mass unrest. Disagreement on the rate, desirability and conditions of self-government among the indigenous elite could facilitate the formation and mobilization of mass nationalist opinion. As one American scholar wrote, 'it is conflict that involves the people in politics and the nature of conflict determines the nature of the public involvement.'[20] The prospect of mass mobilization was both a cause of and a threat to decolonization. Independence was a means (not always successful) of pre-empting the mobilization of mass discontent and maintaining stability at a low cost. The British Colonial Secretary, Iain Macleod, later wrote of his policies: 'It has been said that after I became Colonial Secretary there was a deliberate speeding up of the movement towards independence. I agree. There was. And in my view any other policy would have led to terrible bloodshed in Africa. This is the heart of the argument . . .'[21]

This tacit agreement on the prevention of mass mobilization was to lead to the political irrelevance of the masses. Lavish praise was to be the only political contribution expected of the lower classes. The nationalist elite behaved '. . . to ensure the political superfluity of any political activity other than voting.'[22] The lack of significant mass involvement in politics continued with the formation of one-party states. Reflecting the weakness of their political system, one-party governments acted to prevent the mobilization of the mass base by rival parties.[23] The ruling party and its government were in turn removed from mass involvement and pressures.[24]

This pre-emption or control of mass discontent through decolonization has been noted by a number of scholars. Richard Rathbone, in his thesis on *The Transfer of Power in Ghana, 1945–57*, quoted a letter from Colonial Governor of Ghana, C. N. Arden-Clarke, in this context as remarking, '. . . you cannot slow down a flood – the best you can hope to do is keep the torrent within its proper channel.' Rathbone concluded that the 1930s made clear to colonial officials that gradualism in Asian colonies would have to give way to rapid change if discontent was to be contained and stability maintained.[25] Similarly, in Jamaica, Trevor Munroe found that the advance to self-government had little to do with the growth of nationalism, and that in fact rapid decolonization made mass nationalism unnecessary for the creation of the new state out of the former dependency.[26] Immanuel Wallerstein summed up the pre-emptive strategy of the colonial authorities. Wallerstein wrote that the response of the Europeans in most of Africa 'was to come to terms with the middle-class leadership by arranging a rapid transfer of power to them in the expectation of ending their verbal radicalism before it became coherent, ideological and national in organization . . .'[27]

In the historical context of African decolonization of the early 1960s the effort at pre-emption may have conflicted with the goal of coopting a trained indigenous social class into the political framework. Certainly the British Secretary of State at the time, Iain Macleod, emphasized the unviability of the colonial relationship and the threats of violence in pushing for more rapid devolution. But this was an alteration of timing, not of kind. The political and economic models to be followed, the integration of the indigenous elite into colonial patterns and the forms of the transfer itself were compressed, not altered. Just on the most visible level of the forms of political authority in the English colonies, changes in the 'Westminster Model' were neither sought nor thought needed. 'There was never any seriously sustained attempt, and certainly not at the policy-making level of successive British governments, to consider the possibility of granting independence on any other basis than that of the "Westminster Model." '[28]

Economic criteria for a colony's evolution were more ambivalent than the political requisites. Rathbone listed economic viability as a criterion for Ghanaian independence.[29] But explaining French devolution in Togo or Niger, Belgian in Ruanda, and British in Gambia, under this criterion would be tortuous. More important than the relative viability of the economy would be the relationship of the colonial elite and metropole interests to the economy. Questions of the economic value of the colony to metropole interests, and of the indigenous elite's willingness to maintain the economic structures would be more relevant. The central qualifications, then, were less in the strength of the economy itself than in the political relationships of the involved elites to the colonial economy and their willingness and ability to maintain them.[30]

There were also conditions within the metropole power allowing it to initiate and adapt to the decolonization process. Mention has already been made of a certain slackening of the colonial power's attentiveness toward its colonies, as well as a weakening in its ability to undertake expensive coercive action because of domestic constraints and conflicting foreign interests. Nevertheless, just as important as the weakening of the metropole's commitment to the colonial relationship was its capacity to maintain the fruits of that relationship within an altered authority structure. The question facing the metropole and colonial leaders was: can whatever political, economic and strategic interests which supported and justified the colonial relationship be preserved outside of the colonial structure? Within the metropole the answer to this depended on the strength of its political and economic system; its willingness to maintain financial, personnel and, if needed, military assistance; to exert political pressure; and to mobilize allied states in support of these leverages. In this sense decolonization can be seen as an act of strength by the decolonizing power.[31]

To alter a formal relationship of dominance to a more subtle one of influence (very great, to be sure) not only required domestic control and calculating leadership by the metropole, but also a political economy which could retain its interests in the former colony and protect them both from internal agitation and foreign competition. Perhaps this point becomes clearer in looking at Portuguese Africa, where initiating decolonization has required an overturning of the old metropole regime.

In the early 1960s Portugal appeared to be the colonial power least able to resist the inevitable tide of nationalism. In explaining what appeared to be a residual aberration, scholars have stressed the traditionalism of the Portuguese political economic structure. Ronald H. Chilcote argued that Portugal's 'traditional structural weaknesses' in large part determined the direction of an overseas domination which was the most primitive form of colonialism and the most extreme. He wrote that the intransigence of the industrial and agrarian elites in Portugal to colonial changes was directly attributable to the shortage of capital and labor, ineffective civil administration, and economic and financial instability.[32] James Duffy similarly pointed to the resentment of colonial commercial and plantation industries toward the Portuguese mercantilist policies as forming a significant element in conservative separatist sentiment in Angola and Mozambique.[33]

One can argue, then, that the very weakness of the Portuguese colonizers left them only with the response of forcibly suppressing nationalist movements. The encouragement of settlers and of foreign investment, was an unsuccessful effort by the Portuguese to strengthen the ties between the colonies and the metropole. But the essential dilemma remained: Portugal itself was not economically (and politically) developed enough to maintain its favorable colonial relationships without formal authority. As Amilcar Cabral, the late leader of the nationalist movement in Portuguese Guinea, said in England in 1971, 'The reason that Portugal is not decolonizing now is because Portugal is not an imperialist country, and cannot neo-colonize. The economic infrastructure of Portugal is such that she cannot compete with other capitalist powers.'[34]

· The British experience differed. In Ghana the British reaffirmed in an African setting that they could groom their political successors, and by manipulation of franchises and economic inducements have a large influence over who these might be and what they would be likely to do. As Rathbone concluded, 'Behind a facade of African rule, which of course had considerable substance to it, British interests had been allowed to remain paramount. Ghana had proved that it was not possible to be constitutionally concessive without hazarding major fields of British concerns.'[35]

This represented no great alteration to traditional British imperialist policies. Two leading English scholars, discussing British expansion in the Nineteenth Century, persuasively argued that British policy followed the principle of extending control informally if possible and formally if necessary. Only where informal political means failed to provide a framework of security for British interests (be they commercial, philanthropic or strategic) did the question of establishing a formal empire arise. Power would then be used imperialistically to adjust the situation.

In other words, responsible government, far from being a separatist device, was simply a change from direct to indirect methods of maintaining British interests. By slackening the formal political bond at the appropriate time, it was possible to rely on economic dependence and mutual good-feeling to keep the colonies bound to Britain while still using them as agents for further British expansion.[36]

In tropical Africa, Robinson and Gallagher concluded, the absence of strong indigenous political organizations and the presence of foreign challenges to British paramountcy in the area led to the switch to formal rule.[37]

The calculations involved in British decolonizing policies in the 1950s and 1960s were covered in two studies, J. M. Lee's *Colonial Development and Good Government* (Oxford, 1967) and David Goldsworthy's *Colonial Issues in British Politics, 1945–1961* (Oxford, 1971). The first dealt with the formation of policy by the traditional governing class, while the second attempted to assess the impact of party and group activities on these policies. Both concluded by emphasizing the control and continuity of the British administrative elite over colonial policies. Lee's study stressed the administrative elite adapting not only to changes in relations to the colonies

12

but to England's wider ties in the world. In this aspect the admission of the United States into the system of relationships between Britain and her former colonies loomed large. With its greater resources and similarity of interests the United States was invited to maintain the political and economic patterns established by decolonization. The 'Greenbrier philosophy' came out of a series of informal meetings in 1959 between British and American officials involved in colonial affairs. This 'philosophy' was described as 'the assumption that Britain and the United States had broadly the same interests in aiding the new states of Africa and, in spite of many differences of opinion, common philosophies actuating the formation of policy.' Both groups, for example, thought 'that the chief political problem after independence would be the survival of the political *elites* to whom power was transferred.'[38]

One can summarize by asserting that a successful process of consensual decolonization in Africa in the 1960s was conditioned by a number of factors prevailing in the metropole and colony. In the colony the presence of an indigenous elite capable of managing the inherited political framework, in some pattern of cooperation among themselves, and willing to maintain certain important colonial interests (political, commercial or strategic), enabled the colonialists to pass on the state to their inheritors. At the same time, the quiescence of the colony's populace and the pre-emption of potential agitation of the mass base were important ingredients in the rapid attainment of independence. Similarly, metropole authorities expected that through leverages other than formal political control, such as aid and trade policies, technical advisers, cultural ambience and the assistance of allies, they would have a good chance to maintain most of the advantages of the original colonial relationship. This implied the capacity of the metropole to reassert predominant influence in the crunch, and to exclude foreign rivals from the area.

Process

With the previous conditions satisfied, or with at least a reasonable expectation of their being met, decolonization proceeded as a dual process of bargaining and socialization. Independence was to be the culminating deal. Debate centered on the terms and timing of independence, the position of minorities and loyalists in the new state, the conditions of the post-colonial relationship with the metropole, the political structure of the independent state as encapsulated in a constitution, and even the composition of the new elite to ensure both consensus and moderation.[39] At the same time, colonial officials sought by judicious use of international and transnational ties (aid, trade, advisors) to constrain the new state to remain in the appointed orbit. By such a bargaining process colonial interests came to terms with potentially disruptive elements in the nationalist party, and vice versa.

13

Consensual decolonization

The socialization of the nationalist elite was the dynamo behind the bargaining process. This had both substantive and procedural aspects. The substantive part involved negotiations on issues such as trade policies, constitution-making, judicial norms, pensions for colonial officials and, in the Kenya case, most notably the land issue. But the procedural aspect, the involvement of the nationalists in the colonial forms of governmental authority, was both more subtle and more compelling.

The nationalists were caught in a dilemma by decolonization. Within the colony the essential justification for colonialism was that the colonial subjects were 'unready' for independence. The metropole-educated elite countered by demanding the same democratic procedures as prevailed in the metropole, and their participation in them. The indigenous elite was at some point integrated into parts of the political system with the understanding that constitutional advance was to be based on their ability to act in conformity with the requisites of that system. To deny their inferiority and assert equality, the elite felt compelled to argue for higher constitutional forms. They stressed that refusal to grant these concessions would lead to bad government or even revolt. On the other hand, their competent handling of the colonial machinery enabled them to argue that greater democracy would bring greater efficiency. 'In either event, the frame of reference for the argument and the forms for the test had to be metropolitan. Hence "opposition to Western rule has not usually meant opposition to Western institutions," but rather the affirmation of their necessity.[40]

The cooptive and pre-emptive aspects of this socialization were clearly interconnected. The constitutional participation of the nationalists not only socialized them into the colonial political norms but also deflected nationalist agitation into governmental cooperation and, indeed, created a counter interest to mass rebellion.[41]

In some cases, notably the francophone states of Africa, the transitional phase of decolonization involved bolstering a reluctant local leadership to induce sufficient confidence in their own capacities to survive outside formal colonial authority. (Both Leopold Senghor of Senegal and Felix Houphouet-Boigny of the Ivory Coast were reluctant and tardy advocates of independence for their territories.) Other areas demonstrated the colonial authorities playing the more orthodox bargaining role: citing the problems, the divisions, the inadequate resources – inhibiting a more rapid devolution. (Ghana, East Africa.) In either instance, with independence the functionaries perhaps changed, the functions remained.

Much could be, and has been, written discussing the continuity of the colonial system in sundry aspects of the independent state.[42] The economic system remained based on producing primary products for the metropole and other industrial countries allied to the metropole. The neglect of the rural areas, other than those producing cash crops, and the concentration on the colonial-established urban centers continued, even accelerated. The only change after independence was that the surplus from peasant agriculture was garnered and protected by the nationalist/expatriate bureaucracies. Development strategy was external, based on foreign capital, experts and institutions. African Socialism remained a vague goal seldom restricting the encouragement of foreign capital, the consumption habits of a growing indigenous bourgeoisie, and the pursuit of economic and development policies similar to those of the later 'welfare' period of colonialism.

In almost all areas of the modern state the transnational system once maintained in the colonial structure was continued. After an initial period of activism, the nationalist party sank back to a dependence on colonial forms and institutions, especially those of the bureaucracy. The government and its bureaucracy in turn maintained 'the relational, procedural and substantive norms' of the metropole administrative apparatus.[43] The educational, social, cultural and linguistic models were those of the metropole. Influence was maintained through financial channels (i.e., the franc zone), a metropole education of future leaders, tourism, and the high prestige of the metropole society in the former colony. Even the decision on the use of at least quasi-legitimate force lay outside the independent state. Metropole garrisons, especially in French-speaking Africa, bolstered cordial regimes. When this failed, armed interventions – as in Gabon, Chad, Central African Republic, Cameroon, the Congo, Kenya and Tanzania – were both expected and accepted by the nationalist leaders. In its aspirations, its techniques, its style, the 'independent' leadership remained *plus monarchiste que le roi.*[44]

The result of the decolonization process, then, was the integration of an indigenous leadership into colonial political, social and economic patterns. Decolonization's three themes – adaptation, cooptation and pre-emption – aimed at altering political authority (while perhaps changing the methods of social control), in order to preserve the essential features of the colonial political economy. From this perspective the decolonization process was not so much the *upward* development of an indigenous African political movement, as the *downward* manipulation of that movement into a system. Independence for the new state marked not so much a moving out of the colonial relationship as an enlarging and enhancing of that dependent relationship, with the colonial patterns emerging relatively unscathed.

THE SALIENT ASPECTS OF THE KENYAN CASE

Within these general expectations of consensual decolonization, the Kenyan case will be examined in terms of two salient aspects: the adaptation of the European community and the bargaining and resolution of the land issue. The composition, alignments, divisions and strategies of the European groups bargaining primarily over the land issue can be expected to illuminate the themes and process of decolonization in Kenya.

Consensual decolonization

European adaptation

There was a dualistic division in the European elite over the community's adaptive policies toward decolonization and the political ascendency of the nationalists. European adaptation revolved around the activities of the conservative (or farmer) grouping, and the liberal (or commercial) grouping.[45] The conservative grouping centered on the Convention of Associations and the Kenya Coalition (which effectively merged by mid-1960), and the Kenya National Farmers Union. Support for the conservatives was largely rural-based, most of their members being smaller European mixed-farmers.

The liberal grouping centered on the New Kenya Group, a multi-racial coalition of liberal politicians. The liberals found their strength in the urban areas, among relatively wealthy long-term residents, the European and Asian business and bureaucratic communities, and in support from the colonial administration and British government. The difference in support was based on those least willing or able to adapt to the foreseeable changes adopting harder line, more conservative policies.

Although the two groupings held similar goals, they differed in their priorities. The liberals sought to preserve as much as possible of the colonial economic, social and political system (ties, patterns of behavior, and expectations). This included the preservation of the open colonial economy and the sanctity of private enterprise, the administrative and political structure, the development strategy with the consequent importance of foreign investment, and the colonial legal and social norms of behavior. This overriding goal in turn led to the secondary objective of preserving the assets of the European farmers.

The conservatives, while not disagreeing with the value of retaining the colonial system, were more concerned with preserving their agricultural assets. Hence they pushed for large buy-out schemes which might be destructive to the economy as a whole. Urging the need for British protection and responsibility for their holdings rather than guarantees by the African nationalists, they implicitly stressed the discontinuity between the colonial system and the coming independent state. In this respect their views conflicted with the liberals and coincided with the initial position taken by the nationalists.

The strategies of the two groupings also varied in line with their differing priorities. The liberals sought to preserve the system and their place in it by restructuring the society from one split on racial lines to one divided on a class basis. The thrust of their policy was the building up, and aligning with, a moderate African middle class. The conservatives saw their strength as lying in the re-entrenchment of the European community on racial lines. With this united community the conservatives believed sufficient leverage could be exerted on the British government and the African nationalists to preserve the farmers' property. Each strategy was considered a threat to the other: the liberals viewed racial unity as outmoded and an obstacle to broader alignments, and the conservatives saw multi-racial class politics as unrealistic and hindering the formation of a powerful European lobby.[46]

The land issue

If the adaptation of the European community was a key feature of the decolonization process in Kenya, then the 'Land Question' was the crucial issue. Since the arrival of the European settlers in the first years of the century, and the reservation of 7.5 million acres of the Kenya Highlands (until 1960) for exclusively European use, the land issue had never been far from the center of the Kenya political arena. The sixty-year history of colonial Kenya was replete with petitions, delegations, uprisings and organizations, reflecting a sizeable body of African opinion opposed to settler control of the 'lost lands.' In turn the European farmers' deep sense of insecurity in this threatening environment and their demand for control of the 'White Highlands' was central to their drive for political leverage in the colonial period.

After the 1960 First Lancaster House Conference both independence and African dominance in the political arena were foregone conclusions, though the timing and substance of both remained to be thrashed out in the subsequent period of colonial transition. The most serious obstacle to an 'orderly transition' was neither of these issues. Instead it was the fate of the 'White Highlands.' For the European farmers, their land embodied their future. If their holdings could not be insured then their position in Kenya was tenuous. For the liberals and colonial officials the land issue was both an obstacle to a smooth transition and the test of turning over political authority to colonialism's nationalist heirs. Resolving the land question would not only guarantee the continuity of the economy, but would also stand as a mark of the socialization (maturity) of Kenya's new leaders in managing the inherited colonial system.

The land issue, then, in its bargaining and implementation, inter-related and supported the processes of elite adaptation and consensual decolonization. Its bargaining illustrated the differing priorities and interests of the participants, as well as their compatible objective in a consensual resolution of the issue. The implementation of land transfer schemes demonstrated the schemes' service to the overall process of decolonization. The schemes were adaptive in removing European irreconcilables and retaining the bulk of the Highlands' agriculture under European ownership. They were cooptive in seeking to promote a class of middle-level African farmers and bolstering moderate nationalist politics. And, finally, the schemes were pre-emptive in dissipating African land hunger and inhibiting the emergence of a militant nationalist movement based on the return of the 'lost lands.'

17

The chapters that follow will attempt to fill in the arguments sketched out here. Chapter 2 gives a brief history of the political and economic trends affecting the colonial system and the European community at the time of colonial transition. The history, organization, leadership and bargaining resources of the major European political groupings merit a longer discussion. Chapters 3, 4 and 5 cover the European bargaining on land and the altering political configurations of the transitional period. The chapters deal with the years 1960, 1961 and 1962, respectively: from the announcement of impending African majority rule in early 1960 to the agreement on the Million-Acre scheme and coalition government by mid-1962, which effectively resolved the central tension of the colonial change-over. Chapter 6 is an analysis of the implementation of the land schemes as illustrative of the themes of decolonization and elite adaptation. Finally, the Conclusion attempts to summarize and integrate the study around the expectations of this first chapter.

CHAPTER 2

BACKGROUND TO DECOLONIZATION: TRENDS AND GROUPS IN THE EUROPEAN COMMUNITY

. . . the most common and durable source of faction has been the various and unequal distribution of property. Those who hold and those who are without property have ever formed distinct interests in society.

The Federalist No. 10

Unnatural affection, child-murder, father murder, incest and the violation of the sanctity of dead bodies – when one reads such a list of charges against any tribe or nation, either in ancient or modern times, one can hardly help concluding that somebody wanted to annex their land.

Gilbert Murray

There already exists a large number of books on Kenyan colonial history, many of which are more comprehensive than any treatment that might be presented here.[1] Rather than provide another general approach to Kenyan history, this background chapter will emphasize the trends and policies affecting the bargaining situation which the Europeans faced in the early 1960s.

The first part of the chapter will focus on the political and economic trends which established and altered both Kenya colony and the European community at its center. The parallel political and economic erosion of European farmer dominance and the forces eroding the settlers' position provide the central theme. The thrust toward the separation of the colonizers (European settlers) from colonialism (ties to the metropole) is both a recurring conflict in Kenyan history and an accelerating process up to independence.

The latter half of the chapter deals with the European groups whose bargaining activities during colonial transition are the focus for this study. Details on their organization, composition, leadership and bargaining resources link the trends and conflicts of the colonial period with the negotiations of the early 1960s. The groups themselves reflect the differing European policies and interests visible throughout the history, and thus add another dimension to the decolonization debate over land.

COLONIAL TRENDS

Political trends

The demise of colonial rule in Kenya was not the same as the erosion of European farmer dominance; nor were they necessarily interdependent.

British colonialism in Kenya had to do both with the attempt to colonize Kenya with European settlers and with the maintenance of an authoritative colonial system in the country. Regarding the latter, more important aspect of the term, the European settlers were an important link – perhaps at times the most important – but certainly not the sole one. Colonial officials, commercial interests, tribal authorities, the Asian community and missionaries, were all vital supports to the system. The separability of the two aspects of the colonial system can be seen in a Rhodesia where the settler-dominated political system could survive without colonial authority, and in a Ghana where colonial authority existed without the settler presence.

The distinction becomes important in examining Kenyan colonial history. Although both colonial authority and settler dominance were finished off by independence in 1963, they were not always complementary before that. A common ending did not signify a similar process. In the colony's beginnings European settlement had been encouraged in order to make the railway, built from the coast to Lake Victoria for strategic reasons, a paying proposition. In a sense, the colony created the colonists, rather than vice versa.

Antagonism toward the settled colonizers was more frequent in Kenya's history than was opposition to colonial rule. Indian and African opposition to settler policies on land and labor in the 1920s and 1930s did not mean resistance to colonial rule, any more than did European businessmen's doubts about farmer leadership. Nor did the Devonshire Pledge of 1923 that 'primarily Kenya is an African territory . . . the interests of the African natives must be paramount' question the colonial link, although European paramountcy was thrown, at least theoretically, in doubt. Similarly multi-racialism, as envisaged by Sir Philip Mitchell, Governor of Kenya from 1944 to 1952, was seen as a means of containing both European extremists and African agitators. Multi-racialism, Mitchell wrote, would develop a new political community of civilized men with which the British government should maintain gradually lessening links 'for generations to come.'[2] In theory the policy undercut farmer dominance in order to enhance the colonial structure and ties.

By the 1950s the nationalists had linked their opposition to farmer political influence and colonial authority by their demand for majority rule *and* independence (as well as land). The farmers themselves were not as clear about this identity of interests. In the 1950s farmers' groups pushed for local autonomy in the Highlands while hoping for direct rule of the colony from the colonial office in order to inhibit African political advance. But prior to the 1950s Kenyan political history centered on the conflict between a settled elite striving for autonomy and a colonial government seeking to maintain its control. The process of decolonization itself may be seen as a painful and never quite completed attempt to divide the farmers' interests from the wider imperial ones. Certainly the farmers' groups saw it this way.[3]

20

In explaining the decline of Kenyan colonialism both aspects of the colonial pattern should be kept in mind. The attempt to colonize Kenya with Europeans was probably doomed by lack of numbers if nothing else. Both climate and geography limited European expansion.[4] Basing colonialism on the settler-farmer and then limiting him to some 12,200 square miles of land, some 7,560 of which (receiving thirty inches of rain a year or more) were suitable for intensive farming, signified an upper limit on the immigrant population. The dispersed nature of the Highlands made political separation of the area difficult. The presence of cheap African labor acted as a disincentive for encouraging lower-class immigration, and the unwillingness of the established settlers to sub-divide their holdings for newcomers likewise limited the numbers that could be absorbed.[5] The racial attitudes of both the European and Asian immigrants also made full integration through marriage with an indigenous elite an unpalatable means of preserving the colonial system.[6] Hence by 1960 there were only some 61,000 Europeans, or less than one per cent of the Kenyan population, with almost two-thirds of these living in urban areas. Even including Asians (numbering some 170,000 in 1960), toward whom European hostility was often directed, the immigrant races were only around three per cent of the total population.[7]

With the increasing consciousness of Kenya as an 'abortive' colony came the settlers' rising dependence on the metropolitan links. The government had to bail the farmers out of the depression in the 1930s, and afterward the settler agricultural economy depended on favorable marketing procedures and protective tariffs to maintain itself. The Mau Mau emergency of the 1950s attested to the Europeans' inability to maintain political and military dominance without expensive support from the metropole. Development of the African areas as part of this political support was also requiring a great outlay of British funds. These increasing costs were thus adding to the conflict in the British government's historically divided attitude toward the economic and political value of European colonization.

In the post-World War II environment both European colonization, as the chief support of the colonial links, and the linkages themselves were brought into question. Within Kenya the rise of nationalist agitation and the Emergency brought the first major African challenge to colonial authority. African economic development and increased participation in the colony's political structures were the responses of the colonial government to local political pressure, as well as to the felt need to justify colonialism as a welfare-developmental system. Kenya's multi-racial politics of the 1950s were an unsuccessful attempt to adapt the Europeans to their vanishing political supremacy and to maintain that supremacy with the aid of darker-hued allies. Multi-racialism may also be seen as an attempt to detach the future of the colonial ties (and system) from the political predominance of the settlers. But the ties themselves were under attack, and the nationalists had few reasons for accepting the division between colonialism and colonizer.

21

The Mau Mau Emergency was important in impelling the dismantling of colonial authority in Kenya for two reasons. First Mau Mau was an apparent example of how little colonialism had accomplished of its 'civilizing mission.' As Rosberg and Nottingham commented, 'It was as if a half-century of administration and civilization had been wiped out.'[8] If the claims of the Europeans that Mau Mau was an atavistic reaction against civilization were accepted, then colonial rule had not apparently succeeded even with the reputedly most progressive of the Kenyan tribes. The immediate reaction of 'more of the same' – autocratic government and economic development – could not hide the grave doubts about colonialism's impact and lead to a search for more far-reaching solutions.

At the same time British troops, funds and command reasserted the British presence in, and responsibility for, their colony. The possibility of the Kenya Europeans going it alone was laid to rest not only by the uprising but by the continuing British involvement in Kenya throughout the 1950s. Violence, not directly of their doing, had enabled the nationalist leaders to bring their grievances forcefully to the attention of the British government and public. It was a singular lesson in the art of communication.[9]

In looking, then, at the sixty year history of politics in Kenya, one can draw a useful distinction between the colonization of Kenya and the authoritative colonial system. The colonizing of Kenya with expatriate farmers was probably doomed mainly by the lack of settlers and available land, limitations imposed by climate, and African population pressure. As the failure of the settlers' efforts to politically dominate Kenya became apparent, colonial administrators attempted new solutions to preserve the colonial system and ties. Multi-racialism in the political field and African development in the economic one were attempts to gain new supports for the colonial political economy. Finally, decolonization will be viewed as a continuation of these policies: an attempt to preserve the system and fruits of colonialism without colonial authority or the colonizers. In this context the debate between conservative and liberal Europeans was between one group asking what will happen to the colonizer and his assets, and another worrying about what will happen to the colonial system and its political economy.

Economic trends

Parallel with the erosion of the farmers' political position were economic changes in the colony which reinforced the political changes. From the beginning of the commitment to establish European-directed agriculture in Kenya, there was ambiguity over which of two forms this would take. On the one hand there was the traditional tropical plantation, utilizing European capital and managers, employing large numbers of unskilled native labor, and producing high-valued tropical crops. On the other was the farming system of the temperate colonies, with European settlers practicing the cattle-raising and cereal-growing patterns of the metropole. The plantations would involve the settlers as an aristocracy with supervisory functions over the indigenous population, while the temperate agricultural system implied that the settlers were a separate community with separate institutions and territory, leaving the native populations undisturbed.[10]

The ecological conditions of Kenya enhanced the conflict. The Highlands soil and climate were similar to conditions in such temperate colonies as New Zealand and Canada. The coastal areas, the Lake Victoria lowlands and the lower parts of the Highlands, were attractive to tropical and sub-tropical crops, particularly coffee. Because of the dearth of interest by plantation interests and 'City' money the colony was founded on the basis of mass colonization by European small farmers, in the first years mainly from South Africa. After initially discouraging results, the agricultural economy expanded in the years preceding World War I chiefly from the growing of maize, for which the African laborers provided the best market, and coffee, which combined elements of tropical and temperate agriculture.

However, the basis of the economy was quickly established as plantation agriculture. The two major crops of the plantations, coffee and sisal, accounted for over half the value of Kenya's exports in the late 1920s. The smaller European farmers were increasingly dependent on government protection and market support to compete with the plantations and the lower-cost African producers. Their demands for native land and labor derived not only from the need for these direct production inputs but also from the need to reduce African competition.[11]

From the British point of view the major economic importance of colonies, Kenya included, was their dual role as suppliers of tropical raw materials and as markets for British manufacturers. But the Kenyan settlers were an increasingly expensive instrument for achieving these goals. The major economic contribution made by the mixed farmer was in feeding the urban population and agricultural labor force, and this at inflated prices to the consumers.[12] Through subsidies, tariff protection and market support during the colonial period, the government was bolstering an agricultural sector which could not otherwise survive. The government had early on accepted the doctrine, contradictory to the metropole's economic goals, that those who had contributed capital and enterprise to the colony must not be allowed to fail.[13] This came to mean support for a settler community which, on the economic plane, constituted a dead weight. As Brett comments: 'The real weaknesses of the settler position derived from the fact that they had very little positive to offer in real economic terms – they were essentially parasites upon the Kenyan economy and therefore found it very difficult, even with heavy state assistance, to accumulate the resources required to make their position a tenable one.[14] The settlers' intense drive for political influence and their conflicts with the metropole largely derived from this need to correct the unviability of their economic condition through political supports.

Pressure on the settler farmer came both from the African peasants, and the large plantation and commercial interests. The imposition of colonial policies in Kenya was breaking down the predominance of communal and exchange relations in the African societies. In their place was emerging an essentially individualistic peasant economy oriented to urban markets, wage labor and cash relationships.[15]

At least up to the 1950s, the major colonial policy accomplishing this breaking up of traditional society was the effort to induce Africans to work on European farms. Through expropriation of land, taxation (notably the hut and poll tax), forced labor (often in lieu of taxes), and recruitment, labor was extracted from the indigenous population. It was a migrant work force with ties in the reserves, the large farms and the urban areas, and secure in neither the European world nor the traditional one. The advantages of the temporary labor system were to inhibit the development of an urban proletariat, lower the costs to administrator and employer of social services and wages, and prevent the complete disruption of the traditional social and political order. At the same time the workers gained skills, a greater awareness of the new prevailing order, and perhaps more of an inclination to acquire the education and benefits possessed by the colonizer.[16]

Generally speaking, not until after World War II was African cash cropping actively encouraged. The exception to this was maize, the chief African cash crop, which in the Kikuyu area was worth more than all the other cash crops grown in the area combined. In the late 1930s efforts were made to encourage tobacco, cotton and rice, but the most valuable crop of all – coffee – was prohibited in the Kikuyu reserves.[17] The attempts to promote African growing of coffee in the 1920s and 1930s were opposed by European arguments that the quality of the product would be harmed. More central to the reasoning was the fear that the more attractive profits to be made in the reserves would raise the cost of labor to the farmers. The settlers also worried about the prospect of low-cost African competition. Similar complaints were raised against African cattle raising and marketing.[18]

During and after World War II there was increased government control and support for both European and African agriculture. The government now emphasized that it had a legitimate interest in how land was used in the European areas as well as in the African reserves. In the Highlands this led to the wartime provisions for a guaranteed minimum return to ensure the planting of needed crops, and the multiplication of public boards and committees. Although dominated by the settler-farmers, this extension of public control was to be a Trojan horse subverting arguments for racial divisions with appeals for productivity. In the African areas gardening crops, coffee

24

and tea planting were encouraged, and efforts were made to improve native
cattle stock. Land consolidation, particularly in the Kikuyu areas during the
Emergency period, had the dual purpose of developing efficient farming
practices and promoting a stable landed middle class with interests supportive of the colonial system.[19] These efforts in agriculture may be seen as
the economic side of the multi-racialist politics emerging in the early 1950s.

The development of the African peasant economy was, however, relatively minor compared to the growth of the European commercial and
industrial sectors. Through 1945 Kenya remained an essentially agricultural
economy, in terms of contribution to the money economy. Industrial development was relatively minor, despite the protection given to infant industries by the colonial government. There were a number of secondary industries related to the processing of agricultural products (i.e., flour mills,
bacon factories). However Europeans in the professional and business class
(though many owned small farms) consistently outnumbered the settler-
farmers. Similarly, the Asian community was almost exclusively engaged in
commerce, clerical work and service industries, while of those Africans
employed for hire, much larger numbers were in transport, construction and
domestic service, taken together, than in agriculture.[20]

After World War II the Kenyan economy came to depend increasingly
on commerce and industry. Based in Nairobi, the largest city in East Africa
with an infrastructure and climate suitable for expatriate firms, and selling
to a unified East African market since the 1920s, Kenya's commercial
sector grew rapidly. In 1955 the value of manufactured goods produced in
Kenya was greater than the total yield from European agriculture.[21] By
1967 agriculture, forestry and fisheries contributed K£58.3 million to the
monetary Gross Domestic Product; private industrial and commercial activities (i.e., mining, manufacturing, transport, electricity) added K£97.2
million, and commerce (trade, finance, rentals and other services) was
responsible for K£91.4.[22] There was also a decline in the numbers of
people employed in agriculture relative to the total number employed. In
1946 nearly 50 per cent of those employed were in agriculture, 25 per cent
in industry and 19 per cent in public services. By 1959 persons employed
had risen from 403,700 to 596,900, with the percentages for agriculture,
industry and public services standing at 41 per cent, 25 per cent, and 22 per
cent, respectively.[23] It seems clear that by the time of colonial transition
the business community was replacing the farmers at the top of the Kenya
economic hierarchy.

At the same time the plantations maintained their position as the vital
sector of the agricultural economy. Largely owned by foreign companies,
they specialized in growing tea, coffee and sisal for export. In 1966 these
three crops accounted for almost 70 per cent of Kenya's overseas agricultural exports, and over half of the total exports.[24] The plantations were
also important to the business community. For example, shortly after inde-

25

pendence 74 per cent of agricultural advances from the three major banks went to ranches/plantations, while only 24 per cent were loans to mixed farmers, and 3 per cent went to African small farmers.[25]

This growing importance of commercial interests in the Kenya economy was reflected in the political sphere. Commenting on the replacement of Lord Francis Scott by Alfred Vincent, a Nairobi businessman, as spokesman for Kenya Europeans in 1945, a leading scholar of Kenyan history wrote: '. . . the change in the leadership typified the growing importance of commerce and the relative decline of farming in the post-war European balance.'[26] The colonial government was not adverse to reducing the influence of their settler adversaries. Sir Geoffrey de Freitas, before he resigned as High Commissioner in Nairobi, described the settlers as always having been antagonists of the British government:

This is probably the only foreign country where the British businessmen – bank managers and merchants – are not the leaders of the British colony. One of the things I've tried to do here is give greater prestige and support to the business community. This has been made easier by the decline in the political power of the settlers.[27]

During the colonial period the position of the settled European farmers was being increasingly undermined by political and economic trends. The establishment of European settlers to support a railway built for strategic reasons was restricted from the beginning by policies of the colonial power. In agriculture the farmers were caught between more efficient plantation agriculture and, later, lower cost peasant production.[28] The settlers depended on favorable governmental policies (tariffs, subsidies and market support) to maintain a weak economic position. The post-World War II rise of the commercial community and the increased governmental emphasis on African agricultural development further diminished the settlers' central position in the economy.

In the political field as well, there were conflicts between the settlers' perception of their interests and the colonial government's policies. In fact, Kenyan colonial history was, until the late 1950s, a story of the conflicts between the settlers and the government: The settlers sought political control as the only means of preserving their weak economic position, 1900 to 1930; they compromised by accepting economic concessions and participation in government, with settler dominance over agriculture, 1930 to 1950; and then in the 1950s and early 1960s saw their position eroded by government-supported multi-racialism, the rise of African nationalism, and the divisions in the European community, with more adaptive interests pursuing liberal cooptive policies toward the nationalists.

The settlers' conflict with the colonial power was no mere quibbling between elites. It was one of deciding their position and future in Kenya in the face of forces either disinterested or antagonistic to them. It was also a conflict they were from very early on fated to lose. From the relative quiescence with which the European farmers accepted their displacement in the early 1960s, one could surmise that most realized that the battle had already been lost.

THE EUROPEAN GROUPS

In reviewing the history of the European groups who participated in the debate on land during colonial transition, these trends and conflicts became clear: The decline of the once powerful Convention of Associations and its resurgence in the late 1950s for a final effort to protect the farmers' position; the rise of the liberal Europeans in the New Kenya Group, with governmental and commercial backing, and their key role in undercutting the farmers and other threats to decolonization; and the persistence of a non-political, multi-racial Kenya National Farmers' Union, orienting the farmers toward more submerged, less ambitious policies. The history, composition and resources of the groups provide added understanding of the events under study.

THE FARMERS

History and organizations

The Convention of Associations. The Convention of Associations was the settlers' 'most famous organization.' Established in September, 1910, it brought together Lord Delamere's Colonists' Association and the Pastoralists' Association (originally set up to protest the political dominance of the large European landholders in the Colonists' Association) along with a number of local associations. Despite the European farmers' renowned individualism, the Convention functioned as a 'Settlers' Parliament' down through the 1930s. Accepted by colonial officials as the Europeans' most representative body, the Convention in these years campaigned against 'the antagonistic influence of Asiatic . . . philosophy,' for greater European influence in government, and for the racial sanctity and economic predominance of the Highlands.[29]

From its beginning the Convention was largely oriented to, and led by, rural interests. Ewart Grogan, the Convention's first chairman, was a colorful and wealthy farmer who, in the initial twenty years of the group along with the first Lord Delamere, provided the farmers' leadership. T. H. Harper, the chairman of the Convention in the early 1930s, was chairman of the Ruiru Farmers Association and of the Board of Agriculture. Lord Francis Scott, who served as chairman of the Convention in the 1930s, had come to Kenya following service as a Guards officer, under the Soldier Settlement Scheme. The Convention in the 1930s was a large body composed

27

of individual associations, almost all of which were from the rural areas of the Highlands.[30] In the economic turmoil of the 1930s the Convention shared leadership of the European community with the Elected Member Organization, the representative body of the European members of the Kenya Legislative Council. Especially in the 1930s, with Major (later Sir) Ferdinand Cavendish-Bentinck as secretary, the Convention was considered the more hard-line of the two groups in defending settler interests.

The settler influence on Kenyan politics came chiefly from two sources. Their participation on numerous committees and boards, in the main dealing with agriculture and immigration, enabled them to use their expertise and personal connections in a most effective manner. The Hilton Young Commission had remarked in 1929 that the settler influence on government was being exerted largely through their membership on committees. And during World War II some thirty-one new committees and boards were formed to oversee Kenya's economic life, with a consequent increase in European influence. Beyond this, social connections with the English governing elite were an important settler leverage. The leader of the settlers in the 1930s and 1940s, Lord Francis Scott, had important ties of friendship and blood to the English aristocracy. In 1936 the Permanent Under-Secretary at the Colonial Office was spoken of as Scott's 'old personal friend,' while mention was made of his seeing six Cabinet Ministers, besides George V.[31] Other European leaders such as Cavendish-Bentinck and Sir Alfred Vincent, the post-war head of the Electors' Union, had similar ties. As might be expected, the settlers thrived on publicity in England, as Cavendish-Bentinck wrote to Scott, 'The only thing that seems to have the slightest effect in England is noise and it does not seem to very much matter what the noise is made about provided the word 'Kenya' appears sufficiently frequently.'[32]

By World War II, however, the Convention was moribund. Its lapse has been attributed to the increasingly diverse nature of the Kenyan economy, particularly the rise of commercial and industrial interests within the European community. As a loose confederation primarily expressing farming interests, the Convention was able neither to coordinate with the new groups nor to provide sophisticated information and pressure on the European elected members.[33] To replace it, the Electors' Union was formed of local political associations in March, 1944. Liberal leader Michael Blundell described the Union as a 'natural resting place for failed candidates at any general election.' The Union, Blundell remarked, was apt to discharge political thunder in order to 'stiffen up' the elected representative backing of settler interests, as well as to attract funds for its continued existence.[34] The Electors' Union stressed European involvement in government decision-making, the sanctity of the White Highlands, and the goal of ensuring that European and African interests were complementary. However, by the mid-fifties the Union also declined, in no small part due to the rise of the

Kenya National Farmers Union and the transfer to it of agricultural matters which had figured prominently in the old Convention's platforms.

By 1957 interest in reforming the Convention revived, largely among conservative anti-multi-racialist Europeans who felt alienated from the colonial government and their elected European representatives. The long-simmering divisions in the community had broken out in the mid-1950s over leniency toward Mau Mau fighters and the new Lyttleton Constitution, which sought to promote limited steps toward multi-racial government. Conservatives felt that liberals such as Blundell had lost their loyalties to the settlers, and worried when representatives like Mrs Dorothy Hughes, of Uasin-Gishu, who had won the 1956 election on a right-wing appeal to the largely Afrikaner voters there, showed evidence of a change of attitude. The Convention was to be an effort to formulate and present a united European position.

The reforming of the Convention of Associations was led by Sir Charles Markham, later a rather transient member of the New Kenya Group. Old Kenya political figures such as the seemingly immortal Ewart Grogan were on the platform of the first meeting. Although the local district associations voiced support, the Convention was unpopular with almost all the European elected members, and the organizers found it difficult to get anyone to accept the chairmanship. George Nicol, Member from Mombasa and head of Smith Mackenzie, a long-established trading firm, eventually took over. Upon Nicol's resignation in mid-1959 for personal reasons, C. O. Oates, a man with close connections to Kenya agriculture, became chairman. He was to serve as chairman of the Convention until its demise in 1963.

The Convention's constitution opened membership only to European district associations and other bodies representing Europeans. Its goals were to act as a forum, disseminator and representative of European opinion. The Convention was overseen by a Council composed of the officers elected by the membership, and representatives of the local associations. A narrower Executive made up of the officers of the Convention acted as the key decision-making body. But the organization was never tightly-structured and the Convention leadership felt they had little power over matters before the group. The 'town hall meeting' nature of the group also inhibited a concerted policy program, although the conservative, rural nature of the Convention's membership was clear from the debates and statements of the group.[35]

The Kenya Coalition. The Kenya Coalition began with the resignation of Cavendish-Bentinck as speaker of the Kenya Legislative Council on March 4, 1960. Charging the British government with abandoning their past pledges to the settlers, he felt he must support the people he had encouraged to emigrate to Kenya. On March 20, 'C-B' (as he was referred to by his backers) announced the formation of the Kenya Coalition to promote

29

greater cooperation among Europeans and to represent all endangered minority interests. The Coalition was also described as a 'movement,' stressing economic issues, rather than a 'party,' seeking political office.[36]

But both the non-European and non-political aspects of the Coalition were early casualties of the bargaining process. The Coalition never made more than perfunctory efforts to gain Asian and African minorities' support. With the traditional champion of the settlers as the Coalition's head, and its goal that of re-entrenching the European community, it could scarcely have been otherwise. The support of the right-wing United Party plus the presence of liberal opposition made the Coalition appear as a direct descendent of the traditional vociferous settler politics. The Convention of Associations' backing of the Coalition led to the virtual coalescing of the groups and, although bickering was apparent throughout the period, the alliance held.

While there were real conflicts between the conservatives and liberals, notably on land, their differences were also to a degree a matter of style. The Coalition 'gave an impression of determination, forthrightness and a spirit of do-or-die . . .' Coalition speakers declared themselves to be 'watchdogs' not 'lapdogs,' to which New Kenya Party representatives replied, describing themselves as 'guidedogs.' In appealing to the European electorate in the 1961 elections, both the liberals and conservatives sought the middle ground. They stressed law and order, an independent judiciary, ordered steps toward independence, the need for quality education (with no clear mandate for racial integration in either platform), and security for land titles. After the election the liberals moved toward broader accommodation with the nationalists, and the Convention/Coalition centered exclusive attention on lobbying for a land transfer program.[37]

The Kenya National Farmers Union. The idea of a farmers' union to speak for the European farming community on agricultural policy surfaced in Kenya in the early 1940s. Although various sectors of the agricultural industry had their own organizations, leaders of the marketing cooperatives pushed for a single group to deal with overall policy. Will Evans, later to serve as the first president of the Kenya National Farmers Union, introduced a motion at the Stockowners' Association Annual Conference in 1942 to investigate the possibility of a National Farmers Union. Although the resolution was passed, the war caused a postponement in its implementation.[38]

In November 1947 the Stockowners' Association invited representatives of all the European farmers' associations to a conference in Nairobi. With the backing of the Member for Agriculture, Sir Ferdinand Cavendish-Bentinck, the conference agreed to launch the Union. Meetings were held throughout the Highlands in early 1948, and the National Farmers Union of England and Wales sent a public relations officer to assist the membership drive. By November 1948 the actual work of the Kenya National Farmers Union began.

The Union was organized around two parallel structures with a committee system in between. The fourteen area branches consisted of farmers organized into local groups which sent representatives to the Kenya National Farmers Union Council. Membership came chiefly from the mixed farming areas (the four largest branches being Trans-Nzoia, Eldoret, Nakuru and Mt Kenya) and by 1950 stood at 1,706. The organized industries (i.e., Kenya Farmers' Association, Kenya Cooperative Creameries, Kenya Tea Owners' Association) maintained a loose liaison with the Union by placing their representatives on the Kenya National Farmers Union Council. The standing committees (i.e., Horticultural, Labor, Commercial and Price Fixation) organized around specific areas of concern, and were composed of members of the Union involved in those areas. Authority over the entire structure was vested in the KNFU Council composed of area branch delegates, committee chairmen, representatives of the nine agricultural industries and the officers of the Union. However, power centered in the smaller President's Committee, which met once a month to implement the Council's decisions.[39]

The major problems the Union faced in its early days were gaining organizational predominance in European agriculture, and financial solvency. The two issues were seen as interconnected. Membership dues of £2 annually were not adequate to support the Union's work and a cess of one-tenth of one per cent on all marketed produce, with a maximum of £20, was inaugurated by the Council in May 1950. However, less than a third of the members paid the cess in 1951; the Union had to borrow £1000; and the leadership threatened to dissolve the organization. By the next year the cess was effectively collected, membership declined slightly, and the Union showed a surplus in its accounts.[40]

After securing the financial standing of the Union, the leadership next attempted to amalgamate the organized industries into its structure. The industries had worried from the Union's founding that the KNFU would interfere in their affairs, and their membership on the Council had not allayed these fears. On the other hand, the area branches were concerned that closer integration with the industries would destroy the Union as a representative of individual farmers. Negotiations with the industries in 1952 and 1953 resulted not only in the industries' membership in the Union, but also in the KNFU's reorganization.

The organized industries became members paying an annual subscription of £50. At the same time most of the powers of the Council (except for passing advisory resolutions, meeting twice a year, and electing the Executive Committee), were given to an Executive Committee. The Committee was composed of five members from the area branches and five from the organized industries. While it was argued that the smaller Executive Com-

31

mittee could more efficiently deal with Union affairs, the move also gave the industries a more effective voice in the Union than they could expect in the Council dominated by the area branches. At the same time the internal operations of the industries remained outside the Union's purview, while the area branches were required to confirm with the Executive Committee any action 'not of purely local interest.'[41]

By 1954 the Executive Committee reported the reorganization 'an unqualified success.' The feared division between industries and branches had not occurred. The Union had a surplus of £700, and membership stood at 1700, representing some eighty per cent of the colony's mixed farmers. The Union, having used individual membership to initiate its organization, had broadened to take in commercial members. Paralleling this, the leadership had consolidated powers into a smaller body and subordinated the area branches to the center. The conflict between a loose representative group of farmers and a lobbying instrument, adequately financed and governed, was resolved in favor of the latter by the mid-1950s.[42]

Throughout its life in colonial Kenya, the Kenya National Farmers Union pushed the sort of bread-and-butter issues one might expect from a farmers' lobby. The Union generally argued for guaranteed prices for produce, more money for agricultural research, long term credit at easy terms, and control over agriculture to be placed in the hands of locally-elected committees. The Union claimed credit for the appointment of the Troup Commission in November 1950, and supported the Troup Report's conclusions which set up a procedure for determining the prices of Highland products through negotiations between the industry and government. Increased European immigration was pushed by the Union and emphasis was placed on the Highlands as the focus of increased agricultural production in Kenya. The need for a reduction in taxes was also a constant refrain.[43]

The attempt to gain an African membership had been an unachieved goal from the Kenya National Farmers Union's beginning. In their initial statement of purpose the Union 'hoped that as standards of farming efficiency are reached by progressive Africans, group representation of native agriculture in the KNFU will develop.'[44] But the Emergency served to abort most of the Union's attempts at assistance to and contact with African farmers. However, in March 1957, after lengthy discussion, a formal amendment to the rules was approved allowing farmers of any race to join the Union. Representatives were sent to African District Councils, but results were disappointing. By the 1960 Lancaster House Conference only a half-dozen Africans had joined.[45]

The effort to integrate Africans into the Union's structure accelerated in the early 1960s. Both to blend into the changing political environs and to give credibility to the Union's claims to represent 'the farmer's interest,' Africans were encouraged to join. Through 1962 African membership remained fairly stationary. But in 1962 and 1963 a recruiting campaign was begun (with some £3,000 allocated), dues lowered for small-scale farmers and African field officers hired. By June 1964, 1700 African farmers were paid-up members, with two Africans serving as vice presidents. In 1968, one of these, P. N. Sifuma, a farmer from western Kenya, was elected to head the Union. Though membership dropped by 1967, the rival Kenya African Farmers' Union had dissolved and advised their members to join the Kenya National Farmers Union. Before this Jomo Kenyatta had agreed to become Patron of the Union, thus sealing the organization's preeminence as representative of Kenyan farmers.

Membership in general rose greatly in the turmoil of the early 1960s. From about 1700 paid-up members in 1959 there were over 2400 by mid-1960. Emigrations and a growing apathy among European members reduced the level to 1800 in June 1963. African membership boosted the totals to 2400 in 1964, from which it declined markedly to 1400 in mid-1967 and then rose again to 1600 in 1969. The ratio of large-scale farmers to small-scale stood at almost three to one in 1967.[46]

Leadership

Sir Ferdinand Cavendish-Bentinck had begun his career in East Africa as private secretary to the Governor of Uganda from 1925 to 1927. He moved to Kenya, where he became known as a tough-liner in settler politics and rose in rapid succession from secretary of the Convention of Associations, to a member of the Legislative Council, to secretary of the Elected Members' Organization of that Council. He was later to be the first settler Minister (Agriculture in 1945), and Speaker of the Kenya Legislative Council from 1955 until his resignation in 1960.[47]

One English official who knew Cavendish-Bentinck in the 1930s wrote that he was 'a nice enough fellow, if a little too sure that he's right and the other people wrong.' One of the things C-B was sure he was right about was that the settlers' aim should be 'to secure control by the European element of the Government and the finances of this country.'[48] These words, written in 1933, were apparently still relevant in the mid-1950s when he angrily accused Michael Blundell of destroying his life's goal of 'a white dominion in East Africa.'[49]

C. O. Oates was chairman of the Convention of Associations from 1959 until its demise in 1963. Trained in agriculture at Oxford and Cambridge Oates had spent twenty years as an agricultural officer in the African reserves of Kenya. Retired from that, he owned a mixed farm, served as managing director of one of Kenya's biggest ranches, and as director of, and consultant to, a number of tea companies, including Brooke Bond. In the period of bargaining Oates stood out as a conciliator between the more hard-line small farmers' position and that of the more adaptive European interests.

Peter Marrian was president of the Kenya National Farmers Union from December 1959 until late 1960, when he resigned to successfully run for the Legislative Council as an Independent. Marrian's background consisted of an education at Shrewsbury and Oxford, war service as a Captain in the East African Artillery; he had been a farmer in Mweiga since 1948. His liberal credentials were previously established as an unsuccessful candidate for the Legislative Council on the Capricorn ticket in 1956 (a multi-racial group espousing gradual reforms in Africa). His later switch to the Kenya African National Union (KANU) in 1961 and appointment as parliamentary secretary to the Ministry of Lands and Settlement in 1963, confirmed the mistrust in which some farmers held him. In early 1962 his major economic interests were as chairman and majority holder in Mweiga Estates, Ltd., a plantation raising beef and coffee, director of Buchanan's Kenya Estates, and a shareholder in East African Breweries. He quit his government positions in 1964 for personal reasons, and moved to England.[50]

Cholmondeley Thomas Pitt Hamilton, 4th Baron Delamere, son of 'the founder' of Kenya Colony, replaced Marrian as president of the Kenya National Farmers Union in late 1960. Lord Delamere served until 1963. Educated at Eton, he had come to Kenya in 1945 to assume control of Delamere Estates, Ltd. In 1956 he unsuccessfully contested a seat in the Legislative Council on a moderately conservative platform. His economic holdings were large and widespread. Lord Delamere's ranching lands cover several hundred thousand acres. He also served as chairman of S. H. Benson (Africa) Ltd, Dunford Hall and Partners Ltd, a public relations firm which handled the Farmers' Union missions, and Kenya Cold Storage. He was director of Avon Tyre Remoulding Services, Ltd, Kabuzi Fibre-lands, Ltd, and Kenya Cooperative Creameries, Ltd. During the bargaining over the land issue criticism was heard that while Delamere was urging the farmers to remain calm, he was liquidating several of his commercial holdings and sending the money abroad. Delamere became one of the first Europeans to apply for Kenya citizenship, and today resides at his estate at Elmenteita.[51]

Bargaining resources

The major resource the Convention/Coalition, as well as the Farmers' Union, could call upon in their bargaining activities was their mass base membership of European farmers. In May 1961 the Convention claimed a paid-up membership of three-fourths of Kenya's 4,000 farmers.[52] A memorandum to Secretary of State Maulding in November of that year began: 'As the Convention draws its strength from the rural areas of Kenya . . .' and spoke of the 'Kenya agricultural community.'[53] The terms 'European farmers' and 'European community' were often used interchangeably by the conservative leadership. The general meetings of the Convention attracted wide farmer attention. For example, one on May 26, 1962 had approximately three hundred members of district associations in attendance. The question of rural support was used by the leaders in conflicts among themselves to enhance the standing of their respective organizations. So in arguing for Convention representation at the Governor's Conference in the fall of 1961, Oates claimed that the KNFU presence was insufficient since Delamere lacked the confidence of a great number of farmers.[54]

The Kenya National Farmers Union (KNFU) often appeared better financed than the Convention/Coalition. With an annual income of over £17,000 and a special fund set up for the London missions of almost £10,000 the Union had fairly adequate financial backing, although most of the leaders complained of a shortage of funds. Beyond this, some of the farmers' representatives (such as Lord Delamere) could and did pay their own expenses on the missions to London.

The KNFU's advantages and problems in representing a large rural constituency were similar to those of the Convention. On the one hand, they could validly claim to represent the European farmer in Kenya, while on the other hand the leadership had to assuage these farmers and justify policies which often looked overly liberal to the farmers. A prime example of this was the results of the Second Lancaster House Conference discussed in Chapter 5.

Converting farmer support into influence and viable bargaining tactics was a hurdle never entirely surmounted by the farmers' leaders. The most direct method of conversion was economic sabotage – the threat to salvage the moveable assets on the farms and leave Kenya. In May, 1961, the Convention of Associations threatened exactly this, unless guarantees for land titles were garnered by September.[55] At the Second Lancaster House Conference, in private meetings with British officials, Oates made it 'quite clear' that if Her Majesty's Government did not do anything about land, he would call a meeting of farmers to advise them to salvage what they could and get out.[56] But economic sabotage meant economic suicide, and it remained a threat neither side wished to see implemented.

Most of the funding for the conservative groups appeared to have come from membership dues and a series of fund drives. While it is not known how much money was raised, these drives seemed to have been the major source of financing for the Convention and to have tided them over the period.[57] Appeals to British commercial interests for financial support were not as successful. A request to City firms in April 1961 to donate money for a Convention/Coalition public relations office in London met refusal from a friend in commerce who replied that the City was not prepared to support the Convention on this.[58] Some plantations such as the large tea interests, Brooke Bond, did however support the Convention's activities and multi-national corporation backing was to be a vital ingredient in the ultimate British acceptance of the Million-Acre scheme.[59]

The Union's leadership had access and social compatibility both with the colonial government and the English governing class.[60] Almost all the officers had an English public school education: P. D. Marrian, Shrewsbury and Oxford; Lord Delamere and Michael Robinson, Eton; Jack Block, Loughborough College; Alec Ward, Lancing College.[61] Social and personal contacts were frequently mobilized for political lobbying. When Eugene Black, head of the World Bank, paid a 'private' visit to Kenya in May of 1960, he spent the weekend at the house of Peter Marrian, who was a friend of the family. At the time, World Bank financing for land settlement was being made a crucial ingredient by the British for their commitment of funds. Lord Delamere, by virtue of his title, was able to speak on the floor of the House of Lords, which he did in April 1960, and converse as an equal with influential members of the British nobility. The English National Farmers' Union was a key link in the Union's London activities. The English Union gave their Kenyan associates financial and administrative assistance, as well as access to a number of officials and politicians with whom they had contact.

While not as extensive as the liberals' ties, farmer lobbying found support in Parliament, notably among right-wing Tories opposed to Secretary of State Macleod's decolonizing policies. Among the Conservatives supporting the farmers with advice and lobbying were Lord Salisbury, Lord Colyton, Lord Boyd, Lord Wedgewood, J. Hare, M.P., Patrick Wall, M.P., and Robin Turton, M.P. Most of these were members of the so-called 'Rhodesia Lobby' worried about the precedent not supporting the Kenyan farmers would set for Rhodesia.[62] Patrick Wall, Conservative M.P. from Haltemprice, was particularly active in backing the farmers' efforts both in public support and private advice. Liberally-inclined Conservatives such as Christopher Chataway and Selwyn Lloyd also privately lobbied for the farmers. Lord Carew, President of the British Legion, was another more vocal supporter of the farmers' efforts.

The degree of contact with the English elite led the farmers' leadership (as well as the liberals) to prefer informal private meetings as a forum for exerting pressure. One farmer leader remarked that at the Second Lancaster House Conference the Colonial Office opened in the evenings at the bar after business was over, and it was there that the farmers' proposals were discussed. At the same time, grass-roots pressure was exerted through letter writing campaigns which the Convention encouraged its members to undertake in reaching friends and relations in England. In early 1960 F. T. Thompson, former treasurer of the Convention and an important contact in England for Convention efforts, advised using British domestic pressures to reverse Macleod's stand: 'It is essential to stress in no uncertain practical terms the extent of European settlement in Kenya and its personal connection with constituent residents in Britain.[63]

However, the farmers also encountered antagonism in English ruling circles, and not merely from the Left. Lord Delamere remarked that a number of British officials were unsympathetic to the farmers, apparently associating the settlers with the whip and Happy Valley escapades.[64] Ferdinand Cavendish-Bentinck recalled that both Conservative and Labour back-benchers were more receptive than the Government, and that some colonial officials (with a touch of envy) felt that the settlers had had a wonderful time of it with their climate and servants, and deserved what was coming.[65] In his memoirs, Michael Blundell wrote about a dinner in the House of Commons where a younger Tory M.P. expressed the 'prevailing mood' – in graphic terms: 'What do I care about the f . . . ing settlers, let them bloody well look after themselves.'[66]

THE LIBERALS

History and organization: The New Kenya Group

The New Kenya Group was formed on April 2, 1959, by liberal European politicians seeking to spur their community's slow adoption of multi-racial reforms. The Group was a descendent of the United Country Party, an ill-fated attempt by European liberals to promote limited multi-racialism in the mid-1950s.[67] Founded in July, 1954, by Michael Blundell, the United Country Party supported the Lyttleton Constitution's proposals for increased Asian and African ministerial positions. At the same time, the United Country Party limited its membership to Europeans, supported the 'integrity' of the White Highlands, proposed to restrict Asian immigration and encourage trained European migrants, backed racially separate education, objected to a common roll (Europeans and Africans voting for the same candidates), and pushed for increased authority for local government. African development was stressed and the Party pledged to 'do all that is possible to prevent the creation of a proletariat and to ensure that every man has a stake in the country.'[68]

The United Country Party, because of the attitudes of the European electorate and the contradictions reflected in the Party's positions, was probably doomed from the start.[69] Although formed to counter the right-wing Kenya Empire Party, which was calling for 'provincial autonomy' (which its opponents called apartheid), it alienated European opinion by forming a party (seen as divisive) and pushing multi-racialism (seen as countering the preservation of colonial Kenyan standards). The United Country Party was also frequently criticized as the Government Party because of the leadership's close government connections.[70] In the general election of October 1956, the party moved to the right a bit, won six seats to the rival Independents' eight. The opposition Independents, under Group Captain Briggs, had campaigned against the Lyttleton Constitution, and stressed 'non-racialism' with advancement based on merit and ability, which the liberals viewed as maintaining European dominance. Nevertheless, Briggs, Blundell and Wilfred Havelock, a leader of the United Country Party, accepted ministries in the new government. The two groups then announced their unity in the Legislative Council, and the United Country Party was formally dissolved in January 1957.

The New Kenya Group's origins lay with Europeans closely connected to the colonial government. Michael Blundell recounted being approached by a group of European elected members who urged him to resign the Ministry of Agriculture and lead liberal European opinion in adopting multi-racial reform.[71] Tom Mboya charged that the Colonial Office had clearly given its support to the founding of the Group. He pointed out that of the forty-five members of the Legislative Council who signed the Group's first statement, twenty-one had been selected by the Governor, twelve were Specially Elected Members (selected by the Legislative Council in an election boycotted by the nationalists) and most of the rest (ten) were European elected members.[72] Blundell admitted having written to the Secretary of State, Lennox-Boyd, a month before his resignation, giving him the reasons behind it, and discussing it with Governor Baring and gaining his agreement.[73]

The New Kenya Group was essentially a multi-racial grouping of liberal politicians, heavily dominated by Europeans, and oriented to adapting the European community to integrating Africans into the political and economic system.[74] The three major committees, Executive, Legislative and Financial, were headed by Europeans (Wilfred Havelock, Humphrey Slade and Dorothy Hughes, respectively). The Group expanded into a political party, the New Kenya Party, at a conference in mid-September 1959. The New Kenya Group retained a formally separate organization under the name New Kenya Parliamentary Group. In fact, it remained in Blundell's words the heart of the movement and functioned as the policy-making body of the Party. (The fifteen members of the Executive Committee, nine of whom were European, were all drawn from the Parliamentary Group.) Although the Party set up local branches, these appear to have been rather moribund. The Party (repeatedly referred to as the New Kenya Group) functioned mainly as a lobby group of liberal politicians for the two years of its life.

The Group, in policy statements at the time, proposed the lowering of land barriers in the Highlands to qualified African farmers. It stressed the need to remove the parallel racial and economic divisions in Kenya by raising African living standards and erasing racial barriers. Restoring confidence in Kenya's future was needed to increase foreign investment. Education would be made more available and devolution of 'appropriate responsibility' to local government was rather vaguely backed. The Group proclaimed that through these planned steps their goal of 'a self-governing country within the Commonwealth' could be attained.[75]

Leadership

Michael Blundell, who headed the New Kenya Group in the position of Leader, was clearly the dominant personality of European politics. The son of an English solicitor, educated at Wellington College, Blundell had given up plans to go to Oxford and went instead to farm in Kenya in 1925. His public career began in 1938 when he was elected to the Coffee Board of Kenya. After war service he became Chairman of the European Settlement Board, 1946–7, and initiated the post-war European Settlement Schemes. In 1948, Blundell became the European Elected Member for Rift Valley, and in 1952 Leader of the European Elected Members Organization. In 1954 he was appointed Minister without Portfolio to the Emergency War Council, where he played a key role in evolving strategy toward Mau Mau. In 1955 he left the War Council to hold office as Minster of Agriculture until 1959, and again in 1961–2. He was awarded a knighthood in 1962.

Throughout the narrative Michael Blundell's personality looms large. His very real abilities, as much as his faults, marked the liberal policies throughout the period. A forceful speaker, he was also at times vain and indecisive. A neighbor and political ally of his remarked on Sir Michael's tendency to worry about a decision after he made it, and often to go back on it. Possessed of a keen political mind and at times remarkably prescient, Blundell, another associate remarked, was probably never able to fully jump from multi-racialism to identify with the true nationalists, hence his support for the Kenya African Democratic Union. But at the same time, in a very real sense, Sir Michael Blundell was himself the first Kenyan nationalist: the first Kenyan leader to publicly eschew advantages for his own community in order to better serve his vision of a Kenyan nation. The fact that he equated the long-run interests of Europeans with that of the emerging Kenyan nation should not blind us to the foresight and political acumen he displayed in pushing his own community toward viable adaptive policies.[76]

Other important members of the New Kenya Group included Sir Wilfred Havelock, educated at the Imperial Service College Windsor, a member of the Legislative Council since 1947 and Minister of Local Government, 1954–62. Sir Wilfred served as chairman of the New Kenya Group, and was described by one member as the detail man: Blundell would set out the Group's goals and Havelock would map out the route. R. S. Alexander, born and educated in Kenya, was a former Mayor of Nairobi, and a member of the Legislative Council and of the Group's Executive Committee. Humphrey Slade, educated at Eton, Oxford and Lincoln's Inn, was a lawyer and key member of the New Kenya Group until his election as Speaker of the Legislative Council in 1960. Musa Amalemba was the leading African in the Group, and widely rumored to be their choice to head an independent government. A former member of the Nairobi City Council, Amalemba was a Specially Elected Member of the Legislative Council and Minister of Housing in 1960.[77]

Bargaining resources

The major resources of the New Kenya Group came from the financial backing of British commercial interests and the access to government policy-makers provided by the social contacts of the Group's leadership.

The close commercial ties of the New Kenya Group were both recognized by the farmers' groups and a source of suspicion for them. An ally of Blundell's, Jack Lipscomb, head of the European Agricultural Settlement Board, wrote him shortly after the New Kenya Group was formed, warning that

A major criticism of your group, voiced upcountry, is that much of its original membership and support was commercial and professional, as opposed to country support. This is regarded as a weakness because people feel, rightly or wrongly, that commercial and professional men are not as firmly tied to Kenya by their investments as farmers, and that they are not so vulnerable to nationalism. It is considered that they can, therefore, subscribe more readily to liberal policy.[78]

Financing for political parties is always a sensitive submerged topic. Nonetheless, interviews with New Kenya Group leaders clearly established that most of the funding for the Group derived from British-tied commercial sources. Both Blundell and Havelock attributed the bulk of their financing for the New Kenya Group to British and Kenyan commercial interests.[79] Dorothy Hughes, the chairman of the Group's Financial Committee, was the wife of the head of Hughes Ltd, J. J. Hughes, who had directorships in eleven Kenyan companies in 1966.

Other members of the Group with wide commercial interests would include Lt. Col. S. G. Ghersie, connected with chemicals, pig products, breweries and insurance, who held seventeen directorships in 1967, and Humphrey Slade, with sixteen directorships in the same year, including chairmanship of Canada Dry (E.A.) Ltd. C. W. Rubia, an African member of the New Kenya Group Finance Committee, held sixteen directorships in 1967. Among these was his chairmanship (the sole Kenyan on the board of directors) of Triangle Fertilizers Ltd, which launched the 'biggest single investment of any industrial project in the history of Kenya' in August, 1967, involving a capital of K £5 million. Other directorships held by Rubia were in banking, breweries, hotels (Block Hotel Ltd), insurance, milling companies including the huge Kenya National Mills Ltd, Unga Millers Ltd, and Riziki Ltd. Rubia chaired the Development Finance Company of

Kenya Ltd., which gave loans to large Kenyan companies, and Kenya National Properties, Ltd, which lent funds for construction.[80]

R. S. Alexander was chairman of Kenya Oil Co., Ltd, the main distributor for Caltex Oil (Kenya) Ltd. Sir Charles Markham was a director of Kenya Hotels Ltd, partly owned by Block Hotels Ltd, the largest hotel concern in Kenya, and chaired by Jack Block. Another New Kenya Group member, E. T. Jones, was a director of East African Oxygen Ltd (wholly-owned by British Oxygen Co., Ltd, ranked forty-third in '*The Times* 300' largest companies in England) and of the East African Power and Lighting Co., Ltd and the Kenya Power Co., Ltd. Jones was also chairman of Fitzgerald Baynes and Company, Ltd, holding the franchise for the bottling and selling of Pepsi-Cola and Canada Dry. Both Blundell and Slade served as directors of Fitzgerald Baynes. F. W. G. Bompas was a director of City Brewery Ltd., and of a furniture company. Musa Amalemba held three directorships in the Unga-Riziki Group of millers of East Africa, was a director in the City Brewery Ltd, and presently heads the Kenya Farmers Association (Cooperative) Ltd, which markets nearly all of the Kenyan large-farm grain crop.[81]

Although the owner of a mixed farm near Nakuru, Blundell's major concern had been in government service, and increasingly he became connected with multi-national corporations. By the end of 1967 he held directorships in fourteen companies operating in East Africa, twelve of these in Kenya. The major ones were associated with the English-based Ind Coope Group with which he was allied through his chairmanship of East African Breweries Ltd and Allsopps (E.A.) Ltd, and directorships of Ind Coope Ltd, and Ind Coope African Investments Ltd. The East African Breweries, Ltd, with capital employed of over £9 million, was in 1967 East Africa's largest locally-owned company. The Ind Coope Group in the United Kingdom owned about thirteen per cent of East African Breweries shares.[82] Besides these interests Blundell served as chairman of Saccone and Speed Ltd, the wine merchants, associated with Courage, Barclay and Simonds Ltd, rated fifty-seventh in '*The Times* 300'. Blundell was also a local director of Barclays Bank, the largest bank in Kenya, and the one which the New Kenya Group used.[83]

When Blundell resigned his chairmanship of a subsidiary of East African Breweries Ltd, Allsopps (E.A.) Ltd, in May 1961, to take over the Ministry of Agriculture, it was with the understanding that he would resume the position when his appointment as Minister terminated.[84] Ind Coope had been a major financial backer of Blundell's political career. A number of New Kenya Group members were later associated with the giant brewers.[85] Funding from Ind Coope had been solicited by Lord Howick (former Governor Baring), head of the Commonwealth Development Corporation, and Blundell for use by Kenya African Democratic Union (KADU). Many of the funds coming to Blundell from overseas were channeled through a non-profit educational institution called the Progress Foundation.[86]

The Progress Foundation for Economic Development in Eastern Africa was founded in 1961 by The Earl of Portsmouth, with Mrs Dorothy Hughes serving as Executive Director. It was established as a non-political body to promote the study of economic development and the training of Africans in the field. The Foundation set out a program requiring £75,000 over three years. At its inauguration Iain Macleod, British Secretary of State, sent Lord Portsmouth a letter publicly endorsing the Foundation as a 'particularly welcome' non-political, multi-racial step encouraging economic research and training in Kenya. Among the blue-ribboned list of sponsors were: His Highness the Aga Khan; Lord Colyton, Chairman of the Joint East and Central African Board; Lord Howick, Governor of Kenya 1952–9; Elspeth Huxley, author; Justice Madan, Judge of the High Court, Kenya; R. E. M. Mayne, Company Director, Caltex, Ltd (a financial backer of Blundell's); James Gichuru, former President of KANU; Dr Julius Kiano, Tom Mboya, Masinde Muliro and Charles Njonjo (the last five were all ministers in post-independent Kenyan governments). Members of the New Kenya Group listed as sponsors, besides Hughes, included W. Havelock, C. B. Madan, K. Bechgaard, Musa Amalemba, C. W. Rubia and Sir Philip Rogers, the last two being members of the New Kenya Group Finance Committee. Lord Portsmouth himself was closely associated with the New Kenya Group and attended a meeting of the New Kenya Parliamentary Group on October 25, 1960, apparently as a member.[87]

Contributors to the liberal cause besides Ind Coope included wealthy British–South African interests (£10,000 to both the New Kenya Group and Kenya African Democratic Union), members of the Ottoman Bank Ltd, and Caltex Oil (Kenya) Ltd. The British Standard Portland Cement Company, whose Bamburi Portland Cement Company was the fifth largest public company in Kenya in 1968, gave £500 to the New Kenya Group coffers in 1960.[88] In July, 1960, Blundell met in London with twelve unnamed major financial interests in East Africa to ask them 'for substantial sums for our campaign.' He also planned to go to Rhodesia, apparently for similar purposes, but the delicate political situation prevented it. In late 1961, Roy Welensky, the Premier of the Central African Federation, wrote Blundell a 'Dear Michael' letter citing his own limited finances and regretfully turning down Blundell's request for assistance.[89]

As important as the commercial financial backing for the liberal efforts was the access the New Kenya Group leaders had to the governing class in colonial and English politics. Michael Blundell was again the key figure in this. During Mau Mau Blundell was informed of who the new military commander in Kenya was to be before the Governor himself, because Blundell had been at Wellington College with the man to be appointed.[90] When Sir Patrick Renison was appointed Governor, Secretary of State Lennox-Boyd wrote Blundell to say that he hoped they would get on, adding, 'I regard this as absolutely essential for so much of our confidence in Kenya's future lies in our trust and admiration for you.'[91]

Governor Baring, upon his resignation, referred to Blundell as his 'great standby and advisor' and thought that Macleod, Renison and Blundell would be a 'first class team of three.'[92] Although relations with Iain Macleod were probably not as close as with Lennox-Boyd, they were sufficient to merit a handwritten 'My dear Michael' letter congratulating him on his election in March, 1961.[93] Blundell also had social connections with the Royal family. A November 17, 1961, letter from Lord Boyd (formerly Lennox-Boyd) said how pleased the Queen Mother was to speak with Blundell, and that he should contact her when next in England.[94]

Other members of the New Kenya Group had various ties to circles in both the British and Kenyan governments. Rhoderick Macleod, the younger brother of the Colonial Secretary, and perhaps the major political strategist of the Group, was the most obvious. But almost all the key members of the group were members of the Legislative Council and Wilfred Havelock and Bruce McKenzie held key ministries during the early 1960s. When Dorothy Hughes went to the United States in 1959 attempting to counter Tom Mboya's successful trips, she took with her a personal note of introduction from Governor Baring to the British Ambassador in Washington. Hughes had gone to the United States with her own entrée to the Roman Catholic hierarchy, which apparently wished to draw attention to the threat of communism in nationalism and also to highlight the nationalists' inclination to ignore women's rights.[95]

CONCLUSION: THE FIRST LANCASTER HOUSE COMMENCEMENT

By mid-1960 the European community was divided into two fairly distinct groupings. The conservative grouping, representing the majority of the community, was composed largely of rural farming interests. The conservatives' bargaining resources rested for the most part on their mass-based membership and on the access they had to important right-wing groups in England. The political and economic trends during colonial Kenya gave their subsequent lobbying activities the flavor of an embattled rear-guard movement.

The liberals organized around a core of moderate European politicians in the New Kenya Group. Lacking the conservatives' popularity in the community, the liberals used their commercial backing and close connections in government to pursue their political objectives. Supported by less-threatened transnational corporate interests they could pursue more flexible policies and alignments during colonial transition.

The First Lancaster House Conference in January 1960 brought the conflicts between the groupings to the foreground. The Conference was called by the new Colonial Secretary, Iain Macleod, to devise a new constitution for Kenya. (It would be the third in seven years, with the last one having been hampered by the nationalists' boycott of the Legislative Council.) Lancaster House followed by a few months the ending of the Mau Mau Emergency and the Government's introduction of legislation opening the 'White Highlands' to non-Europeans. The delegates met as the British Prime Minister was traveling through Africa, noting in speeches the 'winds of change' blowing across the continent.

Invited to the Conference were all the elected members of the Legislative Council – Africans, Arabs, Asians and Europeans. The large numbers of New Kenya Group members (mainly Specially Elected Members) gave them an importance out of proportion to the Group's strength in Kenya and made them '. . . the key to the conference.'[96]

The basic issues dealt with by the delegates involved the composition of the Legislative Council and the franchise, the character of the executive, and the question of safeguards. Despite there being no agreement reached by the delegates on any of these matters, sufficient accommodation was produced (chiefly through informal meetings between Blundell and Ronald Ngala, leader of the African delegation) for Macleod to produce a final plan. In the Legislative Council there was to be an African majority. Of sixty-five seats in the Council, thirty-three were to be open (meaning direct African election). Twenty were reserved for minority communities to be selected in primary elections with those candidates receiving a percentage of the vote (later put at 25 per cent) to be selected on a common role. There were to be twelve Specially Elected Members (now called National Members) chosen by the elected members. The Governor retained the right to nominate members in order to produce a government·majority and there was no provision for a Chief Minister or responsible government. Franchise qualifications were significantly lowered.

The issue of safeguards remained unresolved by the Conference. Chiefly in the area of property rights, the Europeans demanded not only compensation for expropriation, but also a strict definition of the 'public purposes' for which the government could expropriate land. The Africans felt this was too restrictive, fearing that it would exclude programs of land reform. The Colonial Secretary's proposals were rather vague in this regard, leaving the Europeans unhappy and ushering in the subsequent bargaining over land.[97]

The decisions of the Conference appeared to be a momentous break in Kenyan history. Though the government was maintained as multi-racial, eventual African control was clear. The Africans had gained four ministries, a majority of elected members, and influence over the elections for the other seats. This meant that Kenya would evolve like its African neighbors toward an independent government under an African majority. As Tom Mboya later wrote: 'The five weeks of the Lancaster House Conference in January–February 1960 not only brought about the declaration we had sought, that Kenya was to be an African country; it also reversed the whole constitutional process.[98]

For the Europeans, including the liberals who reluctantly agreed to the proposals, the Conference was, as one delegate remarked, 'a bombshell.' Future differences between the conservatives and liberals were presaged by remarks of their leaders immediately following the Conference. Michael Blundell was quoted as saying: 'There remains a challenge and a revolution in our thinking which we have got to make in our country on our return. I am certain that together we can meet that challenge and achieve that revolution in our thinking and make a success of our country.' Group Captain L. R. Briggs, leader of the right-wing United Party, said simply: 'I regard the outcome of this conference as a death blow to the European community in Kenya.[99] What the Conference's 'constitutional reversal' was in fact to mean for the European groupings, their economic and political interests (including, most centrally, the land issue), remained for the subsequent period of bargaining to resolve.

CHAPTER 3

1960, INITIATING THE BARGAIN:
THE LOBBYING ON THE LAND
ISSUE AND THE DIVIDING OF
THE EUROPEAN COMMUNITY

Factions arise when the environment provides some new kind of political resource which existing groups cannot exploit.

Lucy Mair

Man is a political animal only by education; he is a racial animal by birth.

H. V. Hodson

When someone steals your ox, it is killed and roasted and eaten. One can forget. When someone steals your land, especially if nearby, one can never forget. It is always there . . .

Ex Senior-Chief Koinange

In the aftermath of the First Lancaster House Conference the European community tentatively attempted to reorganize itself and reformulate its policies. All the groups involved appeared to have underestimated the effects of the Conference in establishing African majority rule. Michael Blundell was told by high British officials that independence remained a decade away, and remarked in May 1960 that independence was much further off than most people thought.[1] Iain Macleod later attested to his surprise at how rapidly Kenya had obtained independence. The leaders of the New Kenya Group three months after the Conference expected to be able to win the coming election and dominate the interim government. The nationalists, as witnessed by their concentration on rapid devolution, still expected the colonial government to pull the rug from under them. The thoroughly disillusioned conservatives, who found their worst fears realized, were closest to the mark in foreseeing Britain's rapid transfer of colonial authority.

Willingly or not, the European groups were drawn into centering attention on the issue most perplexing to their community – the fate of the European Highlands. The farmers' groups followed the traditional channels in seeking British guarantees for their land holdings. Their lobbying missions to London, as a number of farmer leaders remarked, were also symbolic attempts to reassure worried members that their groups could still act effectively. The liberals, using their access to colonial governing circles, backed limited land settlement as supportive of their efforts to bolster European confidence and to integrate middle-level Africans into the Highlands.

46

'Non-political,' primarily economic, arguments were used by all the groups in support of their land proposals. Attempts to remove the land issue from partisan politics included the farmers' plan for trustees overseeing a fund for land, and the British government's attempt to involve commercial and international money in any land scheme. The British hoped that international sources of money, notably the World Bank, would lessen the cost to HMG, while the farmers argued that these funds would also lessen the threat of expropriation. Liberal Europeans, arguing for limited settlements in the Highlands and economic development of the African areas to lessen the attention given to European holdings, did not as yet feel the need to reduce their political activities. They financially and politically backed the moderate African party (KADU) and retained their own key positions in the government.

In 1960 the groups divided most crucially on the question of how the community should be organized. The conservatives encapsulated the mood of the majority of Europeans in seeking to reunite the community as a racial unit pushing 'European' issues. The feeling of betrayal and of an increasingly hostile environment gave the conservative groups a popular backing the liberals could not match. Instead the liberals used their political influence, finances and expertise to maintain ties with like-minded African nationalists and colonial officials. They hoped to use these sources of strength outside the community to neutralize opposition within it. At the same time the liberals sought to move Europeans away from political introversion to positions reinforcing multi-racial policies in the decolonizing state.

FARMERS' INITIAL LOBBYING ON THE LAND ISSUE

The Kenya National Farmers Union initiative

With the ending of the First Lancaster House Conference on February 22, 1960, without a clear resolution on safeguards for European landholdings being adopted, the KNFU felt that it must make a direct representation to Her Majesty's Government. After African majority rule appeared an accepted outcome of the Conference, and while the delegates remained 'land-locked' over safeguards, the leadership of the Union sought to seize the initiative on the issue. The KNFU president, Mr Peter D. Marrian, later to be a member of the Legislative Council and a Minister in the first KANU government, on February 11 backed the liberal European line with two suggestions. He called for a Bill of Rights guaranteed by HMG to remove farmers' anxiety and to insulate any future government from a possible irresponsible opposition. He also suggested setting up a finance pool to ensure a market for land and as a means for financing future development. At the same time he opposed compensation as defeatist and unwarranted.[2]

At a meeting on March 10, the KNFU Executive Committee followed the lead shown by the President and the President's Committee. The Executive Committee unanimously agreed on three main points which provided in the words of the Annual Report six months later '. . . the basis of the KNFU activity since the Lancaster House Conference.'[3] These points were:

(a) European farmers' anxiety as to the future of land values could lead to forced sales, a slump in land values, a slowing down of development, subsistence farming, monoculture and the collapse of the economy.
(b) Confidence that land values would remain stable, both pre-independence and post-independence, would enable the normal business of farming to continue – the European farmer being assured that, if he ever wished to sell for *any* reason, he would be able to do so at a fair and reasonable price.
(c) This could be achieved by HMG guaranteeing a line of credit over a period of years, in the hands of trustees separate from the Kenya Government, for the purpose of purchasing land at a fair price.[4]

These points were incorporated in the plan presented by the farmers' union to the Secretary of State for the Colonies in their April mission to London. Titled 'The Defence of Kenya's Economy,' the plan's stated goals were to allow those who wished to leave to do so with a reasonable return on their income; to permit European farmers to give the transition period ahead a fair trial; and to allow an orderly and controlled resettlement of all races, particularly Africans.[5]

The plan called for setting up a Land Trust Fund with financial backing guaranteed by HMG, spread over several years, and available for the resettlement of all races. In later versions of the plan finances were divided into two inter-related parts: development and stabilization. Development monies were to come from the World Bank, Commonwealth Development Corporation, and similar organizations, while the British government was to provide the funds for stabilization/purchase.[6] The quantity of money needed went unstated but earlier drafts, correspondence and public statements made clear they were thinking in the neighborhood of £25 to £30 million. The leaders stressed that too little money would be worse than none at all. One farmer leader later expressed it as providing too few lifeboats for a ship in a storm. Inevitably a panic would result with everyone dashing for the available boats.[7] The purchase price was to be payable in sterling in any country at the seller's direction. The fund was to be given flexibility in restoring the market by being given money for not less than ten years with 'the amount allocated for any one year to be at the discretion of the trustees in the light of conditions prevailing at the time.'[8]

Control over the fund was clearly a key element in the plan. The fund was to be overseen by four trustees: three from the major Kenyan banks (Standard, Barclay's, and National and Grindlay's), and one from the Kenya government Treasury. Financial transactions were to be administered by an Agricultural Finance Corporation subject to control by the trustees. The fund, though locally administered, would be financed and controlled by those outside the Kenya government for fear that 'if any land purchasing fund was made subject to the control of the Government of Kenya it would fail to restore the confidence of the European farming community in the security of its land.'[9] The Union concluded that if HMG really believed that the new Constitution would bring the long term security and prosperity it claimed, then British funding of such a scheme would result in a healthy profit, as land was always in demand.

The Union's leaders were quick to dismiss the idea that their plan had anything to do with compensation. In a letter to an official of the Colonial Office, Marrian stressed the point: 'This is NOT compensation and I hate the word.'[10] He went on to say that if credit was sufficiently large it would not be used to any extent. In presentations after the London mission the plan was emphasized as a stabilization fund and not compensation. Not only would compensation be an admission of failure but it would involve sums up to £120 million – the estimated total capital investment in the European areas. Giving compensation to the farmers would also start a precedent for commerce and industry and for other countries, a thought which troubled British civil servants at the time.[11]

With these thoughts in mind President Marrian and Vice-President Lord Delamere visited England during the latter part of March and the first two weeks of April. The contacts they lobbied in government and business illustrated the farmers' access to influential sectors in Britain and the scope of the 'Old Boy' system. Some of these contacts within the government were the Colonial Secretary (once before he left for Central Africa); the Minister of State (Lord Perth) a number of times, two being formal meetings; the Permanent Secretary in the Colonial Office; the Economic Adviser to the Colonial Secretary; the Under Secretary for War. In Parliament Lord Delamere spoke in the Lords' debate on Kenya. He reported the atmosphere there was 'helpful' and noted the degree of support from Labour Lords. Also contacted were the 1922 Committee whose chairman undertook to approach the Prime Minister, the Commonwealth Affairs Committee, sundry unmentioned members of the Opposition who were reported as favorable, the Fabian Commonwealth Bureau, the Conservative Commonwealth Council, the Conservative Research Committee, and the Committee for Racial Cooperation in Kenya.[12]

On the commercial, agricultural and financial side, the English National Farmers' Union gave full secretarial help and the advice of its senior staff. Other business contacts included the Federation of British Industries, Sir Percival Griffiths, Chairman of the India, Pakistan and Burma Board, the Colonial Development Corporation, the Vice-President of the World Bank, the President of Barclay's Bank. Also spoken with were Mr Bernard Braine, MP and Chairman of the British Commonwealth Producers' Organization, and Mr Philip Broadbent, Secretary of BCPO and the Joint East and Central Africa Board. The media was involved with Lord Delamere having been, prior to the visit, in 'direct touch' with one of the directors of *The Times*. Delamere carried with him a letter of introduction to Sir William Haley, editor of *The Times*. (A long letter from Marrian was published in *The Times* during the visit.)[13]

At the time the mission was considered a fair success. A Leader (editorial) in the *East African Standard* stated that the mission had succeeded 'probably beyond even its own expectations.[14] President Marrian while declaring the mission only the first shot in the campaign pointed out HMG's acceptance of the principle that it had an obligation to protect immigrant capital and skill. Marrian reported that the British were convinced that European agriculture was the foundation of the Colony's economy and any loss of confidence would seriously endanger the economy and that 'it would be fatal to hand over a bankrupt state at the time of independence.'[15]

As for specifics, to wit: the British acceptance of the KNFU plan, here one senses a certain hollowness in Marrian's report. The £5 million mentioned in the White Paper was an earnest of HMG's intention – the same thing Macleod had said at the end of the Lancaster House Conference.[16] HMG recognized that it was necessary to involve international finance as quickly as possible, but until this occurred it was unwise to make any announcement. The British appreciated the urgency of the situation and hoped to have machinery set up, money available and the scheme operating, before the 1961 Kenya elections.[17]

In the months after Lancaster House, the British government was, in Lord Delamere's phrase, content 'to let things brew.'[18] Inexpensive verbal reassurances to the farmers were preferred to any drastic increase of funds into the unsettled Kenya scene. Hence high government officials attempted to molify in speeches their English 'kith 'n kin' who were angrily accusing HMG of abandonment. The Lord Chancellor, Viscount Kilmuir, at the East African Dinner Club, spoke of HMG as the largest investor in East Africa and remarked that 'we would not invest in a concern which we thought would crash.'[19]

HMG felt that by its actions it would not be able to stabilize land values in the post-independence period. After hedging throughout 1960, Macleod remarked publicly along these lines in an interview in the *Financial Times* in early 1961. Questioned on the British government's refusal to guarantee land titles, he replied, 'The titles are of course fully secured up to independence. However, independence means independence, and it is no good guaranteeing things if you cannot implement those guarantees – should that ever be necessary.'[20] The KNFU countered this with an argument to be widely employed by liberal Europeans – the possible use of international leverages to constrict national policies:

The K.N.F.U. thinks that this [stabilizing post-independent land values] is possible, so long as international finance is involved pre-independence, both in the source of supply and amongst the trustees. The flow of money will not only be stabilising land values: it will also be of vital use in the development of African agriculture. No government is likely to forego such a source of supply, in order to reduce land values by the arbitrary removal of price support.[21]

European unity. Both in the preparation and aftermath of the mission the officers of the KNFU were concerned to unite the various elements in Kenya European political life behind the Union's position or, failing that, to neutralize dissent. In a letter from London to his Executive Officer Alec Ward, the President worried that splinter groups would do much harm.[22] Ward wrote back warning him of the Convention of Associations trying to get into the act and the difficulty ahead of getting them all under 'the KNFU umbrella.'[23] At his first Executive Committee meeting after returning to Kenya, Marrian warned of imperiling the farmers' cause by uncoordinated efforts from small groups in Kenya. To deal with this the President's Committee had scheduled a series of meetings in the Highlands, before his return and without his knowledge, to get people to accept the KNFU handling of the economic effects of the Constitutional Conference.[24]

The Union had already initiated this effort prior to the London visit. Political leaders of the right-wing United Party, Majors Day and Roberts, and Michael Blundell of the NKG supported the Union's brief. Letters of support were received from commerce, banking and industrial groups in East Africa. They were not as strong as hoped for because, it was felt, of political pressures on industry structured on an East African basis.[25] Two letters from the President of the Nakuru and District Chamber of Commerce, Industry and Agriculture were examples of the commercial groups' lukewarm support for the farmers, and hinted at future differences between the European economic sectors on the buy-out schemes. The first letter, clearly for the public record, supported the Union's efforts to restore confidence among European farmers. The second spelled out the objections of the Chamber of Commerce's management committee to the KNFU memo. Basically the committee criticized what they felt was an overemphasis on the farmers who wished to leave. The Chamber of Commerce felt that the emphasis should be on a fund for bolstering the economy rather than as a means for farmers to get out of Kenya 'which would be against the economic interests of the country.'[26]

KNFU apoliticism. To remain out of the growing intra-European fray and to gain support among liberals (and later moderate Africans), the KNFU leadership attempted to adhere to a non-political stance. They projected the Union as a non-political, non-racial body, although at the time there were only five Africans out of some two thousand members. The early attempts to divide political from non-political issues (i.e., guarantees against expropriation from market support) would eventually be dropped. The dynamics of the bargaining process as well as the memberships' own concerns made the division both artificial and counter-productive. 'Non-political' would come to mean non-partisan; the refusal to back political parties on issues other than agricultural ones. However, even this was to be belied by the close cooperation of the Union with the Kenya Coalition and Convention of Associations in representing the European community. Throughout the period apoliticism was a much heralded and often tortured position.

For their April mission the KNFU officers had attempted to project the Union in the broadest non-political light possible. In a letter to Colonial Secretary Iain Macleod, prior to the visit, Marrian stressed that his was a non-political organization with no party affiliation. Further, the Union's work was 'directed towards agriculture as a whole and has no sectional interest.'[27] The public relations firm handling the mission, Dunford, Hall and Partners, emphasized the centrality of this non-political, non-sectional approach.

It is important in all PR activity concerned with the KNFU mission to avoid any suggestion directly or by implication that the mission is concerned with compensation for European farmers. The theme must be pursued that the mission is representative of farmers of all kinds and of all races, that the mission and indeed the KNFU is entirely non-political and that the establishment of the fund is in the national interest.[28]

Apoliticism was designed to enhance the Union's bargaining position, not constrain it. The judgment on whether an issue or an activity was congenial with remaining non-political was rendered pragmatically. For example, the KNFU initially stated that Britain's responsibility for the European farmer was a political matter, therefore the Union should not deal with it. However their press statement at the start of the April mission went on to say that HMG should not permit political change to endanger a national economy 'to the detriment of all Kenya's peoples and in particular the Africans.'[29] Here political responsibility was the premise behind any economic action and it should be noted that the obtaining of HMG's declaration of responsibility was considered the great plus from the April mission.

Apoliticism was also useful in removing the Union from the bitter partisan fray within the European community. Lord Delamere, then President of the Union, issued a circular on the attitude of the Union to the forthcoming 1961 elections. The KNFU was a non-political body, he wrote, 'Therefore it must not give support or encouragement to any part, [*sic*] group or individual who are seeking election. Nor again must it be drawn into official comment on the various policy statements that already have been or will be issued.'[30] Most of the Union's leaders were closest to Blundell's efforts. The two vice-presidents regretfully informed him that due to their position in the Union they would not publicly ally with his campaign.[31] On the other hand, Peter Marrian in explaining his independent candidacy in the elections both used the Union's position as a motivation for running and a reason for not aligning with any group. When asked on a radio show 'Why are you standing as an Independent?' he replied 'Because as an immediate past KNFU President and as a candidate having the intention to project politically many of the economic aims of the Union I cannot give an allegiance to one party or another in view of the non-party status of the Union.'[32]

In private communication to Michael Blundell, Marrian voiced a political position which many Europeans were reaching. The Union's non-political stance was to be extended to the entire European community. European-dominated multi-racial political parties were out; their place must be taken by multi-racial economic organizations.

A European political front is not the correct method of ensuring European strength and influence. This should come through economic organizations (with if possible participation by other races where there is an identity of interest) i.e., Chambers of Commerce, Farmers' Union, Civil Servant Association, etc. Obtain the strength of unity at this level and project it through your political representatives. A European political front as such will get us nowhere.[33]

Similarly John Pollard, soon to be a vice-president and president of the Union, wrote to Blundell assuring him of support but adding:

I have a fear that by having European political parties in the Legislature at this stage every problem between ourselves and the Africans will tend to become a political issue and be magnified out of all proportion to its true importance. I strongly believe we could get much better (and quieter) settlements through our economic and industrial associations.[34]

This effort to lower the political visibility of the community, as well as their contested economic holdings, would become a repeated theme in European political maneuvers.

The Convention of Associations/Kenya Coalition join the effort

The Convention of Associations and the Kenya Coalition attempted to use the mantle of apoliticism for uniting the European community behind their efforts to secure the farmers' property. Because of their conservative leadership and their clear antagonism for the liberals, they met even less success than the Union. While their initial efforts to rally the community behind their leadership were partially achieved, liberal opposition eventually forced them into an explicitly partisan position which increasingly channeled them into fringe lobbyist activities.

At the time of the Union mission to London the conservatives supported the KNFU while hoping to bring it under the Convention/Coalition leadership. At a March 11 meeting of district chairmen the following resolution was unanimously adopted in support of the KNFU moves but with no mention of the mission:

That this Conference of Chairmen of Constituency and District Associations resolves that a scheme backed by considerable finance be inaugurated forthwith by Her Majesty's Government for the stabilization of land values in the Highlands over a period of years in order to minimize the extreme danger of economic disaster to the country as a whole and the ruin of the European farmers who have contributed so much to its development.[35]

At the meeting, besides a call for the Convention to act as a 'European Parliament' with a united European front on a non-party basis, voices were raised for British support of the farmers' holdings. The Chairman of the Convention, C. O. Oates, said that settlers could trust only cash safeguards from the British government, but growing sympathy in Britain for the farmers' position should not be alienated. Sir Ferdinand Cavendish-Bentinck thought that Britain must pay for the change in land policy and that the European community should also get ten years' security for schools and hospitals. He went on to say that self-government was at the most four years away and that talk of friendly contacts with African leaders was brain-washing.[36]

Although representatives of the liberal European wing were present at the meeting the organization was clearly dominated by the conservative element. And from the conservatives came numerous plans and strategies for preserving their economic interests from the perceived chaos ahead. A petition was circulated to all European farmers in support of British responsibility for European land. The KNFU did not officially back the petitition but Marrian supported the wording and said he would not hinder it.[37] There was also an effort to send a delegation of farmers to England to plead their case. This was privately derided and eventually postponed.[38] Criticisms of the KNFU efforts also came from the Right. Captain L. R. Briggs, former leader of the United Party, warned the KNFU not to be narrowed down to asking for certain amounts over a set period. Briggs apparently wanted the money supplied immediately.[39]

Under the leadership of the former speaker of the Legislative Council and European leader in the 1940s and 1950s, Sir Ferdinand Cavendish-Bentinck, the Coalition Party sought economic security for the European farmer in light of what Sir Ferdinand viewed as the British 'betrayal' at First Lancaster House.[40] In his statement on resigning from the Speakership he requested that the British government 'guarantees that those who wish to leave or whose land is expropriated shall receive just compensation, including adequate payment for disturbance.' In the aftermath of Lancaster House and the disgust in the farming community with HMG policies and liberal European support for these, the Coalition party appeared to be 'carrying all before it.'[41]

Under the chairmanship of Cavendish-Bentinck, the Coalition Land and Agricultural Economics Committee attempted to unite the European political groups behind a common land policy to be presented to HMG. The Committee chaired by Cavendish-Bentinck included representatives of the Convention (C. O. Oates), 'independent' members of Legislative Council (L. R. M. Welwood and Clive Salter), United Party (Major Day), and KNFU (Marrian and Delamere). Their meetings were held in the KNFU offices in Nakuru. The NKG was invited to send a representative but did not do so till near the last of the four meetings when Humphrey Slade attended, and was not represented on the delegation to London.

The committee position was essentially the same as the KNFU stand: security of land titles and support for land values by HMG, with compensation in case of land acquisition or other situations, such as a heavy tax, making farming impossible. Money was to be available for ten years at £ 3½ million per annum. One addition to the Union's plan was the call for full compensation to farmers for disturbance beyond the value of the land.[42] The committee also tied European support for Sessional Paper 10, opening the Highlands, to HMG's agreement to provide money for land stabilization.

The KNFU leadership was in a quandary over their relationship to the Coalition's land efforts. On the one hand, they were hesitant to give up their initiative and leadership on the land issue. On the other, Sir Ferdinand's predominant standing in the European community, as the traditional leader, and his espousal of a non-political approach to safeguarding the economy made some sort of accommodation necessary. Thus while working closely with the Coalition Committee the Union's leaders tried to draw lines between the two groups by detaching themselves formally from the mission.

In the Coalition's June mission to London Marrian was part of the Coalition delegation in all but name only. The KNFU president had expressed his fears of political involvement to the Coalition, hence the *modus operandi* of the visit was that the KNFU would remain aloof from the political aspects of the mission (title guarantees and compensation for expropriation). In the matter of land stabilization, the Union would deal as negotiators with 'full and unqualified support' from the delegation. This formal detachment of the Union was practical in two respects: 'This has all been very carefully arranged because it is known that the KNFU must keep right out of politics and also that CB's Delegation may not get as good a reception as the KNFU is now getting in London.'[43]

OPPOSITION TO THE FARMERS' LOBBYING

Opposition to the farmers' proposals arose from the liberal New Kenya Group, the Colonial government with which the Group was closely allied, and the African nationalists. At least in 1960 the conservative groups were able to check most of the public criticism from the liberals and government. At one point a *modus vivendi* was approached where on the issue of land the groups would pursue their own policies while not directly countering the others' activities. However the entrance of the conservative Kenya Coalition into the political arena to contest the forthcoming elections led to direct and acrimonious encounters between the groups. For their part, the nationalists split into two parties over the land issue and other conflicts in 1960. The split was aided by European liberals and illustrated the liberal strategy of dividing the opposition and coopting moderate Africans into their fold.

The New Kenya Group: principled opposition

The New Kenya Group's dilemma on land in 1960 was in resolving the contradiction that had from the time of the emergence of multi-racialism plagued liberal European politics in Kenya: How, on the one hand, to counter their right-wing critics and appeal to the European electorate, and, on the other, to maintain a non-racial posture, eschewing advantage for any particular community? The resolution of the land issue was to stand both as a monument to the success of their policy and as an epitaph for the Group.

The Lancaster House Conference had not been a very auspicious beginning for the Group's efforts to protect European land in the context of an African majority government. Michael Blundell outlined the Group's approach to land for the Conference at a special plenary meeting on February 27, 1960. Oriented to promoting constitutional safeguards to protect European land, Blundell viewed it as impossible to write a clause into a Bill of Rights precluding succeeding governments from nationalizing land. However, what could be done was to insist on the sanctity of all individual property rights so that any such move would involve everyone's land. The crux of the problem was to prevent the use of power in a partisan or discriminatory manner.[44]

This approach had produced notably few results on the land question at the Conference. Probably because of nationalist hesitance to pre-commit an independent government, as well as desires for land in the Highlands, adding to the lack of any incentive for giving up a bargaining point, no statements on land were adopted by the Conference. A draft statement against 'any expropriation of private property in Kenya which was not manifestly just and reasonable' and proposing constitutional safeguards to that end never got anywhere. Nor did a proposal by the Colonial Office, which called in general terms for a more active African role in farming and encouraged the flow of overseas capital with more comprehensive schemes of agricultural development. This apparently died in the Committee on Safeguards.[45]

In a statement on May 5, the Group tried to counter the growing Coalition appeal. They dismissed compensation to those who wished to leave as 'inequitable, impractical and undesirable.' They stressed stabilization of land values through engendering confidence. This could be done by intensively developing the land in over-populated areas, gaining an influx of foreign capital (though the Group's 'considerable influence overseas') for this resettlement of undeveloped land, and providing a Bill of Rights to limit expropriation. They emphasized international leverages, remarking that 'the moral influence of civilized nations upon newly independent countries will grow as modern conditions, especially in the economic sphere where international investment exists, force all nations to recognize their interdependence.'[46]

Other statements of the Group more directly aimed at solving the land problem. In one paper the Group pointed its program toward taking the question of land out of the emotional sphere and putting it in the perspective of an expanding economy based on private enterprise. Therefore, all resettlement must be on an economic basis with stringent control of subdivision. Expropriation was denounced as an 'insidious practice.' Titles should be generally respected with perhaps a case for reinvestigation of a few historical claims.[47] In a draft written at the end of May the Group called for the establishment of an authority to buy land in the Scheduled Areas. This authority, a forerunner of the Land Development and Settlement Board, was to consist of a majority of farmers from the Scheduled Areas. It was to use private and public funds to maintain an economic price for agricultural land, resettle Africans from overpopulated areas, and make better use of land. For these purposes 'very much more' funds wcre needed from HMG for purchasing land.

In a meeting on November 23, 1960, the NKG adopted a draft on land, the last part of which summarized their position. The five points of the summary read:

(a) We believe that *private enterprise* is the right instrument to develop land in the national interest.
(b) We advocate the *support of land values* by the purchase of farms in the settled areas, by the Land and Agricultural Settlement Board, for the creation of Yeoman Farmers, and pledge ourselves to do our utmost to secure the necessary finance.
(c) We advocate the greatest possible *development of agriculture* particularly in the African Land Units.
(d) We advocate the creation of schemes under proper administrative control for small holders to *relieve pressures* from the landless.
(e) We pledge ourselves to whatever measures may be required to *secure land titles*.[48]

This broadly liberal policy of preserving the European farming system and integrating Africans into it with minimal disruption and conflict of interests was part of the Party's general philosophy of Kenya society. In a memo written for the New Kenya Parliamentary Group (probably by Rhoderick Macleod) on May 23, 1960, the Group's leadership sketched out its position. First the memo distinguished between principles – 'matters of belief;' policies – 'matters for argument or advocacy;' and programs – 'matters for tactical maneuver.' It saw most of the political divisions coming from argument on the wrong level. In land, for instance, compensation, degree of subdivision and expropriation for public purposes were not points of principle. The real principles were sanctity of contract and the recognition of private property rights. This was not to argue that basic principles were accepted by everybody.

The plain fact is that there are people who do not subscribe to the belief that contracts should be honoured and private property respected. In Kenya, a pattern has emerged which transcends race, colour, tribe and creed. It is a purely political pattern, that of 'Left vs. Right' . . .

This pattern, present throughout the world, crystallized around an extreme left one-party government with public ownership and redistribution of national assets vs. the conservative belief in the rule of law and order, private enterprise and individual rights. This struggle might soon develop into a conflict in Kenya between the 'Haves and Have Nots,' with KANU the protagonist of the latter. It was therefore in the NKG's interest to allow more flexibility of tactics among its members and independents who accepted the principles and could form part of a coalition based on agreed principles. 'If the NKPG stands on Principles it would be possible for people who at present oppose us, both European and African, to subscribe to our principles and hence be pre-committed to a coalition against the Extreme Left Nationalistic neo-Communist front.'[49] This strategy was to evolve into close ties and support for KADU and other moderate nationalist leaders.

The Kenya Government: conflicted opposition

The Kenya government under a weak governor[50] followed policies at this time generally designed both to diminish conflict among the competing European groups and to reduce the cost of any solution of the vexing land question to the British government. These goals of policy often conflicted, due in no small part to the government's deference to influential members of the New Kenya Group.

Initially government leaders adopted a position of vague general support for the farmers' efforts to 'restore confidence' and 'protect the economy.' Then influential parts of the government (manned by liberal European Kenyans) moved to more direct opposition as they formulated their own land policies and as the political and economic consequences of the farmers' program became clearer. Finally, after bargaining and pressure from the farm groups, the government and the farmers tacitly agreed to pursue their own programs, each unhindered by the other. The uncertain response of the colonial government underlined both the conflicting pressures to which it was subjected and its own dearth of firm leadership.

Kenya's new Governor, Sir Patrick Renison, gave his blessings to the farmers' lobbying activities. In an interview with Marrian in early June, the Governor agreed in principle with the necessity for a land stabilization fund.

He went on to support the KNFU's lobbying attempts. As reported by Marrian to his Executive Committee, the Governor thought that 'whereas it might be difficult for the Kenya Government to obtain any further funds from HMG at present, the KNFU might be able to do so, and that he was prepared to support the KNFU mission and do all that he could to help it obtain its ends.'[51] Marrian had earlier stressed government cooperation in his public report on the April KNFU mission to London: 'We viewed our mission as complementary to that of the Ministers for Finance and Agriculture in that whereas their work lay in the actual negotiation of loans ours lay in creating a climate of opinion that would, over a period, ensure their success.'[52] Before the mission the Minister of Agriculture had privately acknowledged to the farmers the value of the mission.[53]

The warm feelings between the farmers and the Kenya government cooled abruptly when the Minister of Agriculture, Bruce McKenzie, introduced his limited plans for land settlement in the debate on the budget on May 11, 1960. Designed for high potential land in the Highlands, the program set a goal of settling between forty and fifty farmers during 1961 on farms of about fifty acres supported by government loans. The projects were to be economic, in the sense of having all the money coming from loans repayable from the profits made on more intensive farming of the under-developed land. The program was to be administered by a newly reconstituted European Agricultural Settlement Board consisting of a nominated chairman and government officials, six farmers from the Scheduled Areas (Europeans) and two farmers from the Non-Scheduled Areas (Africans). Financing for the program, running for three years through 1963, was to be £3.15 million from HMG for land purchase on condition that £1.5 million could be found each year from international financial sources for development of the schemes. Thus the Minister hoped at least £7.5 million would be available for closer settlement of the Highlands until the end of 1963.[54]

The Minister continued what looks in retrospect like a great overestimate of the economic goals and viability of the scheme by emphasizing the involvement of the private sector in settlement. The government, he said, was considering setting up the government-controlled Land Bank as an independent corporate body 'to help money revolve quicker.' This was to apply in two foreseeable instances. First, when commercial firms and finance houses, under the aegis of the Settlement Board, wished to buy farms on offer and submit subdivisional and development plans for the approval of the Board. And second, when individual farmers wished to operate a subdivisional scheme with the approval of the Board leasing plots to tenant-purchasers. When the purchasers in the two cases had paid forty per cent of the price the Land Bank might take over the liability. He concluded that the development of the Highlands must be seen as only part of an overall plan for development of the colony as a whole.[55]

Several points can be made about the Minister's plans/wishes. The emphasis on economics had several functions. First, he was clearly selling something. To paint a picture of a project not only socially beneficial but economically profitable would increase the attraction to donors public and private, local and international. Secondly, the heat generated from European settlers was already being felt and that from the Africans expected. Cloaking a policy in the sanctity of economic criteria was an attempt to remove it and its administrators from the political fray. Also at this time World Bank assistance was vital to the scheme's promotion, and the Bank insisted on 'non-racial' and 'developmental' characteristics. One could point out that at the £250 a year projected income for the plots it was doubtful that there would be many non-African takers. Also the constitution of the proposed board, with six farmers from the Scheduled Areas and a chairman (who was to be a European farm leader), and two Africans out of twelve members was clearly not non-racial. Rather, it continued the traditional European tactic of maintaining control on administrative levels of political initiatives which might run counter to their interests.[56]

At the close of his speech to the Legislative Council the Minister seemed to go out of his way to throw cold water on the farmers' lobbying activities. He described the farmers' proposals as having the 'taint of compensation' about them. The £30 million (of which the Minister declared he had no idea where it would come from) spent on buying out twenty-five per cent of the Highlands would be a great drain on the national economy and mean suffering for those who stayed. He declared that the economy and society were sound, and that land was likely to double in value in the next five years. He took a hard line in speaking of the exaggerated fears in the farming community, saying: 'If any of the farming community want to leave now, that is their affair and it is up to them to find buyers for their farms.'[57]

The Farmers' Union was quick to take up the gauntlet. In a speech to the KNFU Council, Marrian voiced his 'deep sense of shock' in the government's destroying the KNFU's stabilization plan. He saw the plan as inadequate from the European farmers' view in that it was limited to high quality land growing cash crops (coffee, tea, pyrethrum, or twelve bags plus of maize an acre), and asked: 'Where do the owners of poorer land go?' It was also inadequate to the larger African farmer by confining him to fifty acres. Marrian criticized the Minister for the lack of a trustee obligation in his statement, and thought the lack of any broad responsibility to protect the economy (meaning an obligation to buy land) risked a panic. He denied that stabilization could be equated with compensation. Compensation, he said, involved the arbitrary buying out of land to its total extent, while the KNFU plan was merely an attempt to recreate a healthy market. (An admittedly fine distinction in a situation of no-confidence – just buying from those who *wish* to sell.) Marrian was also disappointed by the small amount of money involved. He concluded in rather self-righteous tones: 'We ask for the bread of understanding and he has offered us the stone of sterile comfortless disdain.'[58]

The Minister came in for criticism from a variety of other groups such as the Convention of Associations which threatened him with a vote of no confidence; the *East African Standard*, which declared the plan inadequate in scope and planning; and the Nairobi Indian Chamber of Commerce, which saw the scheme as much too insignificant in the present context.[59]

The farmers also made their voices heard in high government circles. They quickly got an appointment to see the Governor on May 17. The Union officials were already angry at not being shown the case the Minister of Agriculture had presented to London as the Governor had apparently promised.[60] The Governor, at the meeting, took the tack that there was not much difference between the Minister's plan and that of the KNFU. The impression given to the Union delegation was that the Governor had been too busy to give a great deal of study to the land issue and that he was not familiar with the mechanics of the plan. And in a memorable phrase, Governor Renison declared: 'I have left all these details to Bruce.' This delegation of authority was at least one strand of policy which both pre-independent and post-independent Kenyan leaders consistently followed on land.[61]

On May 25, however, Marrian and McKenzie had a meeting termed fairly satisfactory by the Executive Officer writing to Lord Delamere in England. McKenzie was said to have left active opposition to the farmers' plan but was not yet prepared to openly support KNFU proposals.[62] The government did appear at this time to have moved to more active support of the farmers' position. The Havelock and McKenzie mission to London on June 19, while publicly designed to discuss financing of land matters, was really intended, so farmers were told, to get definite assurance from HMG on the validity of land titles. The ministers sought to have this backed by HMG accepting financial responsibility if expropriation occurred under a future independent African government. At a meeting of the Board of Agriculture (Scheduled Areas), Havelock said he would not be prepared to pilot S.P.10 (the bill opening the Highlands) through Legislative Council unless he got solid assurance on land titles, backed by financial guarantees. He promised to stress to the British government the importance of a five to six year breathing space before independence became a reality. This was in order to allow land settlement schemes time to develop and let some of the steam out of the boiling land kettle. While offering the fullest possible support to the Coalition and KNFU missions, Havelock would not specifically back the Union's plan, as he thought the Ministry of Agriculture's scheme was as much as his shortage of staff would allow.[63]

The African Nationalists: divided opposition

The African nationalists provided the third major focus of opposition to the farmers' plans for preserving their holdings. Although they were by far the most threatening to the farmers' position there were in fact few direct negotiations between them and the conservatives. In part this was simply due to the farmers' lack of personal contacts with the nationalists or with educated Africans at all. The conservative emphasis on traditional channels also played a role, as did the reluctance of some nationalists to have their militant credentials questioned by too much contact with the opposition. The liberals provided most of the links to the nationalists, and it was their policies for splitting the nationalists and aligning with the moderate factions which bore the most fruit in 1960.

Origins, supports and positions of KADU and KANU. The origins of the split in the nationalist movement in 1960 went back a number of years. Even before the First Lancaster House Conference there had been a clear '. . . disharmony between the patterns of urban- and rural-orientated nationalisms.'[64] The urban-oriented nationalist thrust centered in the Kikuyu and Luo tribal areas, and in the major urban area of Nairobi. It tended to be more militant and uncompromising than the rural grouping. The other nationalist pattern found the core of its African support in the rural Kalenjin, Abaluhya, Masai and Coastal areas. These ethnic groups were generally less affected by colonialism and were relative newcomers to the Kikuyu-initiated nationalist movements.

Two other factors exacerbated the split. One was that during the Emergency there had been a ban on all African political organizations and, after June 1955, African parties were confined to one district. This led to the creation of parties and factions along tribal lines. Secondly, the imprisonment of the widely acclaimed nationalist leader, Jomo Kenyatta, in 1952 for involvement in Mau Mau was to lead to the idolization of his legitimacy as leader while depriving the movement of his actual leadership. The militants' attempt to use Kenyatta as a symbol around which to build a mass movement also had the effect of intensifying the non-Kikuyu rural leaders' suspicions of that tribe's dominance.

After the first direct African elections for members of the Legislative Council in March 1957, the attempt was made to use LegCo as a national platform for coordinating and projecting the sundry nationalist impulses. However personality conflicts, varied ethnic interests, and the differing levels of political awareness proved too great. July 1959 saw the founding by the moderates of the initially multi-racial Kenya National Party. Among its leaders were Masinde Muliro, Ronald Ngala, Taita Towett and Daniel arap Moi, all later to be prominent in KADU. The militants responded in August with the Kenya Independence Movement. KIM was led by two Luos, Oginga Odinga and Tom Mboya, and a Kikuyu, Julius Kiano, all later KANU leaders. The need for unity at First Lancaster House resulted in the submerging of these parties and the presenting of a common nationalist front at the Conference.

The unity was short-lived. Allegations and rivalries surfaced again immediately after Lancaster House. Two conferences at Kiambu in March and May 1960 resulted in the formation of a party with Kikuyu and Luo dominating the top positions. James Gichuru, a Kikuyu associate of Kenyatta, was named Acting President; the feuding Odinga and Mboya were Vice President and General Secretary respectively; while the absent Ronald Ngala and arap Moi were relegated to Treasurer and Deputy Treasurer. Significantly the colors and symbols of the Kenya African National Union were those of the Kenya African Union, a militant Kikuyu political party headed by Kenyatta (and, after his arrest, by Gichuru), and banned as a front for Mau Mau.

A number of African political interests and personalities felt threatened by the formation of KANU and moved to form alliances to counter it. Arap Moi had a hand in the merger of four district parties into the Kalenjin Political Alliance. Electing in May not to join KANU the Alliance invited other 'gentle and well-behaved' Africans to join them in developing a national organization. Links were formed with Muliro's Kenya African People's Party (a skeleton of the former Kenya National Party), and with representatives of Masai, Somali and Coastal political associations (the latter led by Ngala). United in the opposition to Kikuyu–Luo domination these groups held a Conference at Ngong on June 25th to form the Kenya African Democratic Union (KADU). Ngala and Muliro became Leader and Deputy-Leader while the original ethnic groups continued to exist as affiliated units of the party.[65]

Throughout colonial transition the most important source of African support for both parties lay in the commitment of the major ethnic groupings to one or other of the parties. The pattern of African politics largely followed in the 1961 elections was of one-party tribes. In some cases the tribal commitment was made quite specifically as when leaders from the two Kamba districts of Machakos and Kitui met on the Yatta plateau, discussed which of the two parties the tribe should support, and opted for KANU. The basis of KANU's majority lay in the support of the Kikuyu, Embu and Meru, Kamba, Luo and Kisii, which represented sixty per cent of the African population. Neither of the parties was able to organize substantial followings in the tribal areas of the other party.

The differences in policy between the two parties were at least afterward considered minimal by the leaders. Both Mboya and Odinga felt that conflict over the distribution of power rather than basic policy differences separated the two. There were, however, four areas of policy disagreement in all of which KADU emphasized positions closer to those of its European allies and the colonial government than did KANU. First, KADU was willing to form a multi-racial government rather than a predominantly African one. Secondly, KADU did not demand Kenyatta's release prior to forming a government. The refusal of KANU to form a government until Kenyatta was released led to KADU entering the government on March 27, 1961 supported by the Governor's nomination of eleven members. Thirdly, KADU was in general less concerned with the return of the Highlands and appeared more anxious to preserve European holdings there. This was due not only to the European backing the party received, but also from KADU leaders' fears of Kikuyu expansion into the newly opened areas. A fourth policy difference, the preference for a regional rather than a unitary constitution, was later to be a major issue separating the two parties.[66]

The nationalist impulse, thus, swung between the poles of unity and division; the thrust toward one was countered by the pull of the other. Whether these divisions would have been concretized into separate political parties with the minority party holding power during much of the period without European aid, is problematic. From these fissures and uncertainties in the African ranks the liberal Europeans would profit. Their ability to coopt parts of the nationalist movement and to prevent the militants from mobilizing a mass following was to be the key to their influence during colonial transition.

Initial African policy on land. At Lancaster House the African delegates had appeared at least verbally united on a hard line policy on land hinting toward radical reforms in the Highlands. Nationalist leaders Dr Julius Kiano and Tom Mboya opposed any bill of rights designed to protect the White Highlands, the latter stating that any such bill must not be used to perpetuate land injustices. Ronald Ngala, leader of the African delegation, sounded exasperated with the subject toward the end of the conference: 'I do not see why the Conference should go any further in discussing the land interests of one race in particular.'[67]

In a strong statement on land issued by the African Elected Members, under Ngala's signature, the nationalist leaders declared that the African people had struggled for many years for 'extensive' land reforms in the Highlands; the African Elected Members' policy on land had not changed from this in any manner. There were 'injustices and economic inequalities embodied in the land alienation system now obtaining in Kenya. No true leaders of their people can close their eyes to such injustices and inequalities for the sake of pacifying the opposition.'[68]

While wishing to make it 'crystal clear' that they would 'always uncompromisingly uphold the property rights of any citizen irrespective of his race or national origin' the statement went on to make a distinction alarming to European farmers.

What we want to clarify is the fact that in the so-called White Highlands claims of land ownership and property rights are in dispute and have been in dispute since the establishment of white settlement in the territory of Kenya. The Bill of Rights that we have strongly proposed cannot be used to overlook the dispute. The Bill can only apply in the protection of property rights NOT in dispute. Disputed ownership cannot be given legal recognition without the issue being thoroughly examined and permanently settled.[69]

The last sentence seemed to provide an avenue of compromise not indicated by the tone of the rest of the statement. This populist tone was carried over in the statement's call for extensive resettlement of landless Africans as the nationalist leaders grabbed for the resettlement bait.

As regards resettlement of landless African families we are positively interested in HMG's offer to provide funds for this purpose. We advise the extensive resettlement of Africans to be initiated immediately. We also state that it is important for HMG to consult with us, the African leaders, in planning and execution of such resettlement schemes. When we can demonstrate to the African people that Government means business regarding this urgent problem of finding some land for the landless then this explosive issue of land will become less explosive and the people of Kenya can then go ahead with economic and agricultural development projects without the emotions and ethnic antagonism which now characterize the land question.[70]

In private discussions with African leaders, New Kenya Group leaders alluded to confusion in their Group concerning this statement and others by nationalist leaders on the land issue. Their questions shrewdly uncovered the contradictions and lack of clear policy in the African position. The nationalists were asked if all land in the Highlands was in disputed ownership, or parts. Ngala's statement of splitting up land too large for one owner was recalled.[71] He was asked whether this meant splitting up underdeveloped land or developed farms as well, and whether this would apply to large holdings outside the Highlands. The liberals inquired as to the African intentions for disposal of the land, a touchy question in tribal Kenya. Would the land be alienated to any particular tribe, or would it be available to any individual who would show need, or show that he could afford to buy it and work it? Answers to these questions were not always forthcoming.

The stand of the nationalists in the bargaining context was an attempt both to 'growl now, smile later' as Tom Mboya put it, and to avoid the trade-off being formulated in Nairobi and London of economic safeguards for constitutional advance. But the position was more tactically sound than politically secure. A 'wide rift' was reported among the African Elected Members by the Minister of Agriculture and Lands, Bruce McKenzie, who had spoken with them about land. At a meeting with several ministers (Finance, Legal Affairs, Agriculture and Lands) and a majority of African Elected Members (excluding Mboya) it was apparent that the nationalists had reached no agreement among themselves on the land question which they were to discuss. They seemed divided with the Kikuyu – Luo faction on one side, who wished for no action on land until independence, and the other tribes whose position was unclear to the ministers. McKenzie later opined to the farmers his view that many of the African Elected Members wished European agriculture to continue on a reasonable basis but would find it difficult to convince the electorate because of rash promises made in the past.[72] Similar views were passed on to a constituent by Marrian. He related the opinion of Taita Towett (a KADU leader) that no two African Elected Members thought alike on land, and that he and ole Tipsis (another member of KADU) were convinced that their respective tribes had stolen land from each other. Marrian drew this conclusion of the African attitudes:

I believe the silence is entirely due to this inability of the Africans to formulate a policy and my guess is that this uncertainty will last right up to the moment of independence. We are therefore working in the dark of ignorance of future intentions and have to try and make provison for every eventuality.[73]

The fissures in the nationalist movement leading to the formation of KANU and KADU were aided by these differing emphases on the land issue and European efforts to aid a more conciliatory African approach.

Liberal Cooptive Policies

The policy of returning the land to the Africans was becoming the problem of 'which Africans?' for the nationalists. The mutual suspicions, especially between the Kalenjin and Kikuyu tribal groupings, as to who would settle in the newly-opened Rift Valley areas were being concretized into political parties. Cherry Gertzel, a student of Kenyan nationalist politics, wrote:

It is difficult to avoid the conclusion that the fundamental source of the divisions within the nationalist movement in 1960 was the land question. Tribal interests were based upon land and thus upon essentially economic interests. The situation seemed to dictate an alliance between the Kalenjin in the Rift Valley and the people at the coast, all of whom were suspicious of the objectives of the Kikuyus and their allies. This alignment of tribal and economic interest was probably the single most important factor leading to the division of the nationalist movement into the Kenya African National Union (KANU) and Kenya African Democratic Union (KADU) in 1960.[74]

Gertzel also mentioned personality factors such as the political ambition of the KADU leaders, Ronald Ngala and Daniel arap Moi, as contributing motives for the split. George Bennett and Carl Rosberg emphasized 'tribal parochialism' as fundamental to this disunity and the absence of the jailed nationalist leader, Jomo Kenyatta, as hindering the emergence of a united leadership.[75] Y. P. Ghai and J. P. W. B. McAuslan as well as John Harbeson stressed the restriction of African political parties during the Emergency to only one district as enhancing divisions in the nationalist movement and leading to the split.[76]

Surprisingly, none of these authors mentioned the liberal European assistance for KADU which preserved and strengthened a rather tentative movement. On May 17, 1960, representative(s) of the NKG met with leaders of a federation of tribal parties intending to form the Kenya African Democratic Union (Towett, ole Tipsis, Masinde Muliro and Ngala). At the meeting the African leaders discussed their need for large funds, and what the NKG members viewed as their conservatively oriented policies. The NKG members felt that given the tribal groupings (Coastal, Wakamba, Masai, Abaluhya and Kalenjin) the land pressure was not so great among them.[77] It was felt that it might be possible to negotiate an agreement with the new organization on the basis of settling a number of specific land claims in return for a general recognition of title for the remainder of the Highlands.

The Africans opposed federation with the NKG before the election for fear of making KADU suspect as a European 'front.' However, close consultation in private at all times was welcomed. The Africans were seen by the liberals as needing encouragement and drive as well as money to bolster a happy-go-lucky attitude. However, their conservative policies, liberal leaders thought, enabled the NKG to find common ground on many subjects sufficient to justify an election truce and subsequent coalition. For these reasons the New Kenya Group leaders felt it was advantageous to finance KADU. This did not mean direct subsidies from Party funds, since that was considered politically unwise. Rather, the liberals would use their influence with private sources of money and sponsor payment to the African group.

The relationship of the NKG with KADU while not entirely clear continued to be more intimate than usually mentioned. The European members of NKG had little doubt about it. One liberal leader declared that KADU was started at the initiative of the NKG and it was only a matter of 'face' that kept them from joining KADU. Richard Slaughter, a member of NKG and treasurer of KADU, called KADU 'the child of the New Kenya Party' and saw it as the natural development of the liberal party.[78] Leslie Melville, the Executive Officer of the NKP, recalled doing the same work for KADU after the 1961 elections that he had done for the NKP. And he said that the central group of planners in the African party were arap Moi, Muliro, Ngala, Havelock, McKenzie, Blundell and R. Macleod (the last four being NKG members), with a shift in emphasis toward actual African control as independence approached.[79]

The contributions of the Europeans appeared to be mainly on the administrative and financial side. Wilfred Havelock saw it as a partnership in which the Europeans provided administrative, management, intellectual and financial resources.[80] Reginald Alexander, former mayor of Nairobi, stressed the contribution of administrative abilities, but as will be shown this ranged into the field of ideas, proposals and, frequently, the writing up of policy statements.[81]

Financing for KADU was not apparently the easiest of tasks. The difficulty of gaining funds from local Europeans derived from the settlers' views that KADU's leaders were 'too nice a sort of chaps' and in the end the Kikuyu would run the show. But funds were garnered from international sources, chiefly through liberals' ties with English businessmen having African interests.[82]

The Liberal–KADU alliance was thus fairly well-established by mid-1960. The affect of the alliance on the nationalists' position on the land issue was difficult to assess. Certainly KADU, fearing Kikuyu–Luo domination, composed of tribal groupings in which the repossession of European lands was not a pressing issue, and enjoying liberal support, could back moderate land reforms and play down land as an issue.

KANU's position on land became increasingly unclear in 1960. Earlier in the year, after the First Lancaster House Conference, both Tom Mboya and Oginga Odinga had strongly denounced the Colonial Government's land policy as an effort to tie the hands of a future independent government.[83] But a later KANU statement took an ambiguous stand toward the land reforms being proposed.[84] The fear of delaying independence as well as being replaced in a future government by KADU was already having its effect.

A CONFLICT JOINED

Summer and fall of 1960 brought the joining of the conflict between the competing European groups. Both in England and Kenya their simmering differences, chiefly on land policy, were to boil over causing public fissures. The liberals used their strong ties with the British government to counter the farmers' proposals. At the same time they sought to enhance their own policies through timely English backing of the limited land schemes. The conservatives responded to these efforts by formally detaching themselves from the liberals and converting the Kenya Coalition into a political party. Given the liberals' opposition and the conservatives' tendency to re-entrench, this move was almost inevitable. Nonetheless the split made the liberal position easier to maintain, with the liberals not having to worry about the accusation, or the burden, of representing 'Europeans.' It also weakened settler leverage in bargaining, thus easing the decolonization process and eventually leading to the isolation and political dismemberment of the European farming community.

London infighting

London in the summer of 1960 found most of the European leaders, official and non-official, pressing HMG one way or the other on the land issue.

Lord Delamere, the Union's vice-president, had spent May and June in London, both on personal matters and 'quietly prodding' influential people on Kenyan land matters. He reported to the Union his feeling that the time was ripe to force definite undertakings out of HMG.[85] Wherever Delamere got this impression it did not seem to have been from Iain Macleod. In a letter on his meeting with Macleod at the end of May, Delamere reported what appear as mostly banal reassurances. Macleod indicated that independence was not round the corner, that he very definitely had no intentions of releasing Kenyatta, and that Cavendish-Bentinck had made a good impression with HMG. Macleod made pleasant references to the farmers' plan, though British government proposals were still not definite.[86]

A month before, Macleod had been speaking to Blundell with a different emphasis. Macleod indicated to Blundell a stiffening of attitude toward release of Kenyatta and said that Governor Renison would shortly be making a strong statement to that effect.[87] Macleod assured Blundell he did not plan the slightest concession to Cavendish-Bentinck's group and stated there was no question of compensation for farmers. He stressed the need for a definite plan for resettlement and a specific sum of money. It was difficult to approach the Treasury with an intangible scheme based on farmers' fears. Blundell for his part declared that he and Bruce McKenzie had no sympathy for either compensation or Cavendish-Bentinck's disturbance allowance, and suggested instead the commitment of loan money for land development and resettlement.[88]

Neither the Colonial Secretary nor Blundell were adverse to making political capital from the schemes for the New Kenya Group. Macleod and Perth suggested that McKenzie's plan should be presented as New Kenya Group policy. Then the Group could secure money from HMG as a definite commitment so that the impact would hit the electorate about September or October. They were worried that an immediate assurance of capital would lose its effect by the time of the elections. This may have been another ingredient in what appeared to be British delaying tactics at this time.[89]

At the same time Blundell was voicing private doubts to Macleod and undercutting the Coalition's efforts, he publicly backed the KNFU activities. Using the KNFU's apolitical mantle he was able to back the Coalition's land policy without supporting the Coalition. In a public letter to Cavendish-Bentinck, Blundell supported the farmers' lobbying for definite assurances on land titles and more money for settlement, adding:

As I told you, since Lancaster House we have had discussions with the President and Officers of the KNFU and support them in their efforts to maintain land values. I have told the President that he has our strong backing in London when he returns there and I understand that you will equally be supporting and collaborating with him.[90]

Blundell's own hesitant backing of the farmers' proposals was reinforced by pressure from African members of the New Kenya Group who, KNFU leaders reported, only mildly supported the Union and were generally unwilling to back the Coalition.[91]

Although Blundell was in London at the time for a 'rest,' and refused to join the Coalition delegation in pressing HMG for more money, he and Cavendish-Bentinck did discuss with Macleod the lack of confidence existing in Kenya. Subsequently Macleod agreed to speak with certain representatives of tea and insurance firms having large interests in Kenya.[92]

The Coalition Delegation visited London in July in a repeat performance of the KNFU with diminished results. Marrian in his report showed the continuity of previous themes – and British reaction. The demand for £30 million was noted and turned aside by government officials. The British were very concerned about security of title and Marrian expected a statement shortly. However this security was more dependent on internal Kenyan politics than on a British guarantee 'which would involve her in a precedent that is unacceptable.' On financing African settlement and stabilizing land values, Marrian linked the two, expecting British financing to continue for as long as necessary to stabilize land. Finally, valuation based on impartial direction was still needed.[93]

Cavendish-Bentinck, in his report to the Convention, viewed his reception as very good. He found 'very senior' English politicians thinking that while plantations and large ranches would be safe, the small mixed farmer would be in for a difficult time. Cavendish-Bentinck said he was not clear on the reasons for this, but suggested that one reason might be the fear of farming and living surrounded by Africans.[94]

A more detached viewer was not as sanguine about the Delegation's success. The *East African Standard* correspondent in London viewed the Cavendish-Bentinck mission as having made three cardinal errors. The delegation was all-European from a multi-racial country. It was ill-timed. Finally, it failed to realize the extent of Conservative Party support for Macleod and Blundell.[95]

The British government's stance of watchful waiting continued through 1960 – and on. After committing themselves to the limited three year scheme the British opted to wait for international money to start flowing. In a letter to Marrian, Macleod made clear his desire to get other foreign capital: 'We will make £3.15 million of Exchequer Loans available (primarily for land purchase) under the present Colonial Development and Welfare Act if a suitable scheme or schemes [are] prepared which will attract international Bank Assistance.'[96] It would however be premature, he thought, to state before the scheme has been approved what measure of assistance would be provided. Though, Macleod added, that beyond the three year period 'I myself contemplate that, in one way or another, there will be continued assistance from Her Majesty's Government after that period and I would hope that the impact of the initial schemes would be sufficiently effective to encourage other authorities to continue assistance also.'[97] He concluded that the government had not yet finished their special study on security of titles.

Kenyan quarreling

The summer's armed truce between the liberal and conservative European groupings ended in the fall. Back-biting and undercutting between the groups erupted in the October 17 meeting of the Conference of the Convention of Associations. With Blundell present ('a rather lonely-looking figure . . .'[98]) Cavendish-Bentinck turned the main address, a report on the London mission, into an attack on his liberal antagonists. He complained of the NKG trying to undercut him in London, and referred to them as having been created by the Colonial government to split the Europeans much like HMG wished to split the Africans. Spelling out his differences with the NKG, Cavendish-Bentinck said it was no use pretending that Europeans and Africans were the same,. and that they would get on better if the differences were accepted. Presenting himself as a realist, he did not believe the Europeans could continue to play a major part in Kenya politics; they could only be an 'acerbation to politics.' The community could be influential if they would unite behind their own standards and traditions.[99]

Although the speech was to herald the Coalition's entrance into the political field, the emphasis was on economic goals. The Vice Chairman of the Convention, L. R. M. Welwood, in supporting the Coalition, remarked that political power would no longer be with the European, his force would be an economic one, and the battle to preserve this leverage was the one to be fought. The resolution adopted by the Conference supported the Coalition's efforts to 'enter the political sphere' in order 'to represent the economic interests of the country.'[100]

Cavendish-Bentinck was also at pains to deny the diehard reactionary label being flung at him by the liberal politicians and press. In his May speech to the Convention he declared his acceptance of an African majority in Legislative Council and inevitable independence. He also said privately that he accepted the Lancaster House Constitution but was constrained by right-wing influence in the Coalition. Nonetheless, the effects of independence on the economy and immigrant communities must be considered, hence European initiative within the present political context must be restored.

The essential difference between the liberals and conservative Europeans was one of strategy rather than goals. Both agreed on the overriding necessity for preserving the economic assets and system of colonial Kenya. The liberals more ambitiously saw this as occurring through a realignment of the Kenya polity from a racial division to a class one. The Coalition's effort at re-entrenchment was a thrust to the heart of this policy. In an earlier reply as to why the NKG would not support the Coalition's efforts on land, Blun-

71

dell said that the General Election would be fought between two ideas – the redistribution of wealth by force vs. the security of private enterprise and property through the maintenance of law and order. The conflict between the two groups representing those ideas was already forming and it was up to Europeans, he said, to see that those Africans who supported a European way of life won that battle. The Coalition did not have a wide enough base to draw the have-nots into the camp of those favoring private enterprise and personal freedom. And Blundell worried that concentration on the land issue would lead to European isolation from the majority of Africans with exactly the same view on land.[101]

The Coalition, for its part, was seeking to maintain Europeans by re-entrenching along racial lines. The realignment called for by the liberals was seen as a threat to both the racial and class position, which were in reality identical. The liberals were derided as idealists who would attempt an alteration in Kenya society which had not occurred in the past sixty years within the limited period of colonial transition. European unity in a threatening environment had a powerful attraction which the class appeal of the liberals never emotionally equalled.

The two parties' initial positions on land illustrated well the differences between them. Both emphasized that their policies were designed to maintain the European presence in Kenya. Cavendish-Bentinck in his October report said, 'My policy is to try and keep people here, just the same as anyone else's policy, but keep them here under conditions that are not only tolerable, but are much the same as they have been used to in the past.'[102] To do this Cavendish-Bentinck wished to maintain the traditional colonial ties supportive of the European economic interests. He worried that the British were going 'to go the whole hog as soon as possible' (independence) in the hope that big business would come into the arena and assist with the economic difficulties. Cavendish-Bentinck did not wish to wait for what was handed out but rather to press for an adequate sum for compensation.[103]

Blundell and the NKG were unwilling adherents to the farmers' efforts to insure their assets. Although they publicly got on the bandwagon, it was likely from political necessity rather than conviction. Even today Wilfred Havelock views land transfer as a 'sop' to the European farmers who pressed for it.[104] Blundell at the time was urging Europeans to forget about compensation and seize the initiative by aligning with the other races. He favored development of the African areas rather than underwriting in the Highlands in order to gain security of title for the settlers. He was willing to forego the immediate interests of his own racial group in order to preserve the greater system. As related by Major Roberts of the United Party, Blundell had supported to senior British officials at Lancaster House the small stabilization scheme of £5 million rather than the £30 million two British government experts said was needed. Blundell declared he wanted to make it as *difficult* as possible for any European to leave Kenya.

The story was told at the October meeting of the Convention of Associations with Blundell present. It was not refuted by him.[105]

CONCLUSION

The hostility of the European farming community in 1960, mainly toward European liberals and the British government, eventually flowed into a broad rather inchoate policy perspective. This was the emphasis on traditional channels and symbols to rebuild the community's ebbing political strength. Politics and divisiveness (the two usually being equated) were to be eschewed. Economic rationality alone dictated unification around the farmers' interests. Not surprisingly, attention focused on London, with emphasis on past pledges and loyalty to 'one's own kind.'

The liberal policy to move the Europeans into broader class alignments went directly against this reaction, and their isolation from the community in the months after the First Lancaster House Conference was manifest. Liberals in the New Kenya Group used bargaining resources outside the farming community to pursue their policies. Access to British governing circles was employed to covertly undercut the farmers' lobbying efforts and gain support for liberal programs. Liberal funds and expertise enabled the Group to establish links with like-minded Africans and stabilize KADU as a moderate alternative to KANU.

The division of the Kenya Europeans into competing political parties, although initiated by the conservatives, was to eventually prove their undoing. Behind the conservative thrust toward re-entrenchment lay another perspective, the consequences of which would become clearer in the following two years. The emphasis on discontinuity was implicit in the importance given to traditional channels and symbols. Stressing British obligations and past actions in Kenya ran directly counter to the process of devolving responsibility on to the nationalist inheritors of the colonial system. In this respect the conservative arguments paralleled the militant nationalist ones: Both groups, toward their own goals, aimed at detaching the independent state from these colonial obligations. Both faced isolation from the process of decolonization because of this, and the later political demise of both reflected the strength of the interests they unsuccessfully challenged.

APPENDIX: THE FARMING ENVIRONMENT (1960)

The widespread pessimism toward the future in the farming community reflected by their representatives was manifesting itself chiefly verbally and by inaction in 1960. In March 1960, the KNFU was receiving letters from members offering their farms for sale. Advice to 'mine' farms – to let the permanent capital improvements (i.e., buildings) run down and only look for investments with a special high rate of return (i.e., more cattle) could be heard. One typical letter from a Molo farmer to the Union began, 'Sir, I have six children and can see no future for them in this country.'[106] In December a KNFU area branch in Western Kenya reported a number of farms were likely to be abandoned after the harvest. The *Standard* reported over forty families, nearly all Afrikaners, in Uasin Gishu had decided to leave but that other farmers in the area were buying up the land.[107] With the influx of Congolese refugees in the summer of 1960 carrying baggages of atrocity stories the climate of opinion darkened. Farmers were reported to have formed self-defense groups in Trans-Nzoia and Uasin Gishu.

Economically a turn-down was evident. The Colonial Office Report on Kenya for 1960 stated: 'Development on farms in the European areas has virtually ceased, except for those projects ensuring an immediate and foreseeable return. . .'[108] An indication of this running down was the report of one European garage in September that it had not sold a single agricultural implement between Nanyuki and Thomson Falls since Lancaster House.[109] Schemes, some a bit harebrained, were afoot to settle farmers in Latin America, and to set up an East African Pioneering Society which would manage existing farms, Africanize the staff and buy land in other countries for the sellers. That sufficient money could be raised within Kenya was the rather crucial assumption.[110] Yet in 1960 there was no significant exodus of people. The *East African Standard* reported early in 1961 that actually more people had emigrated from Kenya in the first three quarters of 1959 than in the same period in 1960. In that period in 1960, January through September, 4,788 Europeans arrived and 4,398 left, resulting in a net gain of 390.[111]

1961, NEGOTIATING THE BARGAIN: ACCELERATING THE BARGAINING, DEEPENING THE DIVISIONS

Every white man in Nairobi is a politician; and most of them are leaders of parties.

Winston Churchill, *My African Journey*

We have met the enemy and they is us.

Pogo (Walt Kelly's cartoon character)

The differing political strategies of the conservatives and liberals (racial re-entrenchment vs. class alignment) led to increasingly divergent political activities in 1961. The conservatives, stressing the preservation of the settlers' assets, found themselves channeled into lobbying on land rather than bargaining on broader political issues. The failure of most conservative candidates to win office in the spring elections further encouraged the narrowing of the farmers' efforts.

The liberals, while privately obstructing the farmers' lobbying, focused their attention on consolidating KADU moderates in government. The land issue was seen by the liberals both as an annoying diversion from their strategy of realigning the political structure and as a problem best solved by retaining their African allies in power. Consequently in the May 1961 discussions with the Colonial Office, New Kenya Group members argued for land transfers as a means of stabilizing the KADU government. Later, at the Governor's Conference, they accepted the lack of agreement on guaranteeing land titles as the price of keeping KANU out of government. Securing the settlers' assets remained a consequence of the liberals' political activities, not an immediate goal.

The lack of support within the European community for the liberals became manifest in the spring 1961 elections. Through a tortuous electoral procedure involving communal primaries, the elections seemed to fulfill the Biblical injunction of the last being first. Most of the New Kenya Group candidates decisively lost their primary election within the European community, but won over 25 per cent of the votes, which enabled them to go on to the general election (on an African dominated register) which they won with KANU backing and ended up in government. KADU equally decisively lost to KANU but formed a minority government, with European liberal support, when KANU refused to do so unless Jomo Kenyatta (the jailed nationalist leader sentenced to prison in March 1953 for allegedly leading 'Mau Mau') was first released from detention. The selection of the liberals as European representatives in the Legislative Council further accelerated the political demise of a community whose official representatives were no longer representative.[1]

KADU emerged from the elections as 'the Great White Hope' for the European liberals and the Colonial Government. However the attempts to resolve the land issue and consolidate KADU in government at least temporarily failed with the Governor's Conference in the fall. Because of liberal pressure, KADU's previous agreement with KANU to form a coalition government was reversed, and agreement on land guarantees delayed. The failure of the Governor's Conference and KADU's introduction of regionalism (the effort to devolve authority from the central government to the regions) both illustrated and accelerated the political weakness of the moderate Africans. By the end of the year colonial officials and liberals were beginning to look to moderates in KANU for support of their policies. At the same time European farmers sought nationalist support on a broad range of economic issues.

FARMERS' BARGAINING PRIOR TO THE GOVERNOR'S CONFERENCE

KNFU lobbying on the land issue

1961 saw the farmers' lobbying activities continue on two levels. Within Kenya there was the attempt to reach local agreement with the African Elected Members. Nudged along by HMG this attempt was to culminate in the failure of the Governor's Conference in the fall. The other strand of farmer politics was the continuation of pressure on HMG for support of land titles and settlement schemes. This latter policy was initially primary to the farmers and frequently the need for local consensus was justified as an important leverage against British inaction. But in 1961 the primacy of the colonial channels was altering.

Alec Ward, the Executive Officer of the KNFU, wrote to a Union member in April, 'I am sure you would agree that the *main* point which is causing the complete absence of confidence is that the emergent African Leaders will not make a statement or act in a manner that causes Europeans to feel satisfied that their security of title is not in jeopardy.'[2] In a public circular of February 16, 1961, on land titles, the KNFU stated that the satisfactory solution to security of title depended on local agreement. The Union therefore intended to canvass for support from the leading European and African agricultural bodies (L.D.S.B., the two Boards of Agriculture, the Kenya African National Traders and Farmers' Union and the General Agricultural Workers Union) before making an appeal to all the Elected Members of the Legislative Council to obtain firm assurances on security of title. This assurance was to include that no restriction be placed on the extent of land ownership provided the land was properly and

76

fully utilized. The KNFU believed that given such assurances from the Elected Members

. . . HMG would be prepared to make additional funds available both for individual land purchases and for development by either individuals or associations of individuals; further, that any lending organizations would take a more favorable view of Kenya as a borrowing country once security of title to all land was assured.[3]

The British stood then, in the farmers' view, as the collateral behind the bribe. Security of title was needed not only to secure an important part of the economy, but for the expansion of land settlement and the development of Kenya as a whole. The farmers had even been brought to the idea (likely by a combination of Government and liberal pressures) that local agreement was preferable to one imposed from outside. But for this London's cooperation was needed, both by calling a conference to discuss land titles and also by various forms of financial aid to take the 'steam out of the land kettle,' hence making the titles more secure.[4]

These local level activities were not initially successful. Marrian, now a Junior Minister, and B. R. McKenzie were having private talks with African members of Legislative Council in March and strongly hinting that 'everything' depended on the matter of titles.[5] The point was also made that Africans were hesitating to take up land in the Scheduled Areas not knowing what validity their titles would be given by an independent government. On April 6 Lord Delamere asked for discussions with the Presidents of KANU and KADU on the question of security of titles. Nearly two months later Union officials reported their requests had been ignored by the African leaders.[6]

Success was also mixed on the African agricultural front. KANTAFU (the Kenya African National Traders and Farmers Union) apparently supported the program and Ward sent a letter to Herman Oduor, General Secretary of the GAWU (General Agricultural Workers Union), which sounded as if their support was in the bag. Ward asked Oduor that when his committee met on land titles to 'write and let me know that your Committee supports the proposals and the submission of these proposals to the Elected Members in Legislative Council after the election is over.'[7] Unexpectedly Oduor could only send his personal endorsement without his Union's mandate. As he phrased it: 'Our Committee members have reluctantly evaded to support the idea openly on some reasonable grounds.'[8]

The major activity in the first part of 1961 on the farmers' lobbying with HMG was Vice President J. A. Seys' visit to London at the end of February 1961. With him Seys brought two requests to lay before the Secretary of State. The first was that HMG should announce fair compensation in the event of expropriation. The farmers saw this safeguard as not necessary if local agreement was reached on land titles and was in fact never directly dealt with by British officials other than by offering vague support for the

Union's efforts to secure titles.[9] The second point, a request for an increase in land purchases under a trustee-managed fund continued the theme set by the 1960 missions, and was more extensively dealt with by both sides.

The farmers argued that the present schemes were on too small a scale to deal with the problem. The estimated purchase of 180,000 acres of high potential land through mid-1963 was only ten per cent of the high potential land available and a mere 2.5 per cent of the Scheduled Areas. This limited amount would make it unlikely that the schemes would have the effect of 'priming the pump' for a market in land. They asked for an acceleration of the schemes, perhaps up to ten years, although the Union admitted, it could not be assumed an independent government would wish to continue the schemes. However, the farming community would gain confidence 'if HMG could give more definite assurances that they will continue to provide adequate funds for the schemes so long as they retain control in Kenya and that they will help and endeavour to persuade an independent Government to continue them.'[10]

This extension was to occur through a 'Private Yeoman Farmer Scheme.' In this new proposal European farmers would subdivide and supervise the transfer of undeveloped parts of their land. The European farmer's proposal and valuation would be approved by the L.D.S.B. (Land Development and Settlement Board) while the Divisional Board would approve prospective purchasers. The purchaser could borrow money on a long term basis from organizations such as the Land and Agricultural Bank of Kenya. Payment to the vendor would occur within a year of purchase. The subdivisions were aimed at a high class of African farmer by allowing a subsistence living, repayment of loans, and an additional net yearly income of £400. Besides speeding up settlement, the scheme would allow the sellers to receive cash for part of their assets and remove the difficulty of finding agricultural advisory officers, which was one of the reasons given by the Kenya government for initiating only limited schemes. The Union also proposed joint European/African companies to run farms, and stressed the importance of increased development in the African areas.[11]

The Union carefully maintained strong administrative control for the European farmer in all its proposals. Having the seller bargain with the European farmer-dominated L.D.S.B. for valuation and subdivisions was not really adversary bargaining. The African buyer had a rather passive role in the proceedings. Most importantly this scheme like the Bond Scheme which followed was still oriented to the question of giving European farmers confidence/capital to continue farming in Kenya or elsewhere. At this point the schemes remained 'stay' oriented.[12] Perhaps inevitably the Union still emphasized British responsibility and financing in their scheme. Local agreement was only a premise to the program, but far from a solution acceptable to the farmers. The schemes themselves while extending settlement horizontally did not look favorably on a vertical extension down to peasant farming. The Union consistently resisted the introduction of peasant farming into the Scheduled Areas as destructive of the agricultural system of the Highlands. Opposition to the original Ministry of Agriculture scheme was not only to its limited nature but its inclusion of subsistence farmers. The fear of stolen cattle/fencing and rural slums reflected a certain class-consciousness transcending apparently outmoded racial views.

Seys' reflections on his interview with high HMG officials showed them trying to be as friendly and noncommital as possible. In his three-quarters of an hour talk with Macleod on March 1, the Secretary of State found an abundance of constraints limiting a change of policy on the settlement schemes. In the first place, Parliament voted the monies in five year periods. The current period for settlement expired in June 1963, and the proposals were due to come before Parliament sometime in 1962. On past experience Macleod thought it automatic that monies would be revoted on a five year basis, but no one could commit Parliament in advance. He did favor a statement saying that, subject to Parliamentary approval, finance for the schemes would continue for five years after June 1963. Seys was convinced that the schemes had HMG backing. 'So far as I am concerned, I was left in no doubt that the British Government will be carrying on those schemes. Macleod was very definite indeed. He said that they think they are worthwhile Schemes; that as they get experience they will try to expand them . . .'[13]

However, Seys could not get Macleod to indicate that HMG would recommend to an independent Government that it should continue to support the schemes. Macleod replied that it was not his policy to say anything that might be construed as an indication that independence was near at hand. Nor did Macleod reply to the Memorandum's request for compensation for expropriation. There was no possibility of expanding the present schemes simply because there was no money available. The development funds now being used were HMG loans which would be repaid from money provided by the World Bank. Macleod promised to look into the private Yeoman Schemes and company farming schemes when B. R. McKenzie visited on March 17.[14]

Is Kenya, new proposals were being churned out by Europeans to meet what seemed a growing crisis. A study group, appointed by the Minister of Agriculture (after the 1961 elections, Michael Blundell) and composed of farming representatives and government officials linked with European agriculture, came out with a Bond Scheme in mid-1961. They referred to the crisis in land coming from the inability to mate the African's desire for the land with the European's wish to sell. They pointed to the possibility of a large-scale European exodus after the next harvest and the movement of capital overseas throughout agriculture: 'A substantial proportion of European farmers are now farming for liquid cash which they are investing overseas with the possible intention of eventually following themselves.'[15]

As a remedy the Group called for a 'clear and definite statement' on titles by HMG and the establishment of a Bond Scheme. The bond issued by a Kenya Land Company (incorporated in the UK) would be given to all landholders for their land and fixed assets based on the last official valuation. The bonds were to be graduated over a ten year period so that the farmer who left his farm early in the period would be penalized, while the farmer who stayed would have protection for his holdings. At the end of ten years the thirty-year bonds which had not been offered to the Corporation would be cancelled. Monies were to be payable in the UK. If a large excess of land was offered to the Corporation, leasing or group farming arrangements could be arranged with those farmers who remained. The scheme would have entailed a private underwriting of £112 million if all farmers in the Highlands participated.[16]

More important than the Plan (it still required a large commitment of British funds, made HMG the largest landowner in independent Kenya, and Under Secretary of State Hugh Fraser in his May visit quickly turned it down) were the principles guiding the future pattern of the Scheduled Areas which the Group laid out. The three guidelines set by the Group illustrated the farmers' attempt to minimize the amount of alteration in the structure and extent of the European agricultural system. The three principles, which were in practice followed in implementing the settlement schemes, were:

(a) Ranching, sisal and wheat farming are only economically viable in extensive units in certain areas and the present pattern should be preserved, though not necessarily under the present ownership. This is also applicable in the areas of low potential.

(b) Farm Economic Surveys carried out by the Government have conclusively proved that the maximum economic return from mixed farming in the high and medium potential [land] in this 'heart' of the Scheduled Areas can only be obtained from fair-sized units. These areas must not, therefore, be broken up into smallholdings on a peasant basis. Where subdivision is necessary, it should be on the basis of yeoman or assisted-ownership holdings.

(c) Peasant settlement should take place on the periphery of the Scheduled Area, preferably contiguous to non-Scheduled Areas. Only in this way can tribal spheres of influence be recognized and peasant settlement schemes be most easily absorbed by existing arrangements for medical, educational and other services. This policy will, however, inevitably mean that some farmland which, for economic reasons, would be better left in large units, will have to be split up. This must be faced. But the possible loss of production must be compensated for by the retention, and even increase, of large units under (b) above.[17]

Within the farmers' lobbying activities the Study Group's proposals in part played a unifying role. Blundell, as Minister in charge of the Group, was almost compelled to support the recommendations of the Group he had appointed – which he only partially and temporarily did. L. Welwood of the Coalition and a member of the Study Group wrote Cavendish-Bentinck that the Group had tended to tie up various efforts by different groups. Yet he seemed to contradict this in the same letter. He mentioned that Blundell was convinced that settling thirty thousand Africans in the next two years would lower the emotional tensions over land. Welwood was 'entirely unconvinced' and implied support for a complete buy-out with his remark on Blundell's scheme: 'It is rather like giving two chops to a lion leaving the rest of the carcass within its reach.'[18]

On the one hand it was important to the Europeans to lower the political visibility of land and any solutions to the land problems. On the other hand they wanted to be sure that the solutions were politically oriented enough not only to solve the politically-charged debate over land but also ensure that the results were a net gain for political allies. Politics was anathema to the Europeans only as a process, not as a consequence. What was economically beneficial inevitably appeared to be that which tampered with the colonial political economy the least.

At the same time that the farmers did not want settlement covering more than selected areas of the Highlands, they did want a British guarantee/underwriting covering all the farms. So whereas the British were beginning to see settlement as the one stone for two birds (European market support and African land hunger), the European farmers were stressing the distinction. Settlement was still a potential danger – burdening the system with uneconomic farms, running the neighborhood down with black rural slums, and forcing out European farmers who did not want to leave. Guarantees against expropriation put the farmers in a position of having their assets and their security. Their economic assets were once again secured under the traditional colonial political arrangements. This *segmental colonization* would allow them to operate economically as before and would give them a powerful ally for leverage on the independent government in the person of HMG. The guarantee would use the colonial channels for safeguarding the economic assets formerly thought secured by settler political power.

Convention/Coalition political bargaining

The conservative Europeans in bargaining within the evolving Kenyan political framework consistently found themselves at a disadvantage. One of the drawbacks flowing from the Convention/Coalition's policy of re-entrenchment was the mistrust of allies/potential allies. The leadership divided between the obvious needs of the European community for wider support, and their mistrust of the goals, methods and personalities of these other groups. Much as the Convention/Coalition would have liked liberal, HMG and moderate African support, they could not overcome their suspicion, partly justifiable, that these groups were obstacles in the path of security for the settlers. 1961 did not see the dilemma resolved.

81

The enmity toward the liberal Europeans continued to burn at a low flame. Cavendish-Bentinck in a letter to a Coalition leader viewed collaboration with the NKP as 'quite useless' and characterized the liberal party as 'untrustworthy.' He was also 'horrified' at people like Marrian visiting Kenyatta.[19] Major B. P. Roberts, a leader of the right-wing United Party and now aiding the Coalition effort, felt that HMG would continue to use Blundell while it suited them and would then discard him. 'He should be disowned by the Europeans at *every* opportunity,' he wrote a friendly English businessman.[20] In a later letter to Oates, Roberts could write that 'Our weakness is the split amongst Europeans in Kenya itself. . . .' implying that the problem was that the community had not re-entrenched sufficiently.[21] Both Sir Ferdinand and Major Roberts felt that Oates' and the Convention's non-party approach was 'futile.' Cavendish-Bentinck wrote to Oates from London that he could not conceive of getting Bruce McKenzie's support or imagine that there was value in such support.[22] In a lengthy letter to Welwood from London, Cavendish-Bentinck spelled out his analysis of the British policy of decolonization. Once direct control was withdrawn the British would establish an interregnum, wrote Cavendish-Bentinck. This was to be 'an era of bogus government' created by HMG using 'flattery, patronage and corruption until some recognizable and definite national movement emerged in Kenya.

The temporary makeshift Government then disappears and is swept away and the country becomes Independent, the hope being that thereafter some of the essential British interests, more especially trade interests, can be preserved. Also thereafter, as far as political control is concerned, they wash their hands. They quote precedents for the success of this policy notably in India and elsewhere.

The NKG were 'minions of this Government,' whom HMG would use for dealing with a difficult temporary situation and then discard. Cavendish-Bentinck viewed this as 'utterly cynical' and entailing moral obligations to communities such as ours.[23]

Similarly another Coalition leader, Clive Salter, saw a sell-out of the small farmers, businessmen and professional people in British policy. He had the impression that HMG thought it could maintain the country by keeping big business houses' trade, and supporting the large plantation companies like Brooke Bond and some of the ranching concerns. Salter predicted that HMG would try to escape from any obligation which was either embarrassing or financially committing. Hence, Salter concluded (and Cavendish-Bentinck agreed), HMG would not be very convinced by the farmers' threats to run down the economy.[24]

But the tactical conclusions flowing from this analysis were not readily apparent. The Coalition leaders dismissed the on-again-off-again Convention attempts at a non-party approach with broad bases of support. They preferred unified support behind the Coalition leadership. But to what end was unclear. Neither Salter nor Cavendish-Bentinck believed that economic threats would get anywhere, indeed Cavendish-Bentinck viewed an economic decline as part of HMG policy.[25] Oates preferred to view the English policy as arising from the erroneous notion that the factor of the European contribution to the economy would remain constant.[26]

The conservatives were also divided as to the wisdom of HMG involvement. Welwood in a June letter to Cavendish-Bentinck saw the advantage in a tripartite conference lying in the involvement of HMG. He reasoned that the British position would become difficult if KANU insisted Crown titles were not valid.[27] Just the opposite view was conveyed by an unsigned August draft presented to the Convention Executive. The draft concluded that the July mission had conclusively demonstrated that Europeans could not rely on HMG for effective assistance and thus had no option but to negotiate directly with African leaders. 'Since, however, Europeans are essential to Kenya and also hold the majority of the wealth in the country their negotiating position is strong *provided* they do *not* allow HMG in Westminster to interfere and sell the pass.'[28]

The two positions were probably irreconcilable. One could not exclude HMG from the process of resolving the land issue and then expect the British to accept responsibility for the results. In practice the conservative Europeans stressed the involvement of the British government in Kenya affairs at practically every opportunity. While the farmers' situation appeared to dictate some accommodation with the nationalists, the Convention/Coalition leaders found their colonialist vision of the Africans (untrustworthy, corrupt, incompetent) too constricting to allow it. The very *raison d'etre* of racial re-entrenchment and their feelings of impotency inhibited meaningful contacts with the Africans. Instead, ambiguously viewing the British as demon and deliverer, they plied the traditional colonial channels to right their grievances. Only gradually did the weakness of their position vis a vis HMG (which the liberals recognized earlier) become apparent.

Nonetheless, by the summer of 1961 the pressure on the British government to do something about land titles was far from abating. In Kenya, KANU and the European farmers maintained their curious identity of views. Bruce McKenzie, who had much to do with keeping these views similar, was now 'Shadow Minister' of Agriculture for KANU. In suggesting a meeting with the British government on land titles, he asserted that HMG should quit the idea of getting African leaders to talk with title-holders. 'Her Majesty's Government is up to her neck in land titles. She gave out the titles to various people in this country and I maintain it is up to her to call this meeting.'[29]

In July a delegation from the Coalition/Convention (Oates, Welwood and Cavendish-Bentinck) joined by Lord Delamere presented a petition paralleling McKenzie's demands. It called for a tripartite conference of HMG, African political leaders, and Kenya European farmers, on land titles. The delegation in talks with Macleod demanded a scheme applicable to the entire Highlands and that HMG assume responsibility as grantor of titles. They called for citizenship to be entirely divorced from land problems and property rights, and stressed the lack of security and representation for minority groups in the present political setup. Macleod replied by asking the delegation to take part in talks under the Governor to endeavor to obtain assurances from African political leaders. The delegation, including Delamere, agreed, adding, 'Whatever the outcome of the talks it must be clearly understood that the ultimate responsibility for titles and the welfare of the European community still rests with Britain.'[30]

LIBERALS AND ALLIES BARGAINING PRIOR TO THE GOVERNOR'S CONFERENCE

The KADU mission to London

The farmers were far from alone in trying to gain political mileage from land settlement. In the negotiations preceding KADU's decision to form a government the land issue had been involved. The *East African Standard* commented that the discussions between the Governor and KADU leaders which culminated in their decision to enter the government had included 'the need for a grant of money from Britain to acquire land for settling landless Africans and for other projects.'[31] A delegation from the new KADU government journeyed to London in April to put their claim for more funds before the Secretary of State. At a meeting on May 1 KADU stressed three major problems to British government officials: unemployment, education, and settlement of landless Africans. The last was described as a serious social problem needing grant money as people did not have the means to purchase lands. The problem was especially acute in Central Province and Nyanza. It was stressed that if the KADU government failed at this the extremists would take over.

In further meetings with Colonial Office officials liberal ministers in the KADU government asked for £5 million annually for the Land Bank over three years. This would be used for land in the 'sore thumb' areas and for settlement on medium potential land. It was stressed that this was not compensation but relief of the landless.[32] Members of the delegation argued that there were three present difficulties. One was KANU raising doubts about land titles. The second was that the settlement system had become too bureaucratic; results took too long. Finally, the assistance from overseas was so expensive that only the highest potential land could afford to carry the charges.

The political side of the issue was stressed in the discussions. In the present proposals money would go further than in earlier estimates because it was not envisaged to do more than purchase the land and settle the tenant

84

farmer. These schemes would be carried out in areas other than those where the World Bank was operating in order to make an immediate political impact. Further, they would be farms of six to eight acres, on medium potential land with planning reduced to an absolute minimum. A charge would be placed on the land to avoid encouraging the view that land could be transferred free. African KADU members stressed the need for projects and settlement in rural areas to raise employment and counter the attraction of 'city lights.'

In reply the British stressed John Bull's financial difficulties as well as Kenya's. The officials warned that the proposed increase would tend to make Kenya permanently dependent on external aid and reminded the delegates of the UK's formidable balance of payments problem.[33]

Despite the money the KADU government seemed to be costing HMG, the British were fairly happy with it. Macleod was described as 'almost jubilant' at the election results in early March which, he said, confirmed his view that it was possible to develop responsible African government in Kenya.[34] The British backed this up with a reception for the delegation at which Prime Minister Macmillan was present, giving newspapers the impression of Britain's whole-hearted support for the KADU government. At the same time the freeze was put on KANU. In late April, Macleod was reported to have told Mboya that he now had a Kenya government to deal with and implied that future meetings with KANU would serve no useful purpose. Later Macleod refused to grant James Gichuru, President of KANU, an interview and, at the reception in London given to the Kenya delegation, members of KANU were not invited.[35]

The liberal political perspective on land

As seen in their treatment of the KANU government mission, the Colonial Office was cooperating closely with the moderate African party and its European backers.[36] In return liberal leaders kept up a flow of advice on the evolving negotiations over the land issue. Blundell took the occasion of Cavendish-Bentinck's summer visit to express his fears about the bargaining pattern which was emerging. He wrote to Macleod on June 20 about Cavendish-Bentinck's delegation:

Whether you see them or not is, I think, a matter for yourself, but I do think that we have to consider whether we should continually by-pass the Kenya Government and accept without expostulation the procedure by which pressure groups can go to the UK and seek interviews with the Secretary of State. This, in effect, nullifies the impact of the Kenya Government, and is a procedure which must, willy-nilly, cease within the next two years at most.[37]

Blundell also felt that the proposed tripartite Conference (HMG, nationalists, farmers) held a danger of isolating the European farmers from Asian and African titleholders. Finally, he put his finger on what was presumably

85

a worry of the British leaders at this time – the coalition of right and left on HMG's responsibility.

Lastly, I feel that by far the most dangerous outcome of such discussions is the likelihood that the African political leaders will be tempted to repudiate all the responsibility for land and place this quite firmly and squarely on the shoulders of HMG. This, I believe, would not only put you in an impossible position but also greatly endanger European farming enterprise out here after independence, as the African leaders would attempt to establish that the responsibility was yours, and yours alone.[38]

The goal of preserving the political economy, even at the expense of the mixed farmers, was uppermost in the minds of liberal leaders such as Blundell. This was the basis of his disagreement with much of the emphasis by the farmers on underwriting schemes. In a letter to a friendly MP Blundell voiced his doubts on guarantees without more political measures. 'The main consideration, in my mind, is as follows: no amount of compensation, underwriting, bond schemes or insurance by HMG or anyone else can protect the settler who wishes to stay unless we can take a lot of steam out of the land question.'[39] These measures to 'take the steam off' included dealing with abandoned farms, developing yeoman farming using cheaper money than previously, purchase of areas in the Highlands which the Africans considered in dispute, and a massive scheme of resettlement to put 25,000 landless families in the Highlands in the next two years. Blundell added: 'I am a little worried because I consider that any ill conceived underwriting of land without the remedial measures which I have outlined above may well precipitate the very thing many of us are anxious to avoid, which is the total elimination, or largely total elimination, of the European farming enterprise.[40]

Later, Blundell explained his views further in a letter to another British MP who wrote asking for his reflections on Kenya and the land issue. The 'remedial measures' previously mentioned were seen as a three-fold aspect to the plans submitted by the Ministry of Agriculture. The first was to buy up the disputed areas (the 'sore thumb' areas), some twenty-two in all: 'Once these are out of the way, many of the tribes will naturally honour individual titles, because they do so anyway in their tribal societies.'[41] Second was 'maximum pressure' behind Assisted Owner or Yeoman schemes for the breakup of larger European farms and their resale on extended payment terms to African farmers on a scale of 100/250 acre farms. Finally,

(3) What we call massive resettlement. This is a real attempt in the next two years before Independence comes to get something like 12,000 to 20,000 African families settled from those areas where over-population most presses on the people. If we can do this then I think African leaders would be able to stand up against the pressure of the unemployed and the landless and justify sanctity of titles and contracts.[42]

The last sentence accurately reflected the close links in liberal thinking between resettlement and the cooptation of an African elite to preserve European interests by preventing mass unrest.

While not viewed as a long-term solution it was hoped that settlement would solve the immediate problem while the economy adjusted itself after the initial pre-independence period. The acceleration of agriculture in the African areas at the time was seen in a similar light. Not only would this aid development and employment but it would also lead to 'less reliance on European agriculture, which means that it is not so highlighted in the minds of African politicians.'

Blundell expanded on the faults of underwriting. Not only was there the danger of encouraging an African government of washing its hands of legal responsibility in favor of HMG, there was also the danger that

. . . unless we look at the root cause of the pressure on land, no amount of guarantees or underwriting will prevent a future government doing something on the lines of Castro in Cuba or Nasser in the Nile Valley. I therefore think that we want the maximum amount of money to buy farms in the Highlands, break them up into units for smallholders and offer them to the smallholder at a price or 'settlement charge' which will enable the prospective smallholder to win out on an economic basis.[43]

By November in a private London talk Blundell opposed underwriting land values altogether. He thought underwriting would make it more attractive for any independent Kenya government to expropriate the land.[44]

English allies' efforts

Conservative backbenchers were also putting pressure on their government for settlement. Fred M. Bennett and Philip Goodhart wrote Blundell of their lobbying Macleod on the need for settlement schemes.[45] Mr G. M. Thomson in a debate on Kenya land in Commons thought the government was putting too much emphasis on fifty acre holdings and too little on family smallholdings. 'I think that the Government are being tempted by a will-o'-wisp to create a well-to-do African landed middle class. Perhaps they feel that in due course, they will become backbencher African baronets in a future Conservative Kenya legislature.'[46] And in a letter to an irate member complaining about the British policy of 'economic blackmail and enslavement of the European farmer in Kenya,' Ward could report in early spring 1961: 'There is much more support to our proposals amongst Conservative backbenchers than there was a year ago.[47]

The visit of the Colonial Under Secretary, Hugh Fraser, to Kenya in late May 1961 provided the European community with an opportunity to vent some of its frustration. During his stay Fraser once again turned down British overall coverage of land titles and said that in the event of abrogation of contract HMG would have to assess its position and do its utmost to meet the problem.[48] He did say that 'massive injections' of financial aid could be expected from Britain to bolster the economy and that HMG would give more aid for settlement schemes.[49] At the same time he disagreed with the Bond Scheme though agreeing to take it back to England for further discussions. He said that by it HMG could become the biggest landowner in Kenya, that resettlement might not be able to keep up with the speed of departing European farmers, and that management of abandoned land might present an insuperable problem. He also implied in a later retracted 'slip' that independence was 'several years' away. This was widely seen as deliberate. The *East African Standard* reported that Conservative MP's felt the government was 'quietly applying the brake' in Kenya.[50]

Fraser was roundly criticized in Kenya. A leader in the *Standard* took the Under Secretary to task for failing to consult all parties, for his paternalistic attitude, and for a general misunderstanding of the Kenya scene.[51] The Convention of Associations announced that unless guarantees for titles were received by September it would advise farmers to adopt a policy of salvaging what they could. (The Convention claimed a paid-up membership of three-quarters of Kenya's four thousand farmers.) The Convention used this as a tactic against what they were coming to see as HMG's sinister intentions toward 'kith 'n kin.' 'There is a widely held view that by economic pressure the British Government is determined to keep the settler here because he cannot leave.'[52] Gichuru called the farmers' threats 'provocative' to Africans.[53]

A FLEETING SYNTHESIS

The Joint Committee meeting (August, 1961)

The European community placed much hope on the Joint Committee talks between KADU/KANU to be followed by the Governor's Conference. In a letter to a Kenyan supporter, Blundell thought it likely that the KADU view on land at the meetings would be 'very similar to our own,' and that out of the meeting might come 'some overall land policy which is reasonably acceptable to the moderate elements of our community.'[54] Writing to his former employer and a sympathetic backer of his political career (Ind Coope), Blundell was more explicit about KADU's similarity of views:

It looks at the moment as if we shall be able to sort out land problems through the joint discussions which are going to take place and indeed my group will play à considerable part by preparing the brief for the KADU members. If we can resolve the doubts and uncertainties over property rights the country will begin to forge ahead again.[55]

Events almost worked out this way but African politics remained the art of the unpredictable.

Between the 10th of August and the 24th of August, 1961, ten meetings were held between KADU and KANU. O. Odinga of KANU was Chairman and P. J. Harbenga of KADU was Secretary of the meetings which included only Africans in attendance. At the first meeting Tom Mboya suggested the formation of a caretaker government which KANU would consider joining. This was opposed by Ngala and Amalemba who retorted with the idea of a more permanent coalition government. Most of the other KADU members also opposed a caretaker government as temporary, apparently from a desire to be part of the government which would take Kenya to independence. By the fifth meeting on August 16, Ngala made a long speech favoring a coalition government with 50/50 KADU–KANU representation, which was supported by Gichuru and Mboya. The Committee then agreed on the desirability of joint interim government. The next two meetings spelled out that the 'Premier' would be chosen by an election before independence, ministries fully reshuffled, and that the Committee would approach the Governor to demand immediate internal self-government. The question of what would happen if the demand for self-government was not met (i.e., would either KANU or KADU pull out of the proposed government) was apparently glossed over.[56]

There were also lengthy debates on two other matters. On August 15 the Committee arrived at an agreed date for independence. After lengthy debate and sundry suggestions establishing militant credentials (names and suggestions were: Mboya – December 9, 1961; Ngala – March 29, 1962; Muliro – first half of 1962, and Amalemba – July 1, 1962), the Committee agreed to demand February 1, 1962, as the date of independence. There was also a prolonged discussion on August 22 on the mechanics of how Kenyatta would enter Legislative Council, which concluded by recommending that he be appointed by the Governor (a moral KANU victory one might surmise by having the Governor appoint the leader unto 'death and darkness').

It was only on August 18 at the third to last meeting that the question of land rights was raised. Muliro had urged at the opening meeting that the European community be maintained for the sake of a sound economy, but nothing else was recorded on this. It was agreed in principle after little discussion that private property and land titles including tribal rights should be safeguarded and that a declaration on land policy in general terms should be issued. At the last meeting on August 23 the following statement was adopted: 'The Committee agreed that land titles including tribal rights and private property rights shall be respected and safeguarded in the interests of the people of Kenya: and that fair compensation shall be paid for any land acquired by any future Government for public purposes, e.g. Schools, Hospitals, etc.'[57]

Throughout the meetings land was a very poor third to constitutional advance and party jockeying for positions in government in both parties' priorities. The issue was only raised at all at the last three meetings and only at the final one was there any extended discussion. This debate over the adoption of the draft memorandum reinforced the view of land as having little priority in nationalist goals at this point. The argument raised in favor of the paragraph was that it was desirable for creating confidence in the country. There was no recorded opposition to this view. Further, even the listing of 'resettlement' in the first draft as one of the 'public purposes' for which the government could acquire land was objected to on the grounds that it was only sometimes a 'public purpose.' It was agreed to remove the reference to settlement.[58]

The paragraph itself made no mention of European lands and indeed put 'tribal rights' ahead of 'private property rights' in the phrasing. It was likely that KANU leaders saw the statement as soothing tribal worries within KADU (especially among the Kalenjin and Abaluhya) over the feared Kikuyu expansion. The lack of any dissent and subsequent European demands for more precise guarantees might also have indicated an agreement to disagree: KANU militants being assuaged by the desire to come to an agreement with KADU, hence to enter the government, speed up attaining independence, and after independence unravel whatever agreements were already made.

The NKG European members were not at all pleased with the Joint Committee's handiwork. They viewed KADU as having 'gone crazy' in agreeing to a Constitutional Conference in 1961 and a General Election before a very early independence on February 1, 1962. Members of KADU replied that they were the government anyway and could not be worse off unless they resigned. Further they saw an opportunity to split KANU. They believed KANU would come across in toto or that its more moderate members would join KADU. Mboya was viewed as exceedingly friendly and 'Ministry-minded.' With Odinga seen as ranked second to Kenyatta, Mboya had no wish to be third.[59]

The Governor's Conference (September–November, 1961)

Farmer hopes on land, at least partly fulfilled by the Joint Committee statement now turned to the Governor's Conference. NKG members were informed that the Governor would start the talks by saying he was glad that the Joint Committee had come to its senses about land policy, because as far as he was concerned it was a prerequisite to any discussions about constitutional advance.[60] Both the Convention of Associations and KNFU submitted drafts to the Conference calling for explicit guarantees on land titles. Chairman Oates wished for separate Convention representation, believing that Delamere, representing the KNFU, lacked the confidence of a great number of farmers. The Governor was apparently following Blundell's lead on keeping the Convention/Coalition out, but relented under pressure. The Convention/Coalition was finally represented at the Conference by

Clive Salter, while the KNFU was to be allowed representation when matters concerning land were raised. The Conference, however, never got that far.[61]

Governor Renison's speech called the Conference 'a great occasion in the history of Kenya.' He said he wished to have the fewest possible points of difference left to be resolved by the Secretary of State. He praised the Joint Committee's work in bringing the parties together into an interim coalition government. However, he cautioned, the grant of internal self-government must be preceded by the resolving of certain problems such as land and property rights, the Coastal Strip, Northern Frontier, Civil Service rights, and economic recovery.[62]

The Governor also delivered an extended lecture to the African representatives. He dismissed the Joint Committee's timetable for independence as 'unrealistic and impracticable,' and projected elections no sooner than eight months after agreement on the constitution.[63] He stressed instead the importance of the economy and land: 'Since I have been in Kenya I have been far more worried about the economy and the economic future than about politics and the prospects of sound constitutional advance.' He praised the African leaders for their statement on land 'though late in the day' and hoped it would be the first step to rapid economic revival. He also hoped it would bring a new atmosphere where all Kenyans might have a secure place irrespective of tribe or race or birthplace. Renison concluded his references to land with the admonition: 'Anyone who runs Kenya will run it to disaster if he does not follow the lead given by the Joint Committee in their immensely important statement on land.'[64]

After the Governor's speech the talks stretched into seventeen sporadic meetings ranging from September 4 to November 3, when the last meeting ended with a KANU walkout. The minutes of the meetings revealed an atmosphere of confusion rather than any great hostility – at least until the end. An example of what appeared as a lack of preparation and party unity by KANU was the question of Kenyatta's attendance at the meetings. Raised by Odinga at the second meeting on September 5, it was disputed by Ardwings-Kodhek (KANU) as liable to involve Kenyatta in contentious events and spoil his role as unifier. The matter was dropped with little debate. However at the fourth meeting on September 7 Odinga again brought up Kenyatta's attendance. This time the split appeared to be along party lines with KANU members falling in behind it while the Europeans and KADU argued against it. The matter was finally ruled out of order by the Governor who said there was no reason to re-open a decision previously taken and that the meeting as a whole did not wish to re-open the matter – this last point being slightly overstated as KANU certainly did.[65]

The major debates revolved around the rate of constitutional advance and the composition of the coalition government. KANU pushed for an immediate conference which would establish internal self-government and a date for independence. KADU, pulling back a bit from their previous accord, still stressed a conference during 1961 but added it could only be rewarding if progress has been made on other problems facing Kenya (i.e., land). The Governor, who made little attempt at playing a neutral arbiter, aligned with KADU and NKG in arguing for a coalition government stage prior to internal self-government.

However, the real obstacle preventing agreement on a joint government, about which KADU, under liberal pressure, was clearly having second thoughts, came out in the discussion on the meaning of KADU/KANU parity in government. KADU argued that it meant equality between the two parties with independent and European members having the extra seats (initially four KADU, four KANU, four non-African). KANU said there should be equality throughout government with non-Africans represented through the party structures. KANU was apparently willing to compromise quite a bit on this by juggling numbers and ministries around, even to accepting a compromise proposed by the Coalition's Salter.[66] But no agreement was forthcoming. Discussions between the Governor, Ngala and Gichuru to reach a private accord at the beginning of October ended in failure.

KADU was clearly concerned about its European supporters losing their ministerial portfolios, but the party was also worried about preserving unity. Their move to split KANU by signing it on to the government was in danger of backfiring. KANU strategy on this point came to light by the revelation of a secret KANU document outlining party thinking on the formation of a coalition government. The handwritten draft, apparently written by a high party official (possibly Mboya) after the Joint Committee meetings, saw KADU as 'shattered' by KANU acceptance of a caretaker government. After outlining the problems of joining the government (the difficulty of working with certain individuals in KADU – Blundell and two ex-members of KANU – and allotting ministries), the draft dealt with KANU goals for joining the government. The two objectives in joining were (1) to obtain dramatic results on the known national issues, chiefly by getting the Finance ministry and (2) to break KADU from within. The draft doubted if KANU could break KADU as such, but thought it would occur when the moderate party found their numbers too great for the ministries allocated under the caretaker government.

This memo was later cited in a brief prepared for Blundell as one of the reasons for the failure of the Governor's Conference. It made clear to KADU leaders that KANU was only interested in a coalition if they could break KADU and seize power. The other reasons for the Conference's breakdown mentioned in the brief were strong tribal feelings (on which it did not elaborate) and the inability of the Governor to influence anyone. The Governor was described as 'unpopular and ineffectual' which seemed to indicate even liberal disaffection from Renison.[67]

92

The bungling of the land issue at the Conference underlined this last point. Land first came up in a formal way at the sixth meeting on September 11. Salter and Blundell raised the question of Paul Ngei's fiery speech on land the day before and asked for a statement reaffirming the Joint Committee's statement and a repudiation of Ngei.[68]

Some KANU delegates thought undue importance was being placed on Ngei's speech and did not wish to repudiate a recently released nationalist hero. Dr J. G. Kiano did not mind reaffirming the Joint Committee statement but most of the other KANU delegates thought it unnecessary. KADU argued for it. At this point there seemed to have developed a consensus for discussing the land issue directly, with Gichuru favoring these discussions. Here the Governor stepped in and moved the discussions in what in retrospect appeared a strange direction. Acting on an overheated report on the deteriorating security situation in the Northern Frontier Province he asked the meeting to discuss this before land matters. After some discussion and over Salter's objections the meeting adopted a watered-down compromise statement on its intentions and dropped the matter. The statement read:

The meeting confirmed its intention to proceed as soon as possible to the consideration of the land question, which will be discussed on the basis of paragraph 4 of the joint KADU/KANU Memorandum.

The consideration of this item will follow after the meeting has completed its deliberations on the position of the Northern Frontier District.[69]

This, however, was not to be.

At the seventh meeting, on September 12, it was agreed to start land discussions on September 15 and to invite the KNFU delegation to attend. However the meetings on the 15th (Friday) and 18th (Monday) were later cancelled to allow the groups to discuss the formation of the interim government. At the tenth meeting on September 20, Argwings-Kodhek brought up a view that was again solidifying into the KANU position as the discussions on a coalition government ground to a halt. He thought that discussing thorny problems might jeopardize the interim government talks and that land might be more effectively acted upon by a broadened government dealing with bodies like the KNFU. The Governor, in reply, pointed out that the Secretary of State would want to know the position on land when examining proposals for a broadened government. And if the trade-off was not being made explicit enough, he replied to a question by Bruce Mckenzie, saying that while constitutional advance and 'land' were not completely tied to each other, there was a close relationship. However at this point Muliro and Mboya joined hands in agreeing on the priority of interim government discussions. The Governor reluctantly agreed, emphasizing once again the importance given the economy and a return of confidence by the Secretary of State.[70]

On September 21, Blundell tried unsuccessfully to bring up property rights. The Governor supported the move terming 'illusory' any constitutional advance without a restoration of confidence and an improvement in the economy. KANU views had stiffened further after KADU's introduction of the 'parity problem.' Mboya at the next meeting viewed further talks as not taking place unless agreement was reached on the formation of a joint government. By the fifteenth meeting on October 6, after the Governor — Gichuru–Ngala discussions had failed, the conference was clearly disintegrating. Blundell, supported by the Governor, tried to turn the discussions to land arguing that agreement on substantive issues might make people less suspicious of each other. Ngala supported this and the Governor spoke in grave terms of the 'deteriorating' security and economic position of the country. KANU delegates called for a conference under the Secretary of State following the breakdown of these talks. To this the Governor retorted that the Secretary of State had hoped for an unambiguous declaration of protection for property rights in the final communique after these talks.[71] KANU declined to participate in discussions on other matters but indicated they would resume discussions on the formation of an interim coalition government when the Secretary of State replied to the Governor's report on the meetings.

The meetings abated for a month while word from the Secretary of State was awaited. On November 3, what was to be the final meeting was held. Ngala, after receiving a memo from the Secretary of State calling for continued discussions, and agreeing to a conference in London early in 1962, proposed immediate talks on land, property rights and constitutional issues. At the same time Ngala expressed disappointment at the Secretary of State's failure to mention internal self-government in 1961.

By this time KANU was having none of it. Gichuru denounced the Governor as an agent of KADU and blamed him for the talks breaking down. He demanded an immediate constitutional conference under the Secretary of State and blamed the Governor for delaying the conference until next year. Property rights and minority safeguards, Gichuru declared, could only be finalized in the context of a constitution for a free Kenya. He saw no useful purpose in restarting the discussions without a joint government having first been agreed to. He and the KANU delegates then walked out. In the half-emptied room the Governor turned down a request that he impose a joint government, saying that the next stage in constitutional advance should only come by the agreement of the parties.[72]

The breakdown of the talks was likely a mixed blessing for the liberal Europeans. It allowed KADU to remain in power. It stretched out the period of transition and pushed back independence placing the onus for both on KANU. The delay also gave the settlement programs more of a chance to 'take the steam' out of the land issue before independence. The one drawback was the lack of confidence among the European farmers and their threats to pull a quick mass exit. The farmers were still demanding written assurances for their assets, so that they could continue farming in

Kenya or elsewhere. The liberals, more ambitiously, wanted a government favorable to their policies, in which they could play a role.

THE LIBERALS CHANGING POLITICAL TACTICS

Whom to support and how to support them

Throughout 1961 the liberals never quite decided whether they wanted KANU's friendship and gratitude or merely the Africans' signature on the dotted line. The trade-off of constitutional advance for economic guarantees was a bargain which Blundell for one wanted while at the same time being afraid the cost of winning might be too high. In a letter to a Laikepia supporter, the liberal leader wrote in July 1961 that independence should not be delayed. He felt that at the most independence was three or four years away, that it was wiser to avoid increasing frustration and bitterness by delaying the inevitable, and that Kenya should get on with it. He concluded: 'We cannot gain more than two years and from the standpoint of making the country more mature, better educated, and with a wide economy, two years is neither here nor there. Proceed swiftly and the Africans may regard our economy as an asset; proceed slowly and they may try to pinch it.'[73] And later in October 1962 he advised the new Secretary of State, Duncan Sandys, along similar lines:

You asked me in what way you could assist and gain the confidence of the Africans, and I explained to you that I thought it was essential to keep moving on towards Independence. The longer we wait, the more opportunity there is for the extremist negative elements to undermine the more reasonable and constructive ones who have taken on the burden of Government at a difficult time.[74]

In a private speech before the Joint East and Central African Board in England, Blundell said it would be a mistake to hold things back by retaining HMG control. Kenya must be kept moving, otherwise the thugs would emerge and seize control from the moderate Africans.[75]

However, these views were not held to be contradictory to the tactical stance of delaying independence in order to gain concessions on security of title. As Blundell wrote to F. M. Bennett, a friendly MP, at the end of June: 'I also feel, and have made it known to the Kenya Government, that we should not make a decisive move forward in regard to the Constitution – as, for instance, the appointment of a Chief Minister with Responsible Government – until this whole issue of security of title has been thrashed out.'[76] At the same time Bruce McKenzie, now a KANU member, had talked to Blundell about the dangers of frustrating KANU too much. Blundell had dismissed this as McKenzie trying to play both sides.[77]

By mid-September as the Governor's Conference was breaking down Blundell was pushing an even harder line. Complaining in a letter to Iain Macleod that KANU wanted 'a ruthless seizure of power' he recommended to the Secretary of State that no commitment be given for internal self-government until Kenya's problems were faced and added: 'I believe that the right course of action is for HMG to put quite clearly to the representatives in the Kenya Legislative Council that responsible Self-Government is available to them tomorrow, but that the conditions for reaching it are amicable solutions of the problems which lie ahead of us.[78] This last letter illustrated Blundell undercutting the policy of the moderate party he supported and in whose government he was then serving. The question then arises as to the importance of KADU in liberal thinking.

KADU was likely never seen as more than a way station by the liberal Europeans. Peter Marrian after deciding to join KANU wrote Blundell on what he believed to be Blundell's overemphasis in supporting KADU.

All I would like to say it [*sic*] that I believe our differences in outlook is fundamental, you believing that you can build round KADU an effective instrument of Government and I taking the view that with all their past intransigence, and unruly tongues the representatives of the 'hot lands' have to form the central core round which other elements can be wrapped. History appears to teach me this lesson and it is a matter for great regret to me personally that we have to part on this issue.[79]

In reply Blundell minimized their disagreement and spelled out some of his own goals:

I do not believe that there is a fundamental difference in outlook between us. There is, I think, a difference in outlook on the best way to achieve the same objective. For the record I would merely like to tell you that I do not believe that a long-term instrument of Government can be built around KADU, any more than I believe it can be built around a Luo/Kikuyu union unless strong elements of KADU are associated with it. I feel that working in the Government established some stability and presented a strong front which would eventually cause the movement to our side of many men who are now in opposition and who really have exactly the same ideas as ourselves.

He was afraid that Marrian's switch might be a permanent setback to this idea, with some unnamed KANU members formerly contemplating switching now 'disappointed and weakened.'[80]

The idea of a moderate black coalition as the best means to preserve the European position was of course an old idea. But frequently caught up in the KADU–KANU rivalry the liberals seemed in danger of losing this perspective in favor of building up KADU. So in late 1960 in a letter to the head of Ind Coope, Blundell classed Odinga as a communist with Iron Curtain financing but was more sanguine about Mboya. 'Although Mboya makes truculent, aggressive and negative speeches, I am increasingly coming to the conclusion that he is a moderate.'[81] But in a September 1961 letter to Iain Macleod he grouped Mboya and Odinga together describing their behavior at the Governor's Conference as 'rude, arrogant and negative' and he alluded to Mboya's 'overwhelming wish for arbitrary power.'[82]

There were other strands of policy weaving their way into liberal thinking. Blundell was being warned of the danger of extremist control of KANU in late 1961. A brief prepared for him read:

KANU is not united, except in its presentation of a hostile front to KADU. Internal stresses and strains pull in many directions, and the tough ex-detainee element as yet outside the Legislative Council wish to gain control. If they succeed, it would mean virtual extremist Kikuyu control of the party. Kenyatta is being lobbied hard by these politically out of date, but tough, elements.[83]

The brief went on to recommend that the Constitutional Conference be held in Kenya because any agreement in London would be valueless as KANU would deny, misinterpret and 'wriggle helplessly' under pressures of their 'thugs.' Holding the meeting in Kenya would force the inevitable showdown, the brief concluded. The process was still seen as a movement of moderates from KANU to KADU. However, others were beginning to appreciate the nationalist party's strength.

Elements in the British government were worried about driving KANU into the extremist camp and were preparing if not to switch from the KADU horse at least to hitch it up. Lord Howick (former Governor Baring) wrote Blundell a very perceptive and prescient letter in early 1962, discussing talks he had with high British government officials. Lord Howick viewed Tom Mboya as the man to back 'since the real danger was those who would look east' whether the old Kikuyu guard or those associates of Odinga supported by the Chinese. The attempt should be made to align three groups: KADU, Mboya and his followers, and other milder KANU followers such as the Kisii and those Kamba not committed to Ngei. This might prove easier, Lord Howick thought, due to Mboya's American funds (chiefly from labor unions) drying up and his position weakening. What Howick feared was KANU winning the election and facing strong opposition from 'eastward extremists' who would prevail on every issue. The prevention of this justified the use of money and of any Bruce McKenzies, etc., who could help to bring KADU and the westward looking half of KANU together, under whatever name and in whatever relationship to Kenyatta himself.[84]

This point of view was reflected by Blundell in an article written at the same time. In it he called on the leaders of African opinion to accept

. . . firstly, that the real menace to the future of Kenya and to themselves is not Colonialism nor Imperialism, nor tribal antipathies and divisions, but the negative atavistic elements in their own midst represented by Mr Odinga with some of the old guard and their associates, supported and refreshed by Communist money. This is a national menace which can only be met by a *national regrouping* [italics added] of those who are dedicated to a free and modern Kenya. Secondly, in an understanding that in this forthcoming battle the energy and enterprise of the resident European and Asian, who have made their homes in Kenya are an asset for eventual success and something to be encouraged . . .[85]

Blundell reflected a similar attitude in a letter written from the Second Lancaster House Conference to a farmer critic. He ended the letter by defending himself from the charge of being out of touch with European farming opinion: 'A Kenyatta-dominated Kenya, with Odinga as his chief lieutenant, must put paid to everything that we have created. I am doing my best over here to help the Africans who oppose these two, so that they can be successful.'[86]

Blundell remained unconvinced however that Mboya was the horse to back. He described Acting-Governor Griffith-Jones as 'obsessed' with the idea of splitting KANU and having Mboya emerge as the national leader. Blundell described Mboya's plan as projecting that after the general election a government would be formed with Kenyatta as Prime Minister. Kenyatta might then feel strong enough to isolate Odinga and invite some of KADU to support his government. Subsequently Kenyatta would be jettisoned as quickly as possible. Blundell viewed this as 'quite impossible.'[87]

Regionalism: politics vs. land

The concept of regionalism was tied up to this liberal concern with ensuring moderate influence in post-independent Kenya. Blundell pointed to this goal of regionalism in a private speech in London to the Joint East and Central African Board: 'The task was to establish a constitution which would enable KADU to remain as a force in it.'[88] The Governor was reported to be backing regionalism in the hope that some members of KANU would form a broader government with KADU and defeat the 'evil elements' in KANU. He viewed any constitution which left Kenyatta on top as meaning the end of everything he had tried to create and the elimination of the European community.[89]

KADU Africans viewed devolving powers to the regions as a protection for the feared Kikuyu–Luo domination of the central government. In viewing the 'Westminster model' as inappropriate for Kenya because it gave too much power to the majority, they paralleled right-wing European arguments of the fifties for 'provincial autonomy.'[90] Similar ideas were earlier circulated among liberal Europeans worried about losing political influence.[91]

In the KADU plan Kenya was to be divided into four or five large regions plus Nairobi. There would be an American-styled legislature sitting for a fixed period and electing the premier and vice premier. The proposed criteria of the four regions (Eastern, Northern, Central, Western) were that they were to be economically viable (except Northern Region), and encourage political and ethnic amity.[92] These were later spoken of as 'natural regions.'[93] The subjects over which the regions were to exercise control were listed in a KADU circular as: (1) Land; (2) Education and other essential services; (3) Appointment of public servants in the Region;

(4) Regional representation in the legislature based on the equality of representation of each region; (5) Amendments to the constitution – to be effected only by a large majority of the people in each region.[94]

Land and regionalism were inextricably linked in the minds of KADU and its supporters. Blundell, perhaps forgetting the history of European settlement in Kenya, remarked at the Second Lancaster House Conference on the impossibility of settling people in a new area without the permission of the people there. 'If you are prepared to back up regionalism it must be based on the one fundamental asset of the region – which is land. I regard this as a serious issue. It may well decide the fate of the Conference.'[95] Later in a letter to Baron Colyton before a debate in Lords on Kenya, Blundell warned that there would 'undoubtedly be a civil war' if a federal system was not instituted. The Kalenjin and Masai would not accept Kikuyu and Luo dominance.[96]

Martin Shikuku, KADU Secretary General, in more flowery language said land belonged to the tribes who won it in battle and other tribes should not be allowed to 'grab' it. KANU's centralized land board was 'just an excuse for grabbing land from others.'[97]

Neither the European farmers nor much of the Kenya government saw it this way, nor were they enthusiastic about regionalism. The farmers were dismayed to see one of their prize offspring, the Central Land Board, being squashed by moderate allies. In a 'My dear Mr Minister' letter to Blundell, Lord Delamere reflected the farmers' dislike for regionalism in regard to land. 'Now I must in fairness tell you that the European farmer regards the formation of a Central Land Authority as his only hope for the future. Any thought that he would be satisfied with some extension of the present settlement schemes under local control should be dismissed from your mind.[98] The Minister was not in a mood to be helpful in replying that the acceptability of regional land control lay in great measure not with the farmers, but with African public opinion.[99]

Colonial officials were also not inclined toward KADU's regional proposals. As early as July 1961 colonial administrators with their tradition of strong central control were advising liberal European politicians against devolving authority to local levels for fear of chaos.[100] In a memorandum prepared for the Governor's Conference, K. W. S. MacKenzie, former Minister of Finance, voiced his doubts on the future of regionalism and its viability as a brake on dictatorship. He pointed out that five-sixths of Kenya revenue came from customs and excise, income tax, stamps and motor vehicle revenue. It was impossible to collect these, except the last, on any but a national basis. He thought that regionalism would work against the very people proposing it – at least economically. The bulk of revenues came from Nairobi and Mombasa, the narrow belt of country on either side of the railroad, Central Province, Nyanza and the Scheduled Areas. Any system whereby revenue was allocated to the areas from where it was derived would work against the areas of lower potential – which, he noted, happened to be those from which the present government's supporters mainly came. MacKenzie concluded that it was unavoidable that the central government would be the principal paymaster and believing 'he who pays the piper calls the tune' left Blundell to draw the obvious conclusions.[101] Lord Howick, while accepting regionalism as a bargaining counter, did not see it as a system which could survive once the British left.[102]

In the arena of land, colonial bureaucrats felt just as keenly opposed to regionalism as the farmers. In discussions with liberal leaders, officials of the Department of Lands listed their reasons: land was a national asset, not a regional one; regionalism would only increase the present doubts on security of tenure as one could expect less responsibility from a regional board; settlement schemes would be complicated as organizations like the World Bank would only lend to the central authority; there were complications over who would get reversionary interest in the Highlands, 11,000 of the 16,000 square miles were formerly Masai; exact boundaries would cause friction; who would own minerals on the land?, would Magadi soda become Masai? The officials concluded that there was little justification for the proposals and very considerable danger and complications arising out of their implementation, even in a modified form.

FARMER LOBBYING AT THE END OF 1961

While the liberals were pushing regionalism, the settlers were plugging away at the land issue — and adding a few new twists. In its presentation to the Governor's Conference, the KNFU stressed again its apolitical nature. The opening line of the memo read:

The KNFU, being a non-political organization whose membership is open to farmers and planters of all races, is not approaching the land question in a sectional manner. (Moreover the views expressed below have been discussed with the Kenya National Traders and Farmers' Union and have that organization's complete support.)[103]

Despite its disavowal the Union's brief went on to deal with the problems of the European seller and the future of the large landowner in Kenya. The memo spoke of land titles as 'an absolute necessity' both for agriculture and democracy itself. It called for no restriction on the extent of land ownership and no discriminatory legislation favoring one group or race of farmers over another, such as a land tax on large acreages or by very high income taxes. It also asked, in a new request, that where land was compulsorily acquired for public purposes, a one year's notice be given and compensation paid in negotiable currency for the value of the land, permanent improvements, and disturbance. Acceptance of these principles would not only bring confidence to Kenya but also attract fresh overseas capital which was 'essential' for future development.

100

In the talks with African leaders both the Convention and the KNFU were preparing to go much further than merely discussing land titles. The Convention leaders thought that assurances on land title would go only part way toward restoring confidence. They wanted to know African views on future agrarian policy, in particular settlement schemes. They proposed an economic survey ('based on commonsense divorced from politics') to decide which land could be most profitably farmed as large-scale holdings and which for smallholders. They sought to have the L.D.S.B. established as a separate statutory body and proposed, in perhaps a flight of political fantasy, that immigrant farmers be encouraged to take over and develop land of which the owners wished to dispose.[104]

Neither the non-sectional approach nor the non-political scope was retained by the Union and Convention in a confidential memo to the Secretary of State during his visit to Kenya in the fall of 1961. They spoke of the need for 'a united voice' representing the Europeans to the Secretary of State. They also asked the British government to assure them, 'their own people' that the principles put forward by the Union would be entrenched in any constitution and fully supported by HMG.[105]

Although the KNFU supported the petition in its entirety, as a non-political organization it said it would discuss with the Secretary of State only the economic points. The three economic points to which the KNFU spoke were: the security of titles and property rights both rural and urban; the scope of the settlement schemes; and the maintenance of the economy. On the question of title they once again called for acceptance of responsibility by HMG, for a conference on titles in Kenya before the Constitutional Conference, and the possibility of the Union president attending the Constitutional Conference. In a new move the farmers pressed for a treaty between HMG and the independent Kenya government 'under which the latter would enter into an undertaking with HMG to respect sanctity of all Crown Grant and Titles and Property Rights.'[106]

The memo called the present settlement program inadequate to restore the land market or European confidence, and discriminatory in favor of lands adjoining the African reserves. The Union also wanted a clarification of tribal areas prior to independence. For maintaining the economy, a pre-independence survey was needed to determine what land was actually undeveloped. Also, there should be no discriminatory taxation, and added: 'Whilst agreeing with the increase of African representation on Producer Boards as a necessity, the Union wishes to point out the undesirability of the present minority Government making sweeping alterations in the very sophisticated structure of the industry.'[107]

The other points mentioned in the memo dealt with internal security, representation of minorities, and interim self-government. The maintenance of law and order meant retention of senior officers of police and administration, and the British service base for several years, as well as the necessity

101

for an independent and impartial judiciary. The administration of police and local armed forces, it was emphasized, must 'remain in European hands till such time as the danger of another Congo in Kenya can be discounted.' The memo also brought up the possible repercussions of enforced citizenship and thought that land ownership and citizenship should be kept separate. The key to representation of minorities in the interim government was that it be by election with the approval of the communities concerned. The interim internal self-government itself must be proved working smoothly prior to granting full independence.

With the breakdown of the Governor's Conference the Union made a half-hearted plea to the leaders of the two African parties for a meeting to go through the joint memorandum on land to answer questions and suggestions.[108] At the same time the Union's leadership doubted whether either of the two African leaders would agree to talk with the Union. In that case they fell back on pressing the matter with the Colonial Office, and talks with European Elected Members 'with a view to achieving a common policy for those Members to adopt at the proposed Constitutional Conference.'[109]

This last position was to lead to a continuation of the working partnership with the Coalition at Second Lancaster House. It also illustrated another difference between the farmers and the liberal Europeans. The farmers' approach to multi-racialism was very ambiguous with a clear emphasis on a pragmatic preservation of their European identity. When it helped it was adopted; when it threatened it was dropped. Hence when the Union was approached with a Convention officer's suggestion that Africans be taken into the Union to fill leadership positions, the Union's reply was skeptical. The Executive Officer wrote: 'Whilst we are in a hurry to get African members on the other hand we do not want to take any step too hurriedly which might cause the whole plan to misfire.'[110] Similar was the resistance to Africanization in the Producer Boards. At the Annual Conference on the 23rd and 24th of November 1961, a resolution was adopted that African residents in the Scheduled Areas be represented on committees of the L.D.S.B. in the Non-Scheduled Areas.[111] This racial criterion seemed to indicate dual feelings toward integrating or merely re-segregating the racially-split society.

The liberals had been tied to multi-racialism a bit longer, were more identified with it and, with their commercial ties, did not feel as economically precarious as the mixed farmer. Hence at the same time the Union was accepting the value of a European front, Blundell was turning down a Coalition request that all European members meet to find common ground prior to Second Lancaster House. He replied that many African Elected Members felt the same way as the Europeans and therefore there was no need to isolate out the particular needs of the community.[112] The liberals were still more interested in politics as a whole in Kenya, while the farmers and friends were essentially lobbyists seeking to preserve certain endangered economic interests.

CONCLUSION

The liberals used their positions in the 1961 KADU government to ensure the stability of the decolonization process and to support their African allies. They also attempted to constrain settler and nationalist opposition. To the European farmers the liberals offered a limited buy-out program and the prospect of negotiating agreement with the nationalists to secure land titles. For KANU the reward of government positions was the inducement, while the prospect of party division and isolation from government remained the threat. The liberals' influence was undermined toward the end of the year with the failure of the Governor's Conference to produce agreement, and the increasing realization, as illustrated by regionalism, that KADU was a minority party in Kenya.

The liberals and farmers were operating in 1961 at two not always compatible levels. The farmers were attempting to preserve their relatively narrow, highly endangered economic interests. This lobbying emphasis justified the preservation of the economy and political stability. For the liberals the motivation was the preservation of the economic-political system which in turn justified solving the land question. The farmers' immediate needs for security were expendable for the greater good of this preservation. Hence the view on underwriting was instructive.

When underwriting was seen as assisting the maintenance of an orderly transition, in say early 1960, it was supported. There was also the factor of the liberal Europeans still needing support from their community to continue in political life. But by 1961 Blundell saw the dangers in underwriting without settlement and opposed it. He was willing to maintain the farmers as 'economic prisoners,' fearing the effects of their departure on the economy and the liberal hopes for a moderate polity. The liberal leaders' concern was with the state; the farmers' with their assets. Settlement as finally evolved in 1962 was seen as preserving the two.

APPENDIX: SECURITY

1961 only brought a darkening of the Kenyan scene for the European farmers. The security situation seemed to be getting out of hand with a feared new Emergency arising. A Kipkabus farmer warned the police in Eldoret that a neighboring farm with an absentee owner was being occupied by Kikuyu from the reserves.[113] Farmers in Sotik reported similar take-overs in their areas, along with a rise in thefts, presumably by Kipsigis tribesmen with long-standing claims to the land. Farmers were leaving, and those remaining asked for a scheme to re-settle the Kipsigis immediately lest the land become vacant and all control lost.[114] The Convention of Associations in a memo to Hugh Fraser, Under Secretary of State for the Colonies, on his visit to Kenya, stressed the deteriorating security of farmers: 'Today the security aspect has assumed more importance and most farmers are not prepared to continue farming if the lives of their wives and families are in danger.'[115]

This lack of confidence by the farmers was reflected in the record of sales of farms in the Scheduled Area. In 'Details of 1961 Sales' by the Commissioner of Lands there were records of a Uasin Gishu 2,063-acre farm sold for Sh.150,000 which the owner had wanted to sell for a minimum of Sh.300,000 in 1959. An Aberdare ranch of over 44,000 acres sold for Sh.380,000 while the unimproved land value alone was in the region of Sh.500,000. A Machakos 4,000-acre coffee and grazing farm sold for Sh.200,000 which was described by the Lands Commission as 'well below the true value of the farm.' Other descriptions of sales by the Lands Commission ranged from 'fairly low' and 'cheap sale' to 'ridiculously low' and 'give away' price. In his covering letter to the KNFU the Acting Commissioner of Lands commented: 'I should be glad if this schedule could be kept as confidential as possible as you will see that as time has passed the market has become more depressed.'[116]

1962, MAKING THE BARGAIN: THE RESOLUTION OF THE LAND ISSUE AND THE DISSOLUTION OF THE EUROPEAN GROUPS

... that in order to save its purse, it must forfeit the crown, and the sword that is to safeguard it must at the same time be hung over its head as a sword of Damocles.

Karl Marx, *The Eighteenth Brumaire of Louis Bonaparte*

'The crowning attainment of historical study' is to achieve 'an intuitive sense of how things do not happen.'

L. B. Namier

The establishment of a large land transfer program and its acceptance by the nationalists within the framework of a coalition government in 1962 stood as a monument to the success of the Europeans' bargaining, and as an epitaph for the groups. Pressure from the farmers had encouraged the British government's growing awareness that the land issue (and the fate of Kenyan decolonization and the European settlers) was not being resolved by their previous programs. The liberals' bargaining, in turn, assisted the rightward movement of the nationalists and their acceptance of the transfer schemes as well as coalition government. But at the same time, the conservatives and liberals had undermined their political rationale. The conservative groups had offered their followers a viable exit and by so doing had reduced the numbers of their supporters. The liberals having groomed their African successors had likewise fulfilled their role. The political climate of the African state further enhanced the demise of the European political groups and the representation of European interests through non-political associations.

The Second Lancaster House Conference acted as a catalyst in fashioning a consensus between the sundry parties. The Conference's origins lay in the failure of the 1961 Governor's Conference. After their walkout the KANU nationalists demanded another Conference headed by the Secretary of State, in order to speed up the transition to independence and ensure themselves a place in the interim government. The farmers still hoped for a clear statement on their land rights and greater British support for land transfers. The liberals and KADU sought a constitution encapsuling regionalism as a means of further limiting the policy options of a nationalist regime. All sides looked to the British government for support of their programs. That the Conference did produce agreement testified both to the ultimate compatibility of the sundry groups' positions, as well as the mediating and obfuscating qualities of the metropole leadership.

A RESOLUTION OF THE LAND ISSUE

An overview of Second Lancaster House

The Second Lancaster House Conference stretched over seven weeks of frequently indeterminate discussions from the middle of February to early April, 1962. The first three weeks of the Conference were largely taken up, at the delegates' request, with extended orations by the members present. The animosity between the tribal groups and what Blundell saw as the indecision of the British as to which way it was going to push the Conference led to negotiations stalling at many points.[1] Blundell did not mention it but KADU did not aid the pace of the Conference.

KADU apparently followed a tactic of not setting out the details of its policy at first, allowing KANU to explain its position and then attacking it. This stalling and blocking in order to assure the priority of its regionalism proposals angered the European farmers. Oates wrote on Feburary 28 that the Conference had achieved nothing after two weeks entirely due to the 'pigheaded attitude' of KADU. On the other hand, KANU had appeared extremely accommodating. A few days later the farmers felt it was scarcely worth sending out more frequent reports as the Conference had been so slow.[2]

By the beginning of March, four committees had been set up: (1) the Structure of Government; (2) Land and Citizenship; (3) Judiciary; (4) Bill of Rights – with a small Steering Committee to regulate matters. This procedure led to conflict between the two parties. KADU wanted discussions on governing authorities to take precedence, while KANU wished to have all the committees meet at the same time. The dispute came from KADU's attempt to give its regionalism proposals priority and KANU resistance. A compromise was reached on February 27 whereby the Structure of Government and Bill of Rights Committees would meet at the same time. By the beginning of March KADU had not yet given detailed proposals regarding regions and means of financing them.[3]

By mid-March Oates was writing that it looked as if KANU would accept the Oates–Delamere land paper but that KADU was balking. He described the Secretary of State as irritated by KADU's firm stand.[4] The Central Land Board, caught in the crossfire over regionalism, became the main sticking point. KADU wished regional authorities to have sole control over land transactions or at least a veto over decisions of the central authority. They feared that land would be transferred to persons [read: Kikuyu] unacceptable to the tribe in a particular area. At the most, KADU leaders were willing to accept the C.L.B. as a resettlement agency only;

once it had settled people the land should revert back to the appropriate regions. Ngala refused to consider entering a coalition government until the issue was settled, and arap Moi threatened that KADU would demand partition if the C.L.B. question was not resolved.[5]

Even the proposal that each region have a representative on the C.L.B. was not immediately acceptable to KADU. Their argument was that the representatives on the Board could not be relied upon to represent their regions as they would be subject to all sorts of pressures. However when a mechanism of appeal was put in so that each region could bring objections to the Supreme Court, KADU acquiesced.[6] Maudling's paper at the Conference's conclusion established a Land Board with regional representation, an independent chairman, and 'the sole responsibility for the formation and implementation of settlement schemes.' Regional authorities were to be consulted on the tribal composition of the settlers and it was to be the Board's duty to 'consider' any objections. In fact the principle of tribal settlement was understood by all the participants and was to become a basic policy in the implementation of the schemes. Private transactions were to be controlled by the regional authority.[7] With some justification the farmers took Maudling to mean that 'there would be an independent board conducting the whole of the settlement exercise getting its finances direct from HMG.'[8]

Farmers' lobbying at Second Lancaster House

Pre-conference problems. The first problem the KNFU faced over the Second Lancaster House Conference was how to get its views represented there. In attempting this the leadership was torn between several conflicting policy goals. In terms of representation the Union clearly wanted: (1) to remain non-political/non-aligned; (2) to speak as part of a unified European voice; and (3) to have its own views presented at the Conference. But it had to choose.

In a press release to the Secretary of State, in conjunction with the Coalition/Convention, the Union stressed its own non-political role in aligning with these clearly European bodies. It wished to ensure that its European members as well as the Africans had adequate representation at the proposed constitutional conference.[9] In a circular to all area branch chairmen, Delamere described the Conference as 'probably the last time where the Europeans will have an opportunity of putting forward their views.'[10] However whether this meant representation through the Coalition (as advisers) was subject to lengthy debate. There was a dispute within the Executive Committee over affiliating with any political group. Some members hoped to garner the support of European members of KADU and KANU for a common land policy. One Vice President (Pollard) thought the land issue should be pressed very hard at the Conference by using those 'patently uncommitted in the political sphere to do it.'[11] The other Vice

President (Seys) thought the divisions between KADU and KANU Europeans were too deep to get agreement and that it was unnecessary for the Union to send its own representative as the questions over land policy were not very complicated.[12]

The Executive Committee, meeting on January 24, 1961, decided that the President, Lord Delamere, should represent the Union in London, that he should not be a member of any committee, and that he need not attend the entire Conference.[13] The latter two points, designed to keep the Union out of politics, were underlined by the Government's permission to attend the Conference. In it the Government allowed the KNFU to present the Union's views on land and property rights but were unclear whether this would be before the full Conference or to a committee.[14]

The Union membership increasingly despaired of British assistance and was ready to play what would seem its last cards. The Annual Conference in the fall of 1961 adopted a series of resolutions expressing dissatisfaction with HMG failure to honor its obligations by safeguarding the farmers. The resolutions cited 'inadequate valuation' by the L.D.S.B. They blamed the British for imposing inadequate finance and terms, and the Kenya government for 'inefficiency, procrastination, and continued changes of policy.'[15] One farmer, on having his land rents raised 643 per cent from the new valuation on land, at the end of a year of widespread drought and floods, concluded a letter to the Department of Lands this way:

I am heartily sick of the Kenya and UK Governments, and have had enough. I assure you I will pay no land rent next year for the very good reason that this worm has turned. I would sooner write off everything, including twelve years' work during which I ploughed back into the farm all I could, under a naive belief in Government promises, than continue under the present chicanery.[16]

Rank and file exasperation at English inaction was only barely beaten back by the more conciliatory Union leadership. At the January 24 Executive Committee meeting a resolution to assist KNFU members to leave by examining the possibilities of chartering ships was opposed by the Union leadership and defeated.[17] However, at the February 21 meeting, with Lord Delamere in London, farmers' frustrations boiled over. There was increasing resentment of the President's public moderation by Union members who believed that he was liquidating his assets and sending them abroad. The resolutions adopted at the February meeting declared that unless the six-point proposal was adopted 'this Union will no longer be able to advise its European members to continue to farm in Kenya,' and further it would assist them in leaving.[18]

The threat was concretized in a letter sent to Delamere by the Acting President John Pollard, giving the gist of the February 21 meeting. There was an underlying criticism of the Union leadership in Pollard writing: 'The Committee believes that our members are anxious to see us take a much stronger line, particularly in London.' It was felt that the British government had only been encouraged in its policy of rapid disengagement without adequate safeguards by the Union's 'patient and responsible attitude.' Pollard made the threat explicit warning that the possible repercussions of not implementing the Union's proposals were:

(a) a large-scale and rapid emigration of farmers and some planters, which has already begun.
(b) strong action by those determined to stay to force Britain to meet at least the minimum obligations relating to personal security and sanctity of title.

Pollard warned that if many people left Kenya in a destitute condition there would be considerable trouble from constituents in the United Kingdom who had friends and relatives in Kenya.[19]

In London Blundell felt the need to reassure European farmers. The Second Lancaster House Conference, he said, was not going to result in the overall administration of Kenya being given up by the British immediately. 'I have no doubt whatsoever that farmers who plant their crops this year will be able to reap them under a stable administration.' At his message's conclusion, delivered four-days before the end of the Algerian Civil War, he discounted the likelihood of a civil war in Kenya when the British departed.[20]

Origins of the Million-Acre Scheme. Up to the Second Lancaster House Conference, the farmers' position had closely followed the brief to the Secretary of State in the fall. The six points in their presentation (internal security and maintenance of law and order; security of Crown grants and titles; expansion of present settlement schemes; representation of minorities; interim internal self government working smoothly prior to independence; citizenship) remained identical. The justifications were also similar, although in commenting on settlement the point was made that the 250,000 Africans employed in European farming would add to the unemployment burden unless the transfer was orderly. The Union used an argument of the liberals in seeing an indigenous middle class arising from the schemes: 'The creation of an African middle class with individual property rights will do much to create stability and to promote an expanding economy.'[21]

In fact this brief was probably never presented to the Conference. On February 28, after two weeks at Lancaster House, Oates sent the Convention Executive a new plan he had written with Lord Delamere. The plan asked for £30 million to buy out all the mixed farmers. Oates mentioned that this was half of what was previously asked for and that it should only be discussed with the senior members of the Executive.[22] The need for confidentiality was brought out in a later report sent by the two leaders to their Executive Committees. It stated: 'In the final analysis African acceptance of the plan must be achieved, and any premature disclosure which might give the impression that the Europeans were hatching up something in their own interests would be fatal.'[23]

The Delamere–Oates plan was presented to Maudling 'on behalf of *The European Community in Kenya.*'[24] The details of the proposal were easily put. After reviewing the economic centrality of the Highlands and the importance of settling the land question for the relief of social tension and attaining stable government, the plan detailed the conversion of part of the Highlands. The proposal concentrated on the conversion of the mixed farming area of some 2,100,000 acres. It argued that the ranches (some 3.6 million acres) were unsuitable for immediate African occupation and could contribute meat produce of all kinds for canning, export or local consumption. The plantations (tea, coffee, pyrethrum, covering two million acres) provided the main export wealth and hence should also be left alone. They contended that HMG should accept responsibility for these branches of agriculture continuing if law and order broke down – in other words, underwriting. The economic importance of the mixed farms was not neglected by the brief, but it added: 'Nevertheless, the settlement of Africans on land of this type is so necessary for political reasons that certain agricultural risks must be accepted.'[25]

The plan called for the buy-out of fifty per cent of the mixed farmers (one million acres) over three years at a rate of £15 per acre with no buying of loose assets. About 100,000 African families could be settled and sufficient money (some £30 million over the next five years) was needed from the British for all the mixed farming land after the initial period (at 390,000 acres per annum). Also £3.6 million in loan money from the Kenya government was to provide subsistence to African tenants in their first year.

The land authority governing this was to be as far removed from politics as possible while embodying 'the maximum African participation, particularly in the matter of settling the people on the land after its purchase from the present owners.'[26] It should also be constituted so as to give confidence to international finance and encourage individual sales to the larger African farmer. If no plan was enacted there would be a rise in African unemployment in the Scheduled Areas, the £15 million worth of produce from the mixed farms would be largely lost, and the mixed farmer himself would either leave or remain discontented, contributing little to the economy and becoming a grave security risk.

The delegation's strategy on land was essentially to make an end run around the deadlocked Conference. Hence, the land paper was discussed first with the Secretary of State before presenting it to the Conference. Other matters affecting the European community were taken up directly with Maudling outside the scope of the Conference.[27] In addition to meetings with government officials, the delegation dealt with unnamed economic interests in Kenya. Delamere and Oates wrote that they had spent much time in the city of London meeting 'important people.' Their purpose was

. . . to explain the advantages of this scheme in taking the pressure off land and as a result their plantations. The Delegation will have to meet many more important people and the way is being prepared in a sympathetic atmosphere for a meeting to be held with all those planting and industrial enterprises who have interests in East Africa. It must not be forgotten that the big plantation companies are committed to work under the African independent government of the future, and for this reason have to be careful in the way in which they can give their support. However, as the land policy has manifest advantages for them we are getting a most sympathetic hearing from people who are large tax payers in the United Kingdom and who might have said, 'if we cannot be bought out why should anyone.'[28]

The leaders found the general reception to their plan encouraging. The Vice Chairman of the Convention wrote of his impression that 'HMG will accept responsibility for the European and will see him through but their thinking is concentrated on rehabilitation rather than compensation. If we want money for farms we must get it on a phased programme for transferring into African ownership.'[29] The leadership described the land paper as having received 'tremendous support' in both Houses of Parliament. Out of two meetings with Maudling, Lord Perth and other high Colonial Office officials had come conciliatory responses from HMG and the request for farmers to be patient. Maudling was seen to be in a difficult position in having to admit the failure of Macleod's policy, while Colonial Office financial advisers described the British Government to the farmers as 'bankrupt.'[30] Oates wrote on March 15 that it looked as if KANU would accept the land paper but he was not so sure of KADU. Some European members of KADU supported it but, Oates warned, Michael Blundell might oppose it out of sheer 'bloodymindedness.'[31]

Farmers' reactions. The really fierce opposition to the land paper came neither from London nor from the farmers' African opponents. It originated from the leaders' supporters at home; from the membership who felt their leaders were selling the pass.

The KNFU membership's increased militancy has already been mentioned. The Convention's stand had been for overall coverage throughout the Highlands. At its Annual General Meeting a resolution had been adopted calling on the Government 'to create a sound and practical scheme for the purchase of farms, based on the partial and temporary nationalisation of the agricultural industry.'[32] The London plan was then a reduction of the farmers' demands in line with perceived bargaining requisites. Opposition both to the substance of the plan and the lack of consultation before submitting it was foreseeable and forthcoming.

On March 1, General Irwin, the Acting Chairman of the Convention, told Oates that the membership should see the plan before it was submitted as Convention policy. On March 6, the General attacked the plan head on, calling it wholly unsound. He criticized the paper for not going far enough, being administratively unworkable, and a mere projection of the present L.D.S.B. Irwin wanted overall protection for the entire farming community. In a bit of red-baiting, he claimed to see the influence of Michael Blundell at work.[33] Later the General moderated his criticism. He complained about the priority it gave to appeasing land hunger, especially in Central Province, and its failure to emphasize African settlement on larger scale farms 'as an insurance against the breakdown of security and towards the maintenance of agricultural productivity.'[34]

On March 10, Convention/Coalition and Union leaders remaining in Kenya met to discuss the plan. The lack of explicitness on the settlement side of the plan was brought out when it became clear that no one was sure whether the schemes envisaged would be high-density or not. The KNFU had worked on the assumption that they were, the Coalition had not. There was no specific indication in the paper. If the paper was a complete land policy rather than only covering high-density schemes, then both the President's Committee of the KNFU and the Convention Executive viewed the paper as unacceptable.[35] The Union disagreed that a reduction in the number of farmers would be economically beneficial to those who remained, citing the decline in internal purchasing power.[36] Doubts were raised whether as many as fifty per cent of the European farmers would stay even with safeguards, or whether loose assets should be left out of valuation, or whether Africans would actually gain a larger share of the economy through the plan.

The leaders at the meeting also felt the plan did not sufficiently enumerate settler conditions for remaining. Besides personal safety and security of title, the meeting added three more: no unreasonable restrictions on the movement of capital, such as currency control; all measures in any land paper to be put into effect pre-independence, unless HMG continued to accept ultimate responsibility for them; and no discriminatory conditions imposed on grounds of race. The meeting concluded that any scheme must cover *all* farmers including ranches and plantations. African involvement was also spelled out in more detail. The groups concluded that the purchasing authority must be created entirely separate from an authority to settle African farmers. The latter should be under African control. 'The former must remain entirely independent, the responsibility of HMG, and must not be dissolved until all European lands offered have been accepted.'[37] This point was to be concretized in the creation of the Central Land Board and Ministry of Settlement.

The question of control was obviously an important one to the settlers. In a letter to Delamere at Lancaster House, Acting President Pollard pointed this out. The phrase 'under African control' in the plan left him dubious. If this meant overall African government control but with a fairly representative authority – O.K. But if this meant executive control of the land authority by Africans he doubted if the necessary confidence in it would be established.[38]

There were then two points of disagreement with the land paper arising from the joint meeting. First was that the authority should be divided, with HMG maintaining control of the purchase side until all the lands were sold, while the Africans could oversee settlement. And, second, that any scheme must cover *all* farmers. If the buy-out was to be limited to the mixed farmers, then ranches and plantations must have their assets underwritten. In fact, the push for an overall guarantee was largely rhetorical as the British had already repeatedly turned this down. Similarly, the demand for HMG responsibility for purchase was to be largely covered by an 'independent' authority.

The London leadership, seeing their home front crumbling, swiftly counter-attacked. Oates wrote to General Irwin that the paper had purposely left the re-allocation of land vague. 'The whole reason for this was that we wished HMG to agree in principle [to] the £30 millions for which we have asked (which in our opinion will cover all the mixed farming areas), and have not stated exactly how it would be spent.' He went on to describe the whole effort as 'a crash programme which will enable the maximum number of people to dispose of their property in the minimum amount of time.'[39] MacAllan, more bluntly, wrote that if people were not satisfied with the delegation's work they were welcome to come over and take up the gauntlet.[40] Oates remarked that 'it is difficult to get people in Kenya to realize that we do not count and that it is only after five weeks of hard work that the papers here begin to mention the Coalition and the European.' He warned that HMG was waiting for an opportunity to tell them that the farmers were not behind their leaders.[41]

The viability of threats was apparently seen differently in London and Nakuru. Oates reported to the farmers that he had made it 'quite clear' that if the British did not intend to do anything about land, he would call a meeting of farmers, as Chairman of the Convention, and tell the Europeans to salvage what they could and get out. At the same time he continued to view British policy as getting out as quickly and cheaply as possible.[42] MacAllan thought that HMG would like nothing better than to see a lot of Europeans quit; it relieved them of a security problem and, probably, compensation.[43] The delegation had in fact taken a plan for massive disobedience with them to London. The 'suggested operation' was to include resignations from government and agricultural boards, refusal to pay rents and interest on government loans, farms to convert to non-union, refusing cooperation with the employees' union, formation of police reservists under Home Guard units, and wholesale bookings by air and sea out of Kenya.[44]

The land paper attempted to bridge the gap between the expectations of the farmers and the bargaining probabilities seen by their leaders. The Kenya farming community was famously introverted and even by 1962 had yet to realize how far down the Kenya political ladder they had slipped. As the Convention's leadership continually stressed, in justifying their program, the farmers were playing with very low cards. The necessity, as the liberals earlier concluded, was to subsume the farming interests under the more adaptive mantle of the policy goals of the moderate nationalist leaders (i.e., prevent land seizures) and of the Colonial Office (i.e., promoting a peaceful transition). At the Second Lancaster House, the farmers essentially climbed aboard the ongoing liberal bandwagon.

Post-Conference perspectives. 'Nothing succeeds like success'; a maxim which made the leaders' problem of gaining their followers' support after the Conference all the more easy. The Second Lancaster House Conference was presented as a success by both the Union and Convention/Coalition leaders. Lord Delamere pointed to the setting up of the Central Land Board as a major farmer victory. 'I consider it a considerable achievement that after some 2½ years of work we have at last succeeded in convincing Her Majesty's Government that a Central Land Board divorced in the main from political control was the only answer to the problem.'[45]

Although the question of financing was not answered by the Conference here too Delamere took heart. He felt there was the 'tacit implication' that funds would be provided. No Secretary of State, he reasoned, would go to the lengths Maudling did to get agreement on the Central Land Board if it was not his intention to support it with adequate finance. Delamere had also made clear to the Secretary of State that unless adequate financial weight was put behind the 'Land Question' the majority of the European farming community would quit Kenya. There were also to be economic and fiscal commissions coming to Kenya to get the economy on an even keel. Delamere advised against 'panic action' and urged farmers to wait. In brief comments, he found proposals on the police 'reasonably adequate' while the question of citizenship was only skated over.[46]

The Convention leaders were likewise succeeding in smoothing out the ruffled feathers of their membership. Shortly after arriving back in Kenya, Chairman Oates wrote a memo to all the members of the Convention's Executive Committee defending the land plan. The thrust of his argument was that, no matter what the farmers wished, the delegation in formulating their proposal had to consider the reaction of four groups. They were the Colonial Office and HMG; KADU and KANU; supporters and others in the Houses of Parliament; and the City Companies, particularly those with plantations, to convince them they would best be served by backing the scheme rather than trying to get bought out themselves.[47] Oates in his April 18 report on the Conference explained that the delegation had intended to send a paper covering the situation as seen in London and explaining their reasoning and suggestions. The need to garner support from the various groups and the lack of time available to draft the brief meant that their proposals were sent to Kenya with no explanation, causing some misunderstanding.

Generally, Oates and Vice-Chairman MacAllan presented a sanguine picture of the Conference. The three European organizations had worked closely together. The regional authorities would have control over resettlement after the C.L.B. bought the land. The leaders thought (wrongly) that titles would be put into the land authority after independence. The British had been told that the L.D.S.B. 'Rolls Royce' schemes were useless and that they must be prepared to accept some rural slums.

Vice-Chairman MacAllan saw both the nationalists and the British increasingly centering their attention on the European farmer rather than the land. KADU and KANU views he said were the same, there were fifty per cent too many Europeans, though KADU favored a slower transfer. KANU wished to give the farmers two years to decide on citizenship and would make it a requirement for owning land. KADU offered five to six years to decide and was willing to allow dual citizenship. MacAllan felt that loss of lives would be more important than loss of lands in a British general election, and consequently influential opinion in London was primarily concerned with the farmer rather than the farm. He wrote at this time: 'If 90% of the European farmers had been able to take up land elsewhere in the Commonwealth, and thus came into the category of absentee landowners, it would be extremely difficult to convince Whitehall that there was any urgency whatsoever with regard to a land purchase scheme.'[48]

At the end of their presentation General Irwin paid tribute to the delegation, saying that the initial unfavorable reaction to the paper was due to the Executive Committee not being aware of the negotiating process in London. The meeting ended by agreeing to set up a Convention/KNFU Working Party on land and other relevant subjects in order to continue the close liaison.[49]

Liberal policies on politics and land in 1962

After the failure of the Governor's Conference the liberal Europeans had returned to attempting to get more finance for the land program and undercutting the KANU nationalists. On October 30, 1961, Blundell flew to London both to argue for better terms in the settlement program and to counter the KANU delegation's visit. With the breakdown of the Governor's Conference, KANU, now led by Kenyatta, decided to appeal directly to the Secretary of State both for a speedup toward independence and for the resignation of the Governor. Fraser and Maudling gave Blundell accounts of the discussions with KANU, and their resistance to African pressure. An instance of this was the Secretary of State meeting the delegation not in his own room but in the Conference room upstairs; a sign, Blundell reported, of Maudling's determination not to open the hospitality of his own room to the KANU delegation.[50] KANU also made a sustained attack on Havelock and Blundell in discussions with HMG, apparently blaming them for KADU's hardening stand.

Blundell wrote to Havelock that the Cabinet had agreed to 'our' recommendation for Kenyatta entering the Legislative Council but would delay an announcement so as not to appear to be under pressure from the Kenyatta visit. Further, he felt that the battle over regionalism had been won, presumably meaning that the officials in the British government had accepted the KADU proposals.[51]

On the settlement side Blundell, as Minister of Agriculture, was cooperating with the farmers to gain better terms for land purchase. He met with Lord Delamere on October 26 and agreed with him on the unsatisfactory nature of the terms. He also agreed to take an unofficial member of the Settlement Board, Mr S. H. Powles, with him to London to press for better terms.[52] In a letter to the Minister of State for Colonial Affairs, Blundell expanded on his fears that the terms of sale were not attractive enough to induce farmers to sell and hence endangered the schemes. He warned:

Unless I can get more attractive terms on which the farmers will sell, we cannot proceed with the Settlement Schemes. These have been so built up in the public mind that it will be a disaster for the Kenya Government and for HMG if we fail to make them a success. I have never moved from the belief that some form of settlement of this nature is absolutely essential to the long-term solution of the agrarian problem. As you know, it also brings into the ownership of land in Kenya organizations such as the World Bank and the CDC. If we cannot get a firm basis of settlement established before independence then much of the thinking which you and I discussed originally after the Lancaster House Conference will fail.[53]

Blundell also wished to discuss the declining European agricultural production leading to unemployment, crimes of violence, lack of security and confidence and hence less production, in a vicious circle. The Minister wanted positive measures to encourage the settlers to go on farming.

The alliance between the Minister and the farmers was a brief marriage of convenience. The farmers were aware of Blundell's ambivalence toward settlement and distrustful of both his motives and goals. In a letter to an Area Branch Chairman, Alec Ward brought this suspicion out in explaining why the farmers pressed for a member of the Settlement Board to accompany the Minister: 'In passing, of course, I should say that the reason why we wanted Mr Powles to go to London was to keep an eye on the Minister.'[54]

The Minister in London fully justified these suspicions. In his memorandum to the Secretary of State, Blundell pointed to the change in European farming from a long term program of a seven to ten year appreciation of agriculture to a three or four year policy. He quoted a recent survey by his Ministry which showed twenty per cent of the European farmers wishing to go in any case in the conditions emerging in Kenya; forty per cent determined to stay; and 'forty per cent are willing to stay unless they can realize a reasonable value for the assets which they have created on their farms.' From this peculiar wording (the farmers would have phrased it along the lines of forty per cent remaining if they were assured their assets could be safeguarded), Blundell concluded that the majority of European farmers were settling down to the new conditions mainly because they had no alternative.[55] This interpretation of settlers' motives was opposite that of the farmers' organizations, and could not help but lead to differing conclusions on underwriting and settlement.[56]

Blundell was also lobbying to secure KADU's place in the evolving political arrangements. In a private speech before the Joint East and Central African Board in London he presented himself as a member of neither KADU nor KANU. At the same time he lobbied hard for KADU. He described them as decent though inarticulate men, disciplined and loyal, but not enjoying the use of any American or Communist money. Their resources were more slender than KANU's. He doubted if Kenyatta without his old enthusiasm and fire was able to control the KANU extremists any more than he could in 1952.[57] Tom Mboya (who was becoming a 'Great White Hope' in Great Britain) Blundell described as constructive in labor and destructive in politics.[58]

In fact Blundell was increasingly worried about the direction of both European and African politics at this time. In an article written for *The Times* in early 1962 he criticized those Europeans looking for 'Emergency Exits.'

The Colonial era is going and our best chance of maintaining a country of reasonable standards and ensuring that our assets, whether businesses, land or property, are a marketable commodity is by working with and helping the new African society which is emerging to be a success. Only when we have failed have we a right to expect Emergency Exits.[59]

By May in a memo to Baron Colyton he was warning about the mixed farmers becoming a 'long term canker to the Conservative Party unless HMG has the courage and funds to deal with the problem.' While Blundell felt there was a future for European businesses, plantations and some of the ranches, he feared the mixed farmer would come under 'intolerable pressure.' At the same time he worried about the 'catastrophic decline' in the economy which would result if a major exodus of settlers occurred in the next two years.[60]

Although Blundell and Havelock declared themselves in retrospect opposed to the post-Second Lancaster House land settlement schemes, the transfers were undoubtedly an extension of their policies.[61] The liberals viewed the program as requiring too much money which could be better used on development projects throughout the country. The liberal leaders emphasized European farmer pressure behind the evolving schemes. But the ex-NKG liberals were weakened and ambivalent at this point. Their attention focused on African politics, specifically regionalism, and the promotion of a moderate (if not KADU-dominated) coalition. The farmers' proposals at Second Lancaster House Conference took a page from the liberals' book and if Blundell opposed them at the time it was neither loudly nor long. By default, the farmers' lobby appeared to have received a wave and a 'nice work if you can get it.' The passing of the Kenyan European liberal from a central political role was neatly illustrated by Blundell's retirement shortly after the Second Lancaster House Conference.

In addition to political factors a certain personal weariness was leading Blundell to resign his Ministry on June 20, 1962. He had been planning to retire for some time. In October 1961 he wrote Lord Alpert of his desire to give up politics the following year to return to his business and family interests.[62] In a letter to Viscount Boyd on May 2, 1962, he delved further into his reasons. Although Ngala had asked him to stay on, there was room for only one European in the Cabinet and he thought Havelock wanted the Ministry of Agriculture. Blundell felt himself to be a direct descendant of a tradition in political life in Kenya, and in England, which was now changing. He felt out of step. He mentioned the need to subordinate his own personality to the new African leaders, and driving to and from Subukia (his up-country farm) over a hundred times a year. The letter ended pessimistically with Blundell writing that he had based his political thinking on the assumption of remaining in Kenya, yet:

I feel that the cry for Africanisation, the compensation terms for expatriate Civil Servants and the general attitude of the African together with the pace at which we are advancing may make it impossible for the smaller European farmer such as myself to continue his activities. In fairness, therefore, to Gerry and Suzie [wife and daughter] I feel I must restore my financial position so that in the event of our having to leave this country, I should be able to offer Gerry and Suzie some future elsewhere.[63]

Two months later he was doubting one of the tents of liberal policy in a letter to the Conservative Party's Research Department. Blundell was dubious if an African government would want 'the disciplines and sanctions which a large European community will impose.' And he did not believe Africans would maintain a Kenya similar to colonial Kenya merely because of the European presence.[64]

Nationalists' positions on land

KANU moderation. By the Second Lancaster House KANU policy pronouncements on land were losing most of their militant tone and coming into line with the other groups' views. Jomo Kenyatta's presence in the high councils of KANU had a moderating effect on the policy preferences at this point. There was still a militant younger wing (the Ginger Group) pushing for expropriation with payment given only for the loose assets and improvements made on the land.[65]

The consolidation of the diverse views on land within KANU around a moderate core may be traced to several factors. Kenyatta's moderating influence has already been mentioned and was undoubtedly central to an explanation. The fear of independence being delayed as well as the hope of unravelling distasteful parts of the land schemes post-independence were also important factors to the leadership.[66] The nationalists had a tendency not to pay much attention to the details of their agreements and Second Lancaster House seemed no exception.[67] There was the worry of KADU moderation leading to KANU being excluded from government – even coalition government. And finally, there was the need to fulfill past promises of land to the forest fighters who were returning disappointed at what their leaders were now doing and threatening to fight against an African government.[68]

In an article entitled 'KANU Policy for Second Lancaster House,' Kenyatta made clear the moderate reformist aims his party would pursue on land:

KANU will recognize and respect rights in private property. As I have often stated, the African people are not robbers. However it is no use pretending that thousands of Africans can go on suffering from landlessness, poverty, hunger and unemployment while vast areas of land lie completely idle and undeveloped.

While we shall maintain and assist farmers who develop their lands and who assist the economy of our country, we shall vigorously pursue a policy of land reform.[69]

This emphasis on a primarily economic argument for taking over 'idle and undeveloped' land was expanded on several days later. The broad policy was that 'maximum security must be given to those – irrespective of race or tribe – who have developed their land.' Security of title would be enshrined in the Constitution. Under-developed land would be subject to government acquisition, with fair compensation, after the owner was given a year to formulate a plan to bring the land into full production. Adequately developed land should not be acquired except for public purposes such as roads and railways. The three basic principles in planning settlement schemes, presumably for those under-utilized areas, were:

1. Particular attention to the landless and unemployed;
2. Increased overall production in the country;
3. Economic viability to enable the new farmer to repay loans and interest without hardship.[70]

What the KANU leadership seemed to be doing was bringing the question of the Highlands under the rubric of development, and, like the other groups, politically defusing it. Explicitly moving away from the political and historical arguments of ownership of the Highlands, KANU emphasized liberal economic arguments designed to minimize conflict. The landless would be taken care of; the hard-working European farmer would be protected;

119

and the economy of the country would flower. All this was to occur by using extra land and external funds to rectify internal conflict.

The obvious contradictions in the program make it difficult to assess how seriously it was put forward as a realistic policy. The contradiction of putting the bottom rungs of the population on undeveloped land and expecting them to pay off loans with a resulting increase in production was likely unresolvable. Though difficult to determine how much of the Highlands KANU leaders felt to be under-utilized (they proposed a land survey commission to determine this), one could point out that the extent of the schemes was to be determined by the availability of land rather than the number of landless. On this point the liberals were more concerned than KANU. The immediate goal of their land policy was to reduce political pressure on land from Africans (and secondarily from Europeans wanting out). Areas transferred were to be a factor of the competing pressures. When the balance was restored in this mechanistic model, the schemes would taper off.

The KANU nationalists, although perhaps thinking along these lines, minimized the idea of competing forces and played consensus politics. Specifics were still scrupulously avoided, though KANU was initially against tribal spheres of interest in apportioning land. At the same time, KANU supported the pre-Second Lancaster House schemes at least to the extent of urging their followers to go ahead with settlement. During the Lancaster House Conference Kenyatta publicly declared; 'There are people spreading rumors that KANU will distribute free land to people when *uhuru* comes. Nothing could be further from the truth.' Even when land was acquired by a free government, Kenyatta said, the persons settled would have to help finance the program.[71]

The disagreements on land between KADU and KANU at Lancaster House boiled down to arguments on regionalism. Specific questions were: Would tribal spheres of influence be recognized in settling Africans? And who would have responsibility for the schemes, the central government or the regions? The outcome of that debate has already been discussed. Although the compromise leaned toward KADU's position, there was apparently some disagreement in the party over accepting it and forming a coalition government. Blundell urged Ngala to accept the Secretary of State's proposals in the hope of strengthening KADU and regionalism for the next constitutional conference. He felt that the dangers in rejection lay in alienating the Secretary of State, causing further economic disintegration in the country, and strengthening the Odinga-wing in KANU.[72]

The liberal Europeans' attempt to undercut the militant wing of KANU remained a constant. Oginga Odinga was seen as the leftist threat while Kenyatta was viewed ambivalently. Often, Kenyatta was portrayed as a weak figurehead unable to control the more militant wing which threatened to engulf KANU. One is not certain how apt a description this was. It may have reflected some liberal and British officials' hopes of having Kenyatta replaced by a stronger, more certain figure – probably Mboya.[73]

The liberals were also not worried about the coalition government failing and indeed thought this likely. If this happened, Blundell felt the Governor should rule by decree with a small body of nominated advisers. In the meantime the Secretary of State would make it clear that elections would be held at the end of the year on the basis of the constitution agreed to in London. This gave added time to the transition period and highlighted the discord among the contending African parties. 'I think that their energies would be so dissipated in fighting each other that the chance[s] are we could continue to rule the country until the elections had decided which part[y] would be in majority, and thus free to resume the task of government.'[74]

KADU reservations. By mid-1962 (after regionalism had been temporarily tucked away) KADU's differing tone in approaching settlement from that of KANU was apparent. Given the strong influence of liberal Europeans with their lukewarm support of massive land transfers, the absence of a mass base of land-hungry supporters (such as those who threatened the KANU leadership's control), and KADU leaders' own fears of Kikuyu expansion, the rather detached, cautious attitude toward land transfers was to be expected.

In July KADU presented a detailed summary of the party's position on land. The plan entitled 'Land Tenure and Agricultural and Pastoral Development for Independent Kenya' made clear KADU's acceptance of many of the liberal European arguments and programs of the previous months. Their development program emphasized the economic production of the Highlands, the necessity for foreign investment, and the limits and low priority of the settlement schemes.[75]

Reassurances for the European farmer were plentiful. Security of tenure was variously termed 'essential' and 'fundamental' to agricultural development. There was a 'vital place' for European and Asian farmers in the economy and Kenya citizenship was not considered 'an essential condition for the development of a farm or ranch to the benefit of the Kenya economy'. The limitations on the size and number of holdings were to be left to the regions. While the document stated that it was vitally important that available land be fairly distributed and that excessively large holdings did not jeopardize the social and economic interests of the rural population, a last sentence on the paragraph added: 'In this connection, it is interesting to note that quite often a large area of land efficiently farmed, supports more people than if it were cut up into small holdings.' Individual tenure was considered the best form of holding for the country, although in some areas it might prove to be impractical.

The constraints and shortcomings of land reform were repeatedly empha-

121

sized. 'Land reforms must be carried through legally and with justice to European farmers and all the tribes,' the paper's summary said. The tone of the document's approach to settlement was brought out by a paragraph on the first page, which demonstrated a singular lack of enthusiasm for settlement, a fear of the process being carried out unlawfully thereby leading to an economic downturn, and faith that development based on the present economic system would lead to greater prosperity for all.

Granted that some reforms are necessary in the distribution of farming land, that some transfers of population from over-populated areas are necessary, and that land must be acquired for them, the seizure of farms and farm property without payment of fair compensation, whether by Government authority in the future, or by lawless persons, and without justice and fair legal procedure, are not only unnecessary in a land reform programme aimed at promoting agricultural expansion, but they would in fact retard development. They would destroy the confidence of all farmers, African and European, Arab and Asian; and they would without doubt cut off investment in our economy through either public or private channels. The solution to the problem of 'land-hunger' is not just in issuing land to the landless; it is in greatly increasing the productivity of farms everywhere.

It was further stressed that the highest returns could be gotten from existing farms. As new farms cost ten to twenty times as much to bring to the same level of production, the 'strictest economy must be exercised in the use of funds for settlement and agricultural development.' All of the farms in the settlement schemes were to be planned to yield a minimum output of £300 a year within ten years, which would seem to belie the concern for the landless as this would reduce the number of plots available and likely presume qualifications. The schemes were to be located in the traditional spheres of influence of the people concerned.[76]

FARMERS' ACTIVITIES AFTER SECOND LANCASTER HOUSE

Efforts at influencing settlement plans

For the rest of 1962 the farmers pushed the urgency of the schemes and the need for finance. Previous ideas of underwriting, private land corporations, and most certainly direct compensation, were dropped as the farmers lent themselves to influencing the schemes being formulated. The Coalition urged the Secretary of State to speed the appointment of the Chairman of the C.L.B. and more than a mere extension of the present inadequate settlement schemes.[77] Maudling replied that the details of setting up the new machinery should not delay the early appointment of an 'independent' Chairman. However by the time of Maudling's visit to Kenya in July he could only report that difficulties had been encountered and he was not yet able to make a suitable appointment.[78]

A delegation from the three conservative groups met Maudling on July 9 and stressed again the importance of having settlement well underway prior to independence.[79] Agricultural development and planning should be left till afterwards, for now it was important to get Africans on the land using tribal authorities. They hoped that the Minister was not swayed by the false impression of prosperous farming as most farmers after the 1961 droughts and floods were planting maximum acreage in hopes of getting enough money to leave Kenya. The delegation also stressed the need to retain the various agricultural marketing organizations. The delegation reported that Maudling was sympathetic but did not appreciate the seriousness of the situation.[80]

The following day (July 10) Maudling announced in Nairobi a one million acre turnover of European land for resettlement. Without giving too many details – which had not been worked out – Maudling saw the schemes running for five years with a likelihood of an extension, and costing more than £15 million. He remarked that there was no question but that productivity would fall. KANU and KADU both welcomed the statement. Representatives of the Coalition and Convention termed the proposals totally inadequate. Delamere backed the scheme stressing that it would provide an opportunity for those whose land was purchased to reinvest in the country if they wished to stay.[81]

A day after the announcement Lord Delamere reported to the KNFU's Settlement Sub-Committee on his visit with Colonial officials. There he had got the impression that HMG was not going to announce a plan for sufficient money for the purchase of the whole mixed farm area over ten years. The reasons given him were the felt impossibility of planning in Africa as far ahead as ten years, and the British Treasury's refusal to pledge all the money necessary to underwrite the scheme. Lord Delamere had urged the first step of a Million-Acre scheme *over three years* which, the Lord strangely reported, the Colonial Office had accepted.[82]

At the end of July a special conference of the Convention met to pass an Executive Committee resolution expressing dissatisfaction with Mr Maudling's 'very vague proposals.' The Conference warned that the lack of urgency and restricted acreage would lead to the large scale abandonment of European farms.[83] In August, two Coalition leaders (Welwood and Cole) journeyed to London to press for a speeding up of the schemes. They wanted the schemes completed in three years, not five. The Europeans still wanted assurance of the continuity of the schemes and thought the British must insist on settlement funds having priority on Kenya development monies, as a lever over Africans after independence. Maudling reportedly replied that 'When Africans began to see the Europeans going and the Africans coming onto the land, it was felt that pressure would be brought to bear on the Africans to stop the scheme.' The delegation attacked the Minister of Settlement, Bruce McKenzie, telling the Secretary of State that having settlement in the hands of a Minister affiliated with KANU was a 'fatal mistake.'[84]

Whether from panic or calculation the farmers were moving to a more short-term political approach to settlement. The previous worry of saddling the economy with non-economic rural slums was now secondary to the immediate need to get Africans on the land and settlement initiated in a manner making it difficult for an independent government to reverse the commitment. In this the Coalition differed from the Union. The latter consistently stressed the importance of making the plots economic – ensuring that they would enhance the large farm system of the Highlands.

This was no small tactical difference. The Coalition/Convention were at this point intent on a 'go' scheme. They wished to have the farmers who chose to leave get sufficient money for their holdings – whether through compensations, underwriting or settlement. They primarily sought to preserve the value of their land and looked for schemes designed to preserve their economic assets, whether they stayed or left.[85]

The Union, though admittedly ambiguous, attempted the much more complicated task of preserving a life-style. The Union leadership was certainly concerned with the settlers' assets. But the hope was to combine this with the preservation of the large farm system. Hence, the interest in integrating the new African farmer into the farming system of the Highlands; the worry over changing the marketing organizations; the concern with the Land Bank so that Europeans bought out under the scheme might settle elsewhere in Kenya.

The Union leadership ran into frequent criticism from farmers for neglecting the needs of those who wished to leave. One member of the Executive Committee resigned in October 1962 saying that he thought the KNFU was being unnecessarily antagonistic to those who might want to leave.[86] And after an October 5 meeting with Bruce McKenzie where the details of the Million-Acre scheme were explained to the Union, President Delamere spoke. He said the role of the KNFU was one of helping farmers who had farms in the settlement area but wanted to remain in Kenya.[87] In a press release, the Union welcomed the Minister's plans and announced it was compiling a list of farms for those in the purchase areas who wished to stay.[88]

Union meetings with Kenyan and British officials in 1962 underlined this concern. The newly-established Settlement Sub-Committee of the Union suggested that Minister of Settlement McKenzie be told the importance of trying to get increased output from the high density schemes. And their recommendation that South Africans be bought out in the early years of the scheme could be seen as a desire to keep visible irreconcilables from rocking a shaky boat.[89]

The Land Bank was a special focus of the KNFU's lobbying activities. In

July 1962 the Minister of Agriculture, Wilfred Havelock, was urged to expand the Bank to allow European farmers who were bought out to purchase farms elsewhere in Kenya. In the fall McKenzie reported to the farmers that he would seek legislation to allow the Bank to lend up to eighty per cent of the land values of the farms.[90] The President pressed the Governor on October 23 to persuade the Treasury, while he was in London, to provide extra funds for the Bank. The Governor agreed to do this.[91] The enabling legislation was passed at the end of 1962, but in early 1963 the Union was still asking for funds for the Land Bank. They denied they were trying to build up the position of the larger farmer or to create an African landed class. The Union stressed instead the settlement farmers' dependency on the large farmer for seeds and stock. Pointing to the increased demand for funds, they wanted a drawing account of up to £4 million (by way of a British loan) for the period of the settlement schemes, adding that the Bank should be regarded as part of the main scheme not a side line.[92]

Despondency and demise of the Convention/Coalition

Increasingly the settlers' hostility toward their old antagonists, the British Government and the nationalists, was mellowing into despair. Cavendish – Bentinck remarked after the Coalition Delegation's August report: 'We had no cards to play really and it must now be a process of attrition.'[93] When a local association (Trans-Nzoia) threatened to pull out of the Convention in the aftermath of the leadership's acceptance of the Second Lancaster House program of settlement, the leaders pointed again to their 'low cards,' the pointlessness of threats, and the possible future necessity of sticking their toes in when ninety per cent of the community was behind the action.[94] An April 1962 appeal for funds by the Convention began: 'While we have time to speak as a community . . .'[95] Governor Renison in a November interview with Oates thought the recent venomous speeches against Europeans were nothing to what one could expect.[96] Cavendish – Bentinck added to the account that those who knew the behind-the-scenes activities were aware of the hatred being built up against the Europeans.[97]

Darkening further the somber-hued environs was what the Europeans saw as the worsening security situation.[98] In a brief apparently prepared for the British Conservative Party Conference, the Convention warned of an 'explosive' situation. The specter of Mau Mau was raised in the person of the Land Freedom Army, which 'composed exclusively of Kikuyu and organized on a cell basis, has the avowed objective of seizing land by force after independence.'[99] These were not isolated gangs, the Convention maintained. They were supplied, fed, informed and assisted by Kikuyu employed on farms and in the forests. The Convention did not believe it could exist if the Kikuyu people 'refused all assistance to the Land Freedom Army and helped the police to locate its members.' The brief also tied in the land schemes to the defeat of this menace: 'if, under the settlement schemes, the Kikuyu receive adequate land to provide them with a good living, there may be no resurgence of the subversive movement in the future.'[100]

Other elements in Kenya political life assumed various postures toward the Land Army at this time. KANU officials were dubious, with one apparently suggesting the Europeans were bribing Kikuyu to make guns. Sir Anthony Swann, the Minister of Defense, in a radio interview pointed to the Army's existence and police raids which had uncovered hidden dumps of home-made and stolen firearms on European farms.[101] In mid-November KADU's President Ngala deplored the tendency to play down the gravity of the Land Freedom Army. He called it a 'vile, subversive movement.'[102]

The Convention was equally bleak over its own future. The leadership realized the impossibility of carrying on after independence as a monoracial organization. Yet the identity of race and interest was so strong that no other avenue but the dead-end street they were on seemed possible. Oates' report at a June 8 Council meeting brought this out:

It needs little thought to realize that Convention in its present form has a limited life, and is unlikely to be able to continue after independence for Kenya has been reached. Up to this time, however, it has a most important role to play for the Europeans and for this reason Council is of the opinion that membership should be confined to them.[103]

At the Council meeting it was felt that after independence any representations for Europeans would have to be made through 'bodies of special interests such as farming, industry, trade, professions, but not by a political body.' In line with this district associations wishing meetings with agricultural and police officers were advised to do it through the KNFU, a multiracial body.[104]

There was, however, thought to be room for an organization 'divorced from party politics and dedicated to the welfare of the community.' A November 30 meeting of Coalition and Convention leaders unanimously adopted a resolution to set up a European organization based on individual membership to amalgamate all existing European groups. It was described as 'a sort of protection association' to meet the risks of the next fifteen or twenty years. While the body would stay out of internal politics, it was needed for representation in England after independence.[105] Although seen as a merger of the Convention and Coalition, by the time this 'Society of Kenya Europeans' was set up its Chairman, R. J. Hilliard, expressed the view that no one who had anything to do with the Convention should have anything to do with the Society. He said this at the last Executive Committee Meeting of the Convention on May 14, 1963, which ended with the Secretary being given the typewriter and Gestetner, and a vote of thanks to the Chairman.[106]

A QUAGMIRE OF MOTIVES

By mid-1962, then, a viable consensus on the land question had been reached by all the contending/not-so-contending parties. KANU was in the government and Kenya was set for self-government and independence on December 12, 1963. The British government had accepted the major responsibility for financing the schemes and for overall charge of them. KADU agreed with the centralized structure of the land conversion and the areas to be converted. KADU and KANU also accepted the presence of the European farmers and the means by which part of the Highlands would be turned over to Africans. The farmers, while still pressing for guarantees of title, were willing to sell their farms under the schemes (the 'goers') or accept settlement as the means for insuring their economic assets (the 'stayers'). All the groups concurred on the necessity of the program for preserving the stability of the independent government. Each had much to lose from rural land seizures and the overturning of the colonial economic structure. The threat from the masses was the cement on the agreement to settlement schemes.

Settlement as a reaction to European farmer pressure

The crucial question remaining was: what were the policy requisites of the two governments involved which they believed satisfied by the initiation of the Million-Acre scheme in the fall of 1962? The answer to this has been usually posed in terms of a reaction to pressures from the European farmers wishing to sell their assets.

Those who argued that governmental concern with the European farmer was the dominant motivation behind the schemes were usually those connected with European liberal politics. Blundell, Havelock, and other members of the liberal European community generally viewed the schemes as a misallocation of funds in the interests of an intransigent settler community. The schemes to them were a concealed form of compensation pushed on the Conservative government by influential Anglo-Kenyan interests desiring to get out of Kenya *avant le deluge.*

Dr John Harbeson presents this perspective in an article.[107] He concludes that: 'The Colonial Office prepared for independence by ministering to the fears of Europeans rather than by helping African leaders to mount social and economic programmes in line with their own national-building conceptions.' This was concretized in the land transfer program by two important terms: '(1) that Africans should not be permitted to receive European land free, and (2) that extensive land resettlement should take place prior to Kenya's independence, in order to minimize the exposure time of European landowners to an African government.'[108] Harbeson stresses the 'sensitivity' and 'preoccupation' of the Colonial Office and British government to European political demands and fears, and concludes that the 'financing, timing, and structuring of land resettlement' was designed to serve 'European interests.'[109]

A phrase such as 'European interests' may be considered a 'Bikini clause': what it reveals is interesting, what it covers is vital. What interests? And which Europeans? 'European' interests were not monolithic on settlement, as the previous chapters have indicated. One must only remember that the European farmers and their families totalled less than 20,000 of a community of 60,000 in order to question the identity of 'farmer' interest with 'European' – were, for example, the resident Colonial officials and European commercial community silent marchers in the farmer phalanx? But even within 'farmers' there were divergent interests: between 'stayer and goer;' large farmer, small farmer; 'mixed farmer and plantation.'

Besides bunching Europeans together, Harbeson consistently overestimates the effects of 'European' interests ('European' here apparently meaning 'settler') overpowering something called 'African interests.' For instance the 1962 regional constitution is designed 'mainly to assuage European political fears,' a conclusion which not only conceals most of the farmers groups' indifference, and bureaucrats' opposition, to regionalism, but also viewing these as 'concessions to the settlers,' ignores KADU Africans (pp. 244 – 5). The Central Land Board is described as one 'in which regional governments and European settlers would have more influence than the Central Government,' a neat legerdemain which obscures the fact that the Board had representatives from *each* region and *one* from the European settlers (p. 241). The other side of the coin is that 'African' interests are slighted in the land policy. 'Except for the policy that all major African communities should be included in the settlement programme, departure from the agricultural specifications for the benefit of African political and social interests was less in evidence.' (p. 242)

This last sentence illustrates much of the fault of the argument. In the first place it is not true. In the next chapter on implementation, this point will be discussed in greater detail. For the present one can point to a number of unmentioned items. First was the emasculation of the settlers' prize, C.L.B., by the Kenya government for a variety of reasons, not least of which was a fear of interference with Kikuyu settlement. The acceleration of the schemes, as made clear by government memos, certainly in 1963, was a direct result of a feared land grab in Nyandarua. The location of the settlements was not, in the main, on the basis of which Europeans wished to sell, but rather which tribes were likely to need buying off. The types of schemes initiated, both high-density initially and later low-density, were designed to dissipate land pressure, maintain the economy, and promote a landed African class.

But there is a more basic fault than a factual one involved in Harbeson's sentence. The remark about settlement seldom departing from agricultural specifications 'for the benefit of African political and social interests' points to the crux of the question which Harbeson merely obscures. Is a program which distributes land to landless Africans *ipso facto* for the benefit of African interests? Is the emphasis on Kikuyu, and former insurgents to be explained as a reward for insurgency? Are the people who are so blatantly the *objects* of a policy necessarily its beneficiaries? Even if Africans were given land free and if the schemes were not initiated until independence, would then 'African interests' be served rather than 'European?'[110] The questions range over the values of the broader political system which, by neglecting, Harbeson has implicitly accepted. Following the nationalists, he has taken up their terms ('nation-building'), their categories ('African interests'), and one might add, their mistakes.

The point is that resettlement in the Kenya Highlands was an integral part of the adaptation of a colonial political economy to the removal of formal colonial authority and the entrenchment of an African political elite. Both the European mixed farmers' threats to abandon their farms and the African (Kikuyu) masses' threats to fulfill by their own hands their leaders' promises of land, were potentially disruptive to this process. Both groups' demands were bought off (sold out) by the bureaucratic, political and economic vested interests of an evolving transnational system. The difficulty of enumerating the interests involved is not sufficient cause for allowing the inadequacy of the African–European dualism to pass unchallenged. In the political sphere, alone, the NKG–KADU merger, the British commercial backing for KADU, the AFL–CIO support for Mboya,[111] and the Colonial Office's efforts to strengthen Kenyatta and isolate Odinga were alliances which were neither one-sided nor limited to racial or national boundaries. The attempt to see racial identification as the crucial analytical category was and is to ignore the pattern of economic and political realignment occurring at the time. It neither reflects the historical record accurately nor does it elicit satisfactory explanations for making sense of the diverse political phenomena under study.

Settlement as a support of decolonization

One seemingly obvious point needs to be stressed. The settlement schemes were initiated and implemented neither by the European farmers nor the African peasantry. They were programs of the Kenya government financed largely by the British government. Both governments were pressured to various degrees by the two groups and especially in the beginning, relied largely on personnel drawn from European settlers to carry out the programs. But the governments also acted to filter out and play off the diverse forces, and to create schemes compatible with the available resources, the demands made on them, and the goals formulated by the governments' bureaucratic-political nexus.[112]

The Kenya government's predominant concern was ensuring stability during the period of transition and after, and preserving the large-farm system. To do this African land pressure had to be relaxed and the European farmers reassured. Internal government documents made this point clearly. In the Government's proposal to the British government for the Million-Acre scheme (completed on July 21, 1962), the Government's own predominantly political goals were made quite evident:

Before going into details of the new scheme, it is necessary to consider some of the implications. The scheme is political and is designed to ensure stability at the time of Independence. It seeks to do this by giving European farmers a sense of security so that they may be encouraged to stay and by removing the tension from the land problems by providing settlement for those tribes which are suffering most from pressure on their own lands, where many have no land or insufficient land, and for other tribes to a lesser extent. If this is not done, a very serious situation could arise in which Europeans would evacuate their farms and Africans walk in. As the economy is an agricultural one to which European farming provides not only the bulk of the exports and of the locally marketed crops (although with the rapid development of African farming under the Swynnerton Plan this preponderance is lessening and will continue to lessen) as well as of taxation, this could bring an economic collapse in the country. It is therefore, imperative to take all possible steps to prevent this and both to give assurances to European farmers and a sense of security and also to settle in the next year or so as many persons as possible from the densely populated African areas. It is hoped that thereafter the pressures will relax, certainly by the end of five years, if not earlier, so that a continuation after five years of this type of scheme may not be necessary.[113]

A memo intended for the I.B.R.D. written to justify a loan revision in the fall of 1963 stated:

2. The primary object of all settlement schemes is to ensure the political stability of the country as it enters independence, through a rapid transfer of land ownership from Europeans to Africans in an orderly way such as will preserve the economy and, indeed, develop it further . . .[114]

The argument against these references, and others, would presumably be that (a) they were justifications for funds from sources favoring a broader objective than buying out European farmers; and (b) the justifications had to be passed upon by African political leaders not overly congenial to compensating expatriate landowners. But there are other references as well. The Permanent Secretary of the Ministry, in turning down a European farmer's proposal for settlement replied to him in part:

The object of settlement schemes is not to buy out European farmers, but to settle Africans so that land pressures, particularly in the more overcrowded African areas may be dissipated, in the hope that it will disappear, and to give some sense of security to the European farmer, who has been promised a successor scheme if there is still a demand for it . . .[115]

In reply to a complaint from the Colonial Office that they did not feel very well informed on settlement, the Ministry sent back an 'Extract from letter from PC [Provincial Commissioner] Nyeri' relating the success of the schemes in countering Kikuyu extremist groups. European farmers' reactions were not dealt with.[116] At least in the correspondence of the Permanent Secretary of the Ministry of Settlement from April 1962–July 1964 (before that he was involved in settlement as Deputy Secretary of Agriculture) the dominant concern was not with buying out European farmers. It was with defusing potential disruptions to the system. This was also the perspective of nearly all the expatriate bureaucrats interviewed who worked on the settlement schemes.[117]

Settler influence was of course felt and likely played a role in evolving HMG support for settlement. This can be seen in the conditions the British government placed on its funding for the Million-Acre scheme. In a memorandum by Bruce McKenzie to the Kenya Council of Ministers, British conditions were listed this way:

These offers are conditional on the Kenya Government accepting that:
i) the settlement schemes will have first priority for HMG's assistance towards Kenya's Development Programme over the five years;

ii) the total aid of £16.3 million towards the 1,000,000 acre scheme (excluding the IBRD/CDS Schemes) will be the maximum financial aid that HMG is prepared to make available to the scheme, and if less is required to settle 1,000,000 acres, that amount only will be available, if more is required, further assistance will not be available and the area will be reduced.

iii) annual negotiations will take place between the Kenya Government and HMG and the Central Land Board on the programme of settlement for each succeeding year and its financing; the Kenya Government will supply any information required by HMG on the operation of the scheme, and will accept occasional visits by experts to examine various aspects of schemes, including land valuation;

iv) HMG's consent will be required to any appointment to the posts of Chairman of the Central Land Board and of Director of Settlement;

v) to the extent that the need arises, the Kenya Government will allocate to the Land Bank up to £200,000 a year during the five years of the scheme to facilitate transfers of land outside settlement areas over and above what it available in its ordinary operations (and HMG will agree to use for this purpose any development funds that it makes available to Kenya).

Although the proposals and conditions have unsatisfactory features the Government appear to have no alternative but to accept and Council is invited to advise accordingly.[118]

The first condition establishing the schemes' priority over assistance had been a settler demand and was probably the least palatable point to the Kenya government. Condition (iii) allowing British leverage over valuation had also been a farmer demand as had been the allocation to the Land Bank in point (v). British consent to the appointment of the two top people in administering settlement was fairly standard in aid projects (the World Bank had a similar clause), but again allowed the British to further protect the sellers' interests.

There was also a certain dynamic in the situation leading to greater British involvement. HMG was following an incremental policy toward land transfers. The schemes evolved as one cautious step at a time proved inadequate, and generated both information and confidence in new, larger schemes. One European leader expressed British thinking on land in 1960–1 as having 'understood, sympathised, and then shied away from the magnitude of the problem.'[119] But the magnitude of the issues was gradually impressed on British officials as the economy continued depressed, the European farmers insecure, and the African masses threatening. On a purely pragmatic basis the early limited settlement 'cures' were seen to be not working, hence a larger dose was needed.

In conclusion, the principal explanation for the resolution of the land issue lay not in assuaging the sentiments of the European farmers, but rather in satisfying the interests of the other groups involved: the metropole government and the nationalist elite, the transnational commercial groups supporting the liberals, and other forces who stood to benefit from the continuity of the colonial political economy. The relevant pressure behind the issue's resolution lay not in those groups removed but in those preserved.

The fear among these groups was that farms left abandoned by Europeans would invite squatter take-overs, troop call-outs, violence and the beginnings of a new Emergency. In 1960 and 1961 when maintaining the European farmers was viewed as supportive of these groups and of the political economy from which they profited (or expected to profit), the settlers were maintained. Indeed they were maintained under such circumstances that they charged that they had become economic prisoners. By early 1962 the farmers (and peasants) were threatening disruption, hence a phased displacement was seen by the political representatives of these groups as a better means of ensuring the continuity of the decolonization process. In both instances European farmers' interests were a consideration, not a goal. The settler was to serve other, greater interests.

APPENDIX: A NOTE ON ACTORS

Throughout the discussion the difficulty of determining viable integrated actors is apparent. The participant groups in this fluid period not only frequently changed policy positions but membership as well. Actors were often a part of two groups at once while heavily influenced by still another. Michael Blundell, for example, was for a time leader of the New Kenya Party, Minister in the Kenya government and, in all but name only, a functioning and influential participant in KADU party politics. Add to this his close associations and frequent visits with members of the British government, and the ambiguity of group membership becomes apparent. Or Bruce McKenzie, who produced the first settlement plan as Minister of Agriculture, was at the same time a member of the NKG. So whose policy did the plan represent? And later when he switched to KANU and continued the same policies, can one make any significant statement about the validity of the groupings at all?

Nevertheless there would appear to have been real and consistent interests represented by the actors, who though they may also have sought other channels, maintained a certain consistency in their views. The KNFU was from the beginning attempting to secure the economic interests of its members – those who wished to stay as well as those who wished to leave – though the change in emphasis from the former group to the latter was gradual in these years. The other conservative Europeans' (Convention of Associations/Coalition) consistency was largely one of tone in the beginning of the period, and their recognition of their weakness as well as their similarity of interests with other non-political groups such as the KNFU, led to their demise as much as did the reversal in political fortunes.

The NKG till its demise held to maintaining a functioning society, and on political and economic levels supported those men and policies who sought a continuation of the then existing political-economic system. Their vacillation on land was no more than an unsteady leadership uncertain whether the system was best maintained with or without the European mixed farmer.

The British government appeared to have been about as consistent as one might expect from a large, frequently unwieldy bureaucratic nexus trying to assuage conflicting political-economic-social interests in a period of apparent great upheaval. The Colonial government similarly found its preference for being an arbiter above the battle fatally hampered by its traditional orientation toward European voices and policies. It pursued an incremental policy on land settlement given its financial constraints, combined with reassuring public speeches and a not-so-private backing of the liberal European positions.

The Africans, in whose name a large number of actions, policies and postures were put forth, were represented by parties of which all the participants were the least concerned by land. While tactically correct in viewing the European position as one of trading economic safeguards (be they underwriting of titles or land settlement) for constitutional advance, the nationalists failed to see, or chose not to, the more important question being answered as to the shape of post-independent Kenya. By putting the form of independence ahead of the substantive questions of the type of political and economic system which colonial Kenya was they missed the forest for the trees. Kenyan independence under an African government was a dead letter by February 1960. (Admittedly which Africans would rule was an important dispute among the personalities involved.) But the type of society that would evolve, the position of the great bulk of Africans in that society and, in a real sense, the reason why one wanted independence in the first place

133

were questions which by their failure to pose at this time the nationalists showed themselves passively accepting the colonialists' answers. They inherited a ready-made state with sufficient resources to make their rule profitable without coming to terms, other than those of the colonizer, with the problems and potentials of Kenya.

1960–1970, SEALING THE BARGAIN: THE IMPLEMENTATION OF THE KENYA LAND TRANSFER SCHEMES

For a colonized people the most essential value, because the most concrete, is first and foremost the land: the land which will bring them bread and, above all, dignity.

Frantz Fanon, *The Wretched of the Earth*

Independence was granted on the basis of the continuation of the system, and not its destruction.

Ahmed Mohiddin

They cost us more now that we don't have them.

Mrs Barbara Castle, M.P. (British Minister of Overseas Development, 1964–5)

The implementation of the land transfer programs in Kenya was lengthy and complex. In this account issues such as valuation of farms and the relative success of agriculture production in the settlement schemes will be ignored. Instead the focus will be on settlement as an integral feature of the process of consensual decolonization. The themes underlined in the transfer schemes will attempt to highlight the perspectives, policies and projections of a colonial bureaucracy attempting to insure the continued functioning of a political economy under an altered political authority. The thread of the narrative lies in this bureaucracy defeating threats from the Right (European farmers) and the Left (Kenyan peasants), mobilizing resources (British and international assistance) and enlisting allies (nationalist leaders, commercial community, African settlers) to stabilize the colonial interests and system of independent Kenya.

The implementation of the land transfer schemes underlined the continuity of the previous themes illustrated in the European bargaining activities. This was not due merely to the largely European personnel involved in administering the schemes. More important was the acceptance by all the parties involved of the values, goals and means propounded in the process of agreement to establish a land transfer program. The value of the colonial economy, the need to stabilize the post-independent regime, and the goal of minimizing the alteration in the inherited political-economic system, all led to a number of perhaps only dimly-foreseen consequences.

The major economic goal of the schemes was a curious dialectic. Briefly stated, it was the desire to preserve the large-farm capital-agriculture system by removing most of the large farmers (or at least, the middle sized, large farmer). The contradiction was only an apparent one. The need was to integrate and stabilize a European-established farming system into an Afri-

135

can-dominated polity. To this end the European mixed farmer was the fatted calf sacrificed on the altar of stability. He was removed either because he wished to leave or couldn't stay. The departure of Afrikaners, the farmers near the Kikuyu reserve (North and South Kinangop), and others who found themselves in a precarious position (Nandi Salient, Compassionate Scheme) reduced the numbers and visibility of the European community.

At the same time efforts were made to insure the continued functioning of the Highlands. By 1968 three-fourths to two-thirds of the former Scheduled Areas remained untouched by either the settlement schemes or private transfers to Africans, including some forty per cent of the mixed farm land.[1] The plantations, 1.5 million acres, were maintained as central to export earnings, too expensive to take over, and intensively employing African workers. The ranches, 2.7 million acres, producing needed cattle supplies, covered land deemed unsuitable for subdivision. Besides these areas, central regions of the mixed farm areas, around Nakuru, Kitale and Eldoret (1.6 million acres of the 3.6 million acres of mixed farm land) were retained as essential to the economy. Along with these retentions went the consequent preservation of the agricultural infrastructure: marketing procedures, pricing system, and farming organizations, all of which favored the products and problems of the large farms.

Both the buy-out of the mixed farms and the preservation of capital agriculture were important to the multi-national commercial interests in Kenya that played a crucial though submerged role in support of the program. From being a predominantly agricultural country Kenya had come to depend increasingly on commerce and industry. What the business community worried about was preserving their own assets including the company-owned plantations and a political structure congenial to their survival. In 1962 commercial interests based in London came to see that a gradual transfer of the mixed farm areas had the advantage of 'taking the pressure off land and as a result their plantations.'[2] Any pressure on the economically more vital plantations could be contained by increased Africanization of their managerial positions. This was to be paralleled by taking Africans into the marketing boards and farming organizations.[3] The trick in the buy-out was to keep the dosage of mixed farm lands slow and never quite complete. A total transfer of these holdings would lead to pressures on the ranches and plantations, with a predicted bill at least three times that required for the mixed farms.

LAND TRANSFERS AND DECOLONIZATION:
THEMES OF AN INTERRELATIONSHIP

Four themes of the land transfer schemes illustrated the program's service to the larger process of decolonization. The first was the maintenance by the

European farmers of administrative and technical control of political initiatives which might run counter to their interests. This was an old theme of Kenya politics dating back to the 1905 Delamere Committee on land transfers, running through the establishment of agricultural marketing organizations in the 1930s dominated by the seller-farmers, to the appointment in post-World War II Kenya of a European farmer (Cavendish-Bentinck) as Minister of Agriculture.

In the transfer schemes this principle was contained in most of the important initiatives taken by the colonial government. The opening of the Highlands in 1959 embodied strict control of transfers by local committees composed of European farmers. The initial overseer of organized settlement was the Land Development and Settlement Board, essentially a re-named European Agricultural Settlement Board, chaired and largely composed of Highland farmers.

Its successor, the Central Land Board, was given authority, under farmer pressure, over the terms of purchase offered to sellers in the transfer program. As independence approached it became less politic for farmers to publicly dominate such quasi-state organizations. European farmers maintained a preponderance in the lower levels of administrative and technical positions needed to carry out the program. This movement paralleled the political submergence of the European community as a whole to economic and administrative positions of influence and decreased visibility.

The defusing of rural unrest, particularly among the Kikuyu peasantry, was a second theme of the implementation of the land schemes. As has been shown, initially this goal was to mean the settling of 'sore-thumb' areas of the non-Kikuyu tribes, both to gain credit for KADU and to garner support among these tribes for the preservation of existing property rights in the Highlands. Later, when consolidating the KANU moderates in government became important, Kikuyu land-hunger was dealt with more directly through the Million-Acre scheme. Government memos, private papers and interviews demonstrated the political motives of the transfers to pre-empt any rural land grabs or threatened insurgency. The Kikuyu-bias of the schemes, in areas acquired, lower qualifications, and timing of the transfers (notably the Jet Schemes of late 1963), illustrated the administrative implementing of these political goals.

Sequentially with this theme, and growing more central as the threat of insurgency subsided, was the trend toward promoting an African landed middle class in the settlement areas. This class having vested interests in private property rights, in maintenance of the Highland farming system, and in the validity of the transfer schemes themselves, was to act as a buffer against agitation by the rural masses. They were also to serve as moderate leaders of rural opinion ('Z' plots), and to Africanize the Highlands (Stamp Program), rather than merely extending the boundaries of the former native reserves as the Million-Acre scheme tended to do.

The political consequence of the scheme in promoting an African gentry was of less importance in motivation than were two other explanations. The first was simply to see the larger plots as rewards for the nationalist elite. The origin of the 'Z' plots likely derived from this impulse. The second, and more important one, lay in the economic criteria used to evaluate the schemes. It was perhaps only to be expected that in a system based on large-scale capital agriculture, in terms of immediate profit and cost, it was perceived as economically advantageous to transfer farms to relatively large scale farmers. Although there was evidence of greater yields from more intensively farmed small plots, the greater costs of conversion and of the development input, combined with greater consumption, at least in the short run made the transfer of larger units appear to be a more economic proposition. This economic bias toward preserving the status quo conditioned the phasing-out of settlement, the encouraging of private transfers, and the holding of 'national farms' by the Agricultural Development Corporation for eventual transfer to large-scale African farmers.

A final theme which ran through the transfer program was the orientation and ties generated by international financial sources. This did not only mean the commitment to repay loans to the sundry lenders of the funds (HMG, World Bank). It implied as well a conditioning process in the lending procedure. Acceptance of the development criteria of I.B.R.D. money meant only using certain land (high potential, under-developed) in a certain way (low density, trained settlers, higher output). It also meant accepting World Bank advice and advisors, and the 'discipline' of repaying the funds through the increased surplus garnered from the settlement areas. Foreign private capital also appeared to be the most immediate source of revenue for the maintenance of these links.

Mention has been made of the colonial government and European leaders' hopes of using foreign investment to bolster the regime and preserve the position of the European community. Beyond this the land schemes were an important link in conditioning the new regime to look favorably on external sources of funding for economic development. Kenya's orientation toward an external development strategy was likely cemented in the land transfer schemes. The inevitable need for external capital to resolve the land question in the terms Kenya's leaders saw it resulted in the setting up of vested channels and experience, personal contacts and inclinations. These were later to be mobilized in approaching subsequent developmental hurdles.

Administrative involvement of European farmers

The opening up of the 'White Highlands' to farmers of all races showed the European farmers undermining at least the intent of the measure. Its general objective was that the basis of tenure and management of agricultural land throughout Kenya regardless of race should be similar, insofar as local economic and agronomic factors permitted. This meant the opening of the 'White Highlands' to qualified African and Asian farmers. The two Sessional Papers (S.P. No. 10 of 1958/59 presented on November 10, 1959, modified in S.P. 6 of 1959/60 presented at the end of June, 1960) dealt with 'Land Tenure and Control Outside the Native Lands,' and hence did not attempt to alter the structure of land holdings in the reserves.

Essentially the Sessional Papers followed the East Africa Royal Commission's 1955 advice in putting land transactions in the Highlands on a nonracial basis.[4] It also allowed European farmers to convert from leasehold (essentially long-term renting) to freehold (ownership), thus seeking to give the settlers added confidence in their continuity. However the bill embodied sufficient checks to ease concern of an imminent flood of black farmers.

Control of subdivisional proposals in the Highlands was transferred from the Commissioner of Lands to Divisional and Regional Boards. Both sets of Boards were to be dominated by local European farmer representatives with several positions open to colonial administrators. Besides weighting the composition of the Boards, their functions similarly leaned toward minimal alterations in the agricultural system of the Highlands. The grounds for refusing consent to a transaction in land were broadly spelled out. The Divisional Board could refuse consent on the grounds that the applicant already had sufficient land, that the area of land was unlikely to be economic, that the terms of the transfer were onerous, and, finally, 'that the proposed transferee is unlikely, for any reason, to be a good farmer of the holding.'[5]

At the time this local administrative control of transfers and the lack of financing for Africans was seen as taking away much of the impact of the 'opening of the White Highlands.' The Executive Committee of the Federation of Chambers of Commerce and Industry of Eastern Africa thought the Sessional Paper would be unlikely to eliminate racial barriers because of the lack of Asian and African representatives on the boards controlling transfers.[6] Tom Mboya earlier described the legislation opening the Highlands as an effort to entrench even more firmly the European farmers' position. He pointed to the control procedure, the Africans' inability to compete on a basis of willing buyer–willing seller, and the opportunity given European farmers to convert from leasehold to freehold.[7] And the Permanent Secretary of the Ministry of Land Settlement later wrote: 'In 1959 when the European Highlands were opened to all races it was obvious that changing the law would have no effect. Europeans would be unlikely to sell to Africans and Africans with sufficient money and experience to buy and operate a large farm were rare.'[8]

However after the First Lancaster House Conference of early 1960 the need for an organized transfer program was widely acknowledged. The program was to meet the needs of those Europeans who wanted out, those

Africans who wanted (and could afford) in, and those Europeans who wished to stay in a stable environment with a restored market for land. To administer the schemes, the Minister for Agriculture, Bruce McKenzie, announced the establishment of a Settlement Authority, an independent statutory body operating on a non-racial basis.[9]

The Land Development and Settlement Board (L.D.S.B.) was formally set up in January 1961 as a reconstituted European Agricultural Settlement Board (E.A.S.B.).[10] Its Chairman, J. F. Lipscomb, had served as Chairman of the E.A.S.B. and the Board of Agriculture (Scheduled Areas).[11] The L.D.S.B. was designed to purchase land and to approve and initiate settlement schemes under the 'New Scheme.' This scheme sought to settle the 'sore thumb' areas in the Highlands among neighboring African tribes and to maintain European confidence by insuring a market in land through the phased buying of farms offered to it. Composed of a majority of European farmers, the Board was established, in the words of its first chief executive officer, to gain the confidence of the European settlers worried about being sold downstream. The two African representatives on the L.D.S.B. in his words 'didn't mean a thing.'[12] At the time, the Kenya government justified the European preponderance on the L.D.S.B. as necessary to gain the cooperation of the local Agricultural Committees for the schemes.[13]

The L.D.S.B. quickly ran into trouble due largely to the inadequate administrative and financial backing it was given. From its beginning the Board, and perhaps land settlement itself, was seen as rather peripheral. The L.D.S.B. had a part-time Chairman and Executive Officer, and was supposed to meet all of its costs out of the interest on the loan monies re-lent to the African settlers at a rate of seven and one-half per cent per annum. The Settlement Board immediately concluded that these terms of finances made the schemes 'unrealistic and unworkable;' both because the interest rates were too high for the African farmers, and because the European sellers objected to the terms of sale.[14]

Talks were held in London in late August 1961 between the Minister of Agriculture Michael Blundell, and the British government to obtain grants for subsidizing the cost of land purchases and of administering the settlement schemes. This resulted in the L.D.S.B. holding up negotiations until firm purchase terms could be communicated to the vendors.[15] The British offered increased loans for land purchase and administration but the terms remained unacceptable to the European sellers. The land-owners argued that having one-third of the purchase price paid in cash and the remaining two-thirds spread over seven years made it impossible for them to liquidate their indebtedness and finance a start elsewhere. This was modified to allow for one-half immediate payment and the remainder spread over three years. A further concession was that payment could be made in sterling to meet the landowners' fears of exchange control. This offer of the British government was accepted by the European farmers 'reluctantly and with suspicion' and land purchases began on November 1, 1961.[16]

From the start of the L.D.S.B. European farmers dominated its administration. Not only did they have a majority on the Board itself but all of the twenty-one settlement officers were European and most of these were drawn from the farming community. The practice of recruiting settlement officers from local European farmers who were anxious to see which way Kenya was going was continued throughout the life of the schemes.[17] The effort to transfer land in the South Kinangop, though finally rejected at the time, was felt to have come from personal connections of members of the Board with settlers in the area. However efforts were made to phase out the L.D.S.B. almost as soon as it actually began. Besides farmer resentment of the Board's terms, personal conflicts within the Board and with the government, the main reason stemmed from the need for a full-time administrative unit closely linked with the government to carry out the much larger transfer schemes being formulated. There was also the felt need of recognizing the increasing African political influence through greater administrative representation in the land transfer program.

The Central Land Board, agreed to at the Second Lancaster House Conference but not established until April 1963, sought to fill this need. The 1963 Constitution (Chapter XI) gave the C.L.B. the status of 'an independent constitutional Board' and the function of selecting land, buying it, and conveying it to the new plotholders. The C.L.B. was to have an independent chairman (agreed among the parties to be from outside Kenya), a deputy chairman, a member representing the Kenya government, one member from each of the seven regions, and a member representing the European sellers.[18]

Even the formal duties and composition of the C.L.B. showed how far the political fortunes of the farmers had slipped. Their effort to directly dominate governmental boards was dropped in favor of pushing for 'independent' non-governmental authority. This combined with moderate African support from the regions, European expertise on the lower administrative levels, and British leverage through funding stipulations, was hoped to accomplish the same thing.[19]

However soon after the Second Lancaster House Conference ended, the Ministry of Lands and Settlement initiated efforts to reduce the authority of the C.L.B. The importance of this effort derived from the C.L.B. being, in the words of one participant, 'the final battle ground for European control of the settlement schemes.[20] On April 13, 1962, the Council of Ministers asked the head of the new Ministry of Lands and Settlement, Bruce McKenzie, to present detailed proposals on the composition and functions of the C.L.B. This resulted in a memorandum submitted to the Council of Ministers on May 26.[21]

In the memorandum the Ministry argued that the Kenya government was 'vitally interested not only in settlement as a general project but also in the details of execution.' The likely conflict in the existing arrangement and the unwieldiness of the Board carrying out its functions were pointed to:

6. It [C.L.B.] is charged with the sole responsibility for the formulation and implementation of settlement schemes in the scheduled areas and with purchasing land for settlement. Except for purchasing it is unlikely to be the kind of body that can, in general, initiate settlement activities of this kind, although it can give advice and guidance. If it were to be responsible for planning then settlement policy as a whole would be split between it and the Government.[22]

Further the memo stated that new, wider and long term transfers would 'begin before the constitution is in force and the Central Land Board established.' This was to be a self-fulfilling prophecy brought about by the Ministry's efforts to delay the establishment of the C.L.B. and ignoring the farmers' understanding with the Secretary of State to appoint a chairman and to set up the Board's machinery at an early date.[23]

The Ministry recommended that the Board's functions be limited to buying land based on government approved conditions and plans, to consulting with the regions on the tribal composition of the settlers, and to advising the Ministry on any aspect of settlement policy. Further, the representative of the sellers on the Board would only be allowed to vote on issues involving purchase. The memo concluded 'that the actual detailed planning and execution of settlement schemes should be a function of the Government through the Minister responsible for settlement taking cognizance as he must, of the expressed views of the Board.'[24]

Opposition to this move came chiefly from the farmers and the British government. The chairman of the L.D.S.B., J. W. Howard, had written the Ministry pointing out the difference between the constitutional requirements and the Ministry's views of the C.L.B. functions. The Permanent Secretary replied that there had been very little discussion at Lancaster House on this part of the framework of the constitution and that, if consensus could be reached on what the C.L.B. should do, the White Paper of the Conference would not be important.[25]

The problem the Ministry faced with the farmers was, as one high bureaucrat put it, nothing had ever been done in the European areas without farmer permission. The C.L.B. stood, for the farmers, as protection against the government spending settlement money for other purposes. Discussions between Ministry officials and farmer representatives in the spring of 1962 made clear that the European concern centered on the purchase of land. They would settle for the C.L.B. supervising only this. Although the Ministry accepted this position, the Colonial Office didn't.[26]

In correspondence with the Colonial Office, Ministry officials argued that the C.L.B. would become 'a Government within the Government;' that for political and other reasons it could effectively stifle settlement.[27]

British officials feared that the Minister for Settlement would have responsibility without authority and pressed for the early appointment of a Chairman of the C.L.B. and an interim board. The Ministry replied through the Governor that the Board would result in administrative duplication and added expense, that the government had a vital political interest in settlement, and that it was responsible for the money it had borrowed abroad.

The Ministry argued that the Kenya Coalition had accepted these arguments, as long as the functions of land purchase and settlement were divided, with the C.L.B. supervising the former and the Government the latter. 'We have given it the executive function only of buying land and giving title. This is to ensure that the European farmer's interest is looked after by an independent body.'[28] However by mid-September a Ministry official reported there still remained a 'large difference of opinion' between the Colonial Office and Kenya bureaucrats over the functions of the C.L.B.[29]

The conflict between the Colonial Office and the Ministry came to a head in late 1962 with the appointment of Sir Geoffrey Bourne as Chairman of the C.L.B. HMG, under continuing European farmer pressure to appoint a chairman, selected Bourne without consulting with the Kenya government. Adding to his problems, Bourne rather recklessly proposed to take over from the Government the Department of Settlement.[30] Correspondence flew hot and heavy in early 1963 over the appointee and his ideas. Bourne was clearly unacceptable to the Ministry and other important political elements in the Kenya government.

By mid-March the Ministry could write that the Chairman-designate would not be taking up his post.[31] Bourne's non-appointment also signaled the acceptance by HMG of the Kenya government's definition of the C.L.B. The Ministry's victory was complete. A brief prepared for the Minister of Land Settlement read in part:

. . . it has now been decided that the Central Land Board will confine its attention to the buying of land in consultation with the Regions and the Government, and will have a very limited function, and further that the settlement schemes should be controlled by a Central Settlement Committee under the chairmanship of the Minister.[32]

There were a number of levels of explanation for the downgrading of the C.L.B. The personal one of a strong Minister not having his domain invaded by inexpert outsiders was certainly one. This was closely aligned to a desire for bureaucratic autonomy within the Ministry; entrenched administrators wishing to retain their position and program. Perhaps of central importance was that both the nationalist-political and expatriate-bureaucratic elements in the Government felt the C.L.B. to be an inhibition on their scope of action. Settlement was viewed as a Government responsibility, hence for practical and political reasons it should be under direct Government control. For the nationalists in the government the emasculation of the C.L.B. paralleled their own efforts to remove regional constitutional constraints which they considered an unneeded legacy of colonial transition.

On the level of settlement policy there was concern that the Board would not emphasize Kikuyu settlement sufficiently, a crucial point discussed below.

For the farmers, although they had hoped to limit further a Minister they viewed as unfavorable to them, the results of the C.L.B. debate were not necessarily antagonistic to their interests. The division of purchase from settlement left them dealing with an 'independent' board to sell their land to, rather than representatives of a nationalist government. Although the Minister would have liked to amalgamate this function he was not in a position to change it.[33] So, for the duration of its life 'The real function of the Central Land Board is to protect the interest of the European farmer over the sale of land on the one hand and the interests of the different Regions over their proportion of settlement on the other hand.'[34]

In fact, the delay in setting up the C.L.B. and the entrenchment of the Ministry's direction over settlement limited the Board's functions even more than these formal restrictions. Until the Board was set up on June 1, 1963, the Ministry, with the L.D.S.B. as a very silent partner, continued to run the schemes.[35] Even after being established the C.L.B. was not called on to select any farms scheduled for purchase before July 1964. Selection of settlement areas for the crucial Kikuyu-dominated Central Region had already been decided on for the twelve months after July 1, 1964.[36] As seen in the chart below this left the C.L.B. dealing with some 161,000 acres of the 1.2 million acres under the scheme. By the time the C.L.B. began operating, the

Statistics of Land Purchase Program

	1961/62 land purchased			1962/63 land purchased			
	Farms	Acres	£	Farms	Acres	£	Farms
Region:							
Rift Valley	13	23,266	241,051	25	41,757	281,236	49
Western	1	19,377	75,000	23	43,679	291,141	23
Nyanza	4	12,054	114,038	11	14,180	179,400	23
Eastern	15	99,010	216,613	8	19,540	62,731	13
Central	29	28,962	380,345	89	127,672	1,407,220	187
1st List-Compassionate	–	–	–	57	44,903	498,843	–
2nd List-Compassionate	–	–	–	–	–	–	103
Nandi Salient	–	–	–	–	–	–	19
Totals	62	182,669	1,027,047	213	291,731	2,720,571	417

Kenya Cabinet was considering a paper to remove the Government's priority for settlement on the basis that 'the back of settlement has been broken.'[37]

The counter-insurgency thrust of land settlement

Breaking 'the back of settlement' referred to the effort to stabilize the new government by weakening rural unrest primarily among the Kikuyu. For the bureaucrats involved in the land scheme the dissipation of land-hunger was both the great threat to the transfers and the motive force behind them. The two co-authors of *The Million-Acre Scheme*, who served as administrators for the schemes, J.R. Goldsack and C.P.R. Nottidge, stressed the centrality of land hunger in the planners' minds. Especially in the Kinangop, the chief area of settlement for Kikuyu, there was a great fear of land seizures. Government officials expected a land grab in the first six months after independence. The Land Freedom Army (a Mau Mau grouping) appeared to be very powerful among Kikuyu, with the atmosphere in their areas 'at the boiling point.'[38]

Other accounts at the time supported this impression. The Provincial Commissioner at Nyeri focused optimistically on the political effects settlement was having in the Kikuyu areas.

Had we not at long last made a start with the settlement of Kikuyu it [the die-hard Mau Mau element] would be much bigger and it would be growing daily. As it is, the fact that resettlement has started has had an exceedingly good effect in Kikuyu country . . . What we now have is on the one hand a large and grow-

1963/64 land purchased		Farms	1964/65 (purchase under negotiation figures provisional)		Farms	Totals 1961/65	
Acres	£		Acres	£		Acres	£
60,355	616,509	47	71,066	710,660	134	196,444	1,849,456
33,505	264,924	21	51,416	514,160	68	147,977	1,145,225
31,534	397,979	33	28,267	282,670	71	86,035	974,087
32,529	192,592	3	11,319	113,190	39	162,398	585,126
149,351	2,051,530	113	144,193	1,461,320	418	450,178	5,300,415
–	–	–	–	–	57	44,903	498,843
84,846	886,991	–	–	–	103	84,846	886,991
14,701	160,063	–	–	–	19	14,701	160,063
406,821	4,570,588	217	306,261	3,082,000	909	1,187,482	11,400,206

Source: Central Land Board, *Annual Report, 1963–64.*

ing group of non-violent Kikuyu, which includes loyalists, Government servants, farmers and now the new settlers, and on the other a small very hard, very resolute violent group, but which, if properly watched, should not be more than a temporary embarrassment should it later decide to take some sort of action.[39]

The Central Land Board in its Final Report referred to the African peoples' demand to find accommodation and security for their numerous impoverished and landless people. 'An explosive situation existed and would have detonated if this demand had not been at least partly satisfied.'[40] In his book *The Anatomy of Uhuru* the former Permanent Secretary of the Ministry of Land Settlement, N. S. Carey Jones, repeatedly mentioned the danger of land seizures, and the fear that at independence Africans would simply move onto the Highland farms and effectively drive the Europeans out.[41]

The land schemes were the Government's major method of 'letting steam out of the boiling kettle.' And the Kikuyu Central Region was on the hottest burner. The reasons for this pressure on land in Central Region, besides population increase (around 3.2 per cent) could be listed: the land consolidation program displaced many people; the release of some 60,000 Mau Mau detainees; the regional pattern of Government pressured Kikuyu to return to their homeland; the economic downturn caused unemployment; and a heightened political awareness in the Kikuyu areas brought on by the nearness of independence. There was the fear that these people would not only agitate but be attracted by the bright lights of the cities. Settlement was to cope with this also. As one high-ranking European in an agricultural agency put it, 'the masses were to be diverted from the cities to the fields.'

The response of the Government to the worsening security situation in the Kikuyu areas was to initiate the Accelerated Kikuyu Settlement Program. In a draft written in late 1962 seeking permission from the Kenya Council of Ministers for the accelerated program, the goal of the schemes and the danger in the situation were spelled out.

The object of this is to prevent a flood of Kikuyu from other parts of the Central Region and from Rift Valley Region (driven by unemployment and pressures from other tribes) into the parts of the Central Region west and north of the Aberdare Mountains, which could effectively drive out the Europeans, and replace them with squatters. This would destroy the economy of the area, [and] remove all prospects of orderly settlement either there or in other parts of Kenya.[42]

In a meeting of the Colonial Office in December 1962, Bruce McKenzie proposed to compress Kikuyu settlement under the five year Million-Acre scheme so that all land purchases for Central Region would be completed by the end of July 1965. Local Kikuyu leaders had agreed that if this was done they would try 'to hold the position.' This meant 'that they would support the eviction of illegal squatters and strictly apply the Trespass Ordinance in this area, and give full backing to the authorities in applying the law.'[43]

146

There was another reason for speeding up the Kikuyu purchase program. Because of the limitation put on total finance for the Million-Acre scheme and the Kenya government's agreement not to make any further demands for funds during the five year duration of the scheme, the purchase of more land for Kikuyu settlement would mean the reduction in the other tribes' share. The Central Land Board was expected to present a stumbling block to this. 'It's extremely unlikely that the Central Land Board, composed of representatives of each Region would agree to more Kikuyu Settlement at the expense of other tribes.'[44]

Another problem with the Accelerated Kikuyu Settlement was the lack of suitable land for the new schemes. The other tribes, worried that independence under Kikuyu leadership would mean expansion into their spheres of influence, were unwilling to accommodate Kikuyu in their areas.[45] The areas in the Highland closest to the Kikuyu reserves, North and South Kinangop, had previously been rejected as unsuitable for settlement. The L.D.S.B. although under strong pressure from European farmers in the South Kinangop who wished to sell had rejected that land as unsuitable for small-scale farms.[46] As late as March 31, 1962, the Permanent Secretary of the Ministry had written a memo strongly advising against settlement in the South Kinangop. He stated it would be uneconomic, expensive and unproductive. He argued that more labor would be displaced from the large-scale farms there than would be employed in the new schemes.[47] Nearly all the technical advisers consulted on the area's potential for settlement had recommended against it as unviable given the climatic and soil conditions existing in most of the area.

The constitutional path had been previously cleared for Kikuyu settlement in the Kinangop by the Regional Boundaries Commission Report of December 1962. The Commission initiated by the Second Lancaster House Conference was set up to design the boundaries for the various regions and, although denied by the Commission, to judge tribal regions between competing claims to land. For Central Region, the Commission 'endeavoured to make reasonable provision for the numerous, hard-working and progressive Kikuyu people, by including in the Central Region areas of land capable of being made available for settlement schemes.'[48] These areas, including the Kinangop and the Ol Kalou Salient, were deemed 'eminently suited to the agricultural pursuits of the Kikuyu.'[49]

The British agreement to the Accelerated Kikuyu Settlement for 1963/64 was apparently quickly garnered. But concurrence for the 1964/65 plan was slower in coming. At the end of May 1963 the Governor sent the Secretary of State an urgent telegram asking for an immediate go-ahead. The worry in the Kenya government was over the C.L.B. responsibility for the purchase program of 1964/65 beginning on June 1, 1963. The telegram repeated the previous arguments that the C.L.B. was: 'unlikely to agree on its own to accelerated purchase for Kikuyu in 1964/65. It is essential that your approval be given now, before the 1st of June to the accelerated programme in 1964/65 so that there can be no argument about it later.'⁵⁰

Despite the accelerated settlement of Kikuyu the security situation appeared to worsen in 1963. The local Kikuyu leaders had proven unable to check the movement of people into the Highland areas, and indeed many minor leaders continued to promise free land up to independence. A Ministry memo in late August 1963 proposed a 'Second Million-Acre Scheme' (later to surface in the Stamp Program), and warned of the 'real possibility of a breakdown of farming in the Central Region.' It stressed that the acceleration of land purchase had not checked the uncontrolled movement of Kikuyu into Central Region. There was a rise in crimes, squatting, unemployment, and oathing 'mainly directed against the new African government.'⁵¹

In early November 1963, the Kenya Cabinet was presented a memorandum from the Settlement Fund trustees (the Ministers of Lands and Settlement, now J. H. Angaine; Agriculture, B. McKenzie; and Finance, J. Gichuru) warning of the serious security situation in the new Nyandarua District (the Kinangop). The Ministers pointed out that in settling some 12,000 persons in the District, 6,000 laborers had been displaced and were now squatting on the land. There were some 30,000 people in the District without land and some 10,000 in interim settlements who, although promised land, would not get it. Twenty-four South African families in an area of 111,000 acres in neighboring Ol Kalou were planning to abandon their farms with the rise of anti-South African propaganda. The expectation among the landless in the District was that they would be able to seize land free at independence.

If this happened, the Ministers warned, the Government would either have to forego the development of the country, or mount an unpopular major anti-squatter military operation. Instead, they recommended a number of measures to counter the deteriorating situation. First was needed an immediate announcement of Government plans for Nyandarua. This would be combined with a statement that there could not be land for all, that no land would be free, and that there was no point in moving into the District. Complementing this would be an approach to HMG for the purchase of Ol Kalou, and for the British to announce the broad outlines of a Second Million-Acre scheme. Proposals were also mooted to settle people in the forest areas, and to take over abandoned or semi-abandoned farms with the laborers there. This last step was designed to ensure that 'there will be a large number of persons interested in seeing that the land is not seized or squatted on by others.'⁵²

These alarms resulted in the so-called Jet schemes of late 1963. Mzee Kenyatta ordered that the Kinangop scheme be completed in the weeks remaining before independence (on December 12, 1963). Every agricultural officer available was engaged in what one participant described as an army-type operation. In a few months the increase in plots allocated per month rose over five fold and the total number of plots allocated doubled, as shown in the chart below.

Progress of settlement 1963/64

Period ending	No. of plots ready	Plots allocated	Monthly increase in plots allocated
November 1	9,083	6,929	515
December 1	11,935	8,759	1,830
January 1	13,815	11,429	2,670
February 1	14,529	12,774	1,345
March 1	15,510	13,712	938

Source: Republic of Kenya, Department of Settlement, *Annual Report, 1963–64.* The rise was also partly due to the pattern of the bulk of settlement occurring during the Kenya dry season November to March. By June 1964, 15,682 settlers were 'on the ground.' (p. 9)

Many of the advisers involved in the program had doubts about the utility of the program at the time, pointing to the previous economic objections to converting the Kinangop. Even the Department of Settlement reported that because of the crash program there were problems in planning and phasing, adding, 'Wastage was high and administration suffered.'[53] But in retrospect all the Settlement officials spoken with viewed the crash program as an absolute political necessity for the new government, without which a major land grab would have occurred shortly after independence.

Ministry officials held few illusions about the economic benefits accruing from either the Kinangop crash program or from at least, high density settlement. A Ministry draft in March 1963, on labor discharged from European farms in the Central Region, found that some 25,000 families were employed in the area. Even if the whole of the land was suitable for High Density Settlement (and much of it was not), and the lowest standards of settlement were applied, not more than 33,000 families (in fact double the actual number settled by the Jet schemes) could be settled. 'The implication here is that in relation to the size of the problem of Kikuyu unemployment and landlessness, settlement schemes can make only a small contribution, but one hopes a significant one, and that the main object of policy is a transfer of landownership.'[54] A report to the Kenya Cabinet a few months later from the Minister for Lands and Settlement was even more pessimistic.

The qualification 'landless and unemployed' was introduced when it was thought that settlement schemes could make a large contribution to the problem of landlessness and unemployment. It is now known that they can be no solution to this problem, although they do, of course, help to resolve it, since the number of labour employed on European farms is high.[55]

This conflict arose from competing political pressures to settle as many Africans as possible and the expectation that the relatively larger-scale plots would be the only ones on which the settlers could make farming an economic proposition. So in the Central Region the Government had set the yearly target income at between £25/40 while other areas with less pressure for land would aim for £60/70.[56] The African ministers in the Government were described as anxious to get away from high-density settlement as soon as possible.[57] Throughout the period settlement officials held to the expectation that as soon as immediate political pressures were alleviated settlement would move to transfers of larger plots.

The question of squatters and of Africans *de facto* receiving free land remained a threat to the settlement program throughout the life of the schemes. The prospect of Europeans abandoning their farms crystalized this fear. Persuading European farmers to wait and sell their land through settlement came, at least by late 1962, less from European political leverage than from the Ministry's fears of the consequences arising from abandoned farms. In a request to the British Secretary of State for funds to buy up farms in the Ol Kalou area, the Minister for Settlement stressed that 'the farmers in the Ol Kalou area are likely to abandon farms in large numbers and this presents a danger to security and settlement schemes generally, if vacant land is squatted on and squatters, in effect, obtain land for nothing.'[58] Earlier in requesting approval from the Kenya Cabinet for the accelerated Kikuyu program, the Ministry warned: '*Any failure to insist* on repayment of debts or any suggestion that land has been obtained free, would destroy all settlement schemes.'[59]

This was also the basis within the Ministry for the interest in the compassionate Case farms. These were farms occupied by elderly or infirm Europeans who could not maintain their farms but were not able to sell them.[60] The Compassionate Scheme has been seen as a bit of a 'pork barrel' for the Europeans and certainly pressure on HMG was being exercised on this point.[61] But within the Ministry the scheme's importance lay in inhibiting the occupation of the farms by landless Africans. The original Kenya government proposal for a Million-Acre scheme did not mention the European needs in the matter of the Compassionate farms, but argued 'they must be bought, since if the owners are incapable of running them, they will be largely occupied by squatters.'[62] European objections that the farms were being sold by the government at lower prices than they were bought, thus hindering the market in land, were brushed aside as less important than that these farms should not lie unoccupied and abandoned.[63] The British attempt to limit the scheme to British citizens was termed 'highly unsatisfactory' for apparently similar reasons.[64]

150

Transferring large-scale plots: Landing the gentry

With the perceived easing of pressure on the land from the Kikuyu masses, government officials sought to move settlement in a direction they had always preferred – the transfer of large-scale plots.[65] There were a number of reasons for the move. Primary was their view of the greater economic gain derived from the preservation and Africanization of the large-farm system than from its transformation. Settlement officials, despite the Swynnerton Plan, were still attuned to the needs and advantages of the European system and sought the minimal alteration in it.

The African leadership used the large-scale transfers not only to bolster the economy but also as a means of rewarding followers (and leaders). Having an indigenous gentry was seen, in a rather muted way, as a means of consolidating the rural populace around a moderate government and stabilizing the society by giving important elements in it a vested interest in property rights and the economic structure. The movement and creation of middle class Africans in the Highlands was, if not a conscious object in the planners' minds, a foreseeable consequence of their policies.[66]

To view the move from high-density schemes to large-scale transfers as a change from political priorities to economic ones would be a mistake. The preservation and Africanization of the Highlands agricultural system clearly had political objectives foreseen at the time. On the one hand the scattering of African farmers throughout the Highlands would reduce the visibility and precariousness of the European farming system. As the Deputy Secretary for Agriculture wrote in 1960; 'The survival of the good European farmer depends on his having Africans in various parts of the Highlands.'[67] He added that confining settlement to the periphery of the Highlands invited expropriation. Beyond this, officials hoped that large-scale African farmers throughout Kenya would stabilize the potentially disruptive rural society. This was to stand as a justification both for the 'Z' plots and increased funding for the Land Bank. And in just these terms the Director of Settlement, J. W. Maina, argued for lower-density transfers in general.

We should aim at a land reform programme whose main ingredients are divorced from temporary political expedients and should endeavour to create a land owning, stable rural society with enhanced social status, rights and privileges. In the long run this has the most important stabilising force upon which the rest of our Nation can be built.[68]

Not surprising in the initial proposal for a 'Second Million-Acre Scheme' the emphasis was on low-density transfers, with finance given to an agricultural corporation 'for the conversion of large-scale holdings in their entirety.' In listing the reasons for large scale farm transfers the planners returned to many of the ideas of the early schemes. The new program would allow European farmers to leave; there would be no purely-owned European block; there was a strong African demand for large farms

151

('. . . which has political implications . . .') but no loan finance; and it would bring stabilization to the large-farm sector by having African ownership scattered widely over the area.[69]

Throughout 1964 representatives of the Kenya government and the European farmers pushed for an extension of the Million-Acre scheme along these lines. In lobbying activities both groups stressed the political repercussions likely to ensue if the schemes were not continued. One farmer leader wrote from London that: 'They [HMG] are realizing that orderly land take-over is the only way the present government can survive, and the only alternative is an extremist set up a la Zanzibar which would be a disaster to all the three parties [HMG, Kenya government, European farmers].'[70] By August 1964, Bruce McKenzie, now Minister for Agriculture and Animal Husbandry, felt assured enough of future British finance to outline the Kenya government's plans for buying out the some two million acres remaining of European mixed farms. In a speech to the Nairobi Chamber of Commerce, McKenzie thought 200,000 to 300,000 acres would be farmed by Europeans who became citizens. Another 400,000 to 500,000 acres would change hands privately with finance from the Land Bank. The remaining 1.2 to 1.4 million acres would be bought by a commercially-run Agricultural Development Corporation. The Corporation would manage those farms whose produce was considered vital to the economy (i.e., pedigree cattle, hybrid maize seed), and hold others for eventual transfer, in their entirety, to experienced African farmers. No mention was made in the Minister's proposals for a continuation of settlement.[71]

However British money for the buyout of the remaining mixed farm areas was not forthcoming in 1964. Although apparently high level political support had been garnered for the buyout (including the Prime Minister, Alex Douglas-Hume; Secretary of State, Duncan Sandys; and Leader of the Opposition, Harold Wilson), the Treasury and the British High Commission in Nairobi remained opposed, and agreement was delayed.[72] With the Labour government taking over from the Conservatives in the fall of 1964, further delay resulted. The new British officials, likely feeling they needed more time and information before committing themselves to new schemes, appointed the so-called Stamp Mission in January 1965.[73]

The still-secret report of the Mission in October 1965 was not very encouraging to hopes for further transfers of European farms. Not only did the Report doubt whether the transfer schemes made any contribution to Kenyan development, but thought transfers resulted in a large scale outflow of capital and that the diverting of scarce resources and personnel to the schemes harmed more useful development projects. Further, Kenya was saddled with a heavy debt burden, and Britain with a heavy aid commitment, for little economic advantage. The Mission reported that the Kenya government was preoccupied with the mixed farming areas and pointed out that the settlement proposals did not reflect the government's own priorities as set out in the paper on African Socialism.[74] They stressed that the European mixed farms were not of central importance to either the Kenyan commercial sector or to earning foreign exchange, and warned that the Kenya government was getting into a situation of feeding a 'white elephant' at very high cost.[75]

The Mission recommended that the Kenya government be encouraged to de-emphasize the land transfers. Concentration was better placed in those areas outside the former European Highlands '. . . in which the vast majority of the population live and work.'[76] If continuing purchases were necessary for political reasons then the slower and smaller the transfers the better. The money available for transfers should be tied in with development aid; more transfers meaning less aid for development. A pause in settlement for at least two years was necessary to enable past results to be analyzed. The Mission thought a reduced level of land purchase should be continued at a rate of around 95,000 acres per annum with the emphasis placed on encouraging private transfers under the Land Bank and moving away from high density schemes.

In the fall 1965 negotiations, the Kenya government and European farmers confronted HMG with political arguments to rebut the Stamp Report. They stressed that the transfers, and with it the expectation of land among Kikuyu, had enabled the government to hold its position. But unemployment, cattle thefts and squatters remained to make the European farmers' position untenable.[77] The Kenya government objected to the two year pause and the transfer schemes being tied in to development monies. Their representatives emphasized the political angle and the potentially explosive nature of the land question in Kenya. One participant in the talks between the two governments remembered McKenzie saying to British officials, 'Do you want to be dealing with Leftists next time? If we don't get the money that's what will happen.' Throughout the negotiations the Kenya government and the European farmers, in the words of the *Financial Times*, worked 'hand-in-glove.'[78]

The British offer though not entirely to the Kenya negotiators' liking went further than the Stamp Report in subsidizing land transfers. Some £18 million in interest-free loans were provided Kenya for agricultural development from 1966 to 1970. Of this over one-third was to be used to finance the transfer of 100,000 acres per annum over four years, with 20,000 acres per annum of this to be used in low density schemes. Notably absent from the discussions was the use of the remaining £12 million, which was to be devoted to development projects, subject to further bilateral talks. The Kenyans objected to the amount of money for transfers (they had wanted twice the figure offered), the linkage with development aid, and the lack of a grant element (which Europeans felt would mean a reduction in the prices the government paid for farms).[79] The British were also not certain how famous a victory they had won. A farmer leader

153

remembered Mrs Castle remarking after the negotiations on the high price of Kenyan independence for the British. She is reported to have said, 'They cost us more now that we don't have them.'[80]

Despite the political arguments used in the negotiations, the implementation of the new land program demonstrated a reversal of political priorities from settling potentially disruptive elements, to maintaining the large farm system and integrating Africans into it. The Peers Report, written by the Deputy Director of the Ministry of Agriculture and later General Manager of the Agricultural Development Corporation, A. W. Peers, stood as the Kenya government's interpretation of what became known as the Stamp Program. Peers set out that 320,000 acres were to be bought by the A.D.C. (the remaining 80,000 to go for low density settlement) in areas producing those agricultural commodities considered vital to the economy.[81] The farms within these National Farming Blocks would be managed by the A.D.C. for transfer to trained African tenant farmers and eventual sale or leasing arrangements.

The stress of the report was on the maintenance of vital national agricultural production. British farmers within the Farming Blocks who wished to sell would have first priority. On the other hand political pressure to buy out farmers outside the Blocks should be resisted.[82] Peers also hoped that the presence of neighboring large-scale African farmers would encourage many Europeans to stay. Certain areas not set aside for large-scale farming in the national interest might remain large mixed farms – Naro Moru, Nanyuki, Mweiga, Lumbwa, Kericho, Londiani, Nandi/Lessos, and Nyandarua. Since there was only £6.4 million in the British loan for the transfer of 400,000 acres and the average purchase price of farms had been around £18 per acre (as opposed to the new projected £16 per acre) Peers speculated that money might have to be taken from the funds allocated for overall development.[83]

In fact the acreage goals of the Stamp Program under the A.D.C. program and the low density schemes came nowhere near being fulfilled. By 1969 the *Development Plan* expected the A.D.C. to purchase only some 170,430 acres of land with £3.6 million of Stamp Funds. Of this figure only 149,200 acres had been purchased by mid-1970.[84] Settlement schemes were even more drastically curtailed. Of the 80,000 acres allotted settlement only some 16,000 acres had been settled in one scheme at Ol Arabel under the Harambee Settlement Program.[85]

The failure of the Stamp scheme to reach its acreage goals could be attributed to the higher-than-expected costs of farms, bureaucratic inefficiency, and the Kenya government's desire to de-emphasize land transfers and settlement. On the last point the *Development Plan* pointed out that in 1963/64, three-fourths of all agricultural development money had gone into land transfers. By 1968/69 this had fallen to less than fifty per cent and within the projected plan period, 1970–74, only about twenty-two per cent of agricultural development monies would be used for transfer programs. The reasons for this were similar to the Stamp Mission's arguments four years earlier. Economic benefits were marginal as was the rise in employment. Transfers had an adverse effect on the balance of payments; there were better ways to use the funds; and time was needed to evaluate the lessons learned from the previous schemes.[86]

The high costs of the transfers were demonstrated in the A.D.C.'s spending of some £2.5 million (or over two-thirds of their budget for 1966–70) in buying 170,430 acres by the end of June 1969.[87] A.D.C. officials in 1970 complained that they were unable to assimilate any more farms due to budgetary and personnel restraints. However other parts of the Government had an apparent surplus of funds. Of the £8.69 million for general development covering formally approved projects in the Stamp package, only £3.7 million had been disbursed as of July 10, 1970.[88] The Kenya government apparently had more money than its bureaucracy could use.

Perhaps two of the best examples of the schemes' tendency to promote an African landed class could be seen in the 'Z' plots and the activities of the Land Bank. Both these projects sought to settle Africans on relatively large-scale farms in the Highlands. Both were motivated by a desire to preserve the large-farm economy and to reward politically important elements in the government. Both in fact created conditions for the movement of middle-class Africans on to large farms. This was the long-term social side of the political-economic coin the planners were examining. Cementing a social class into the agricultural system with an interest in its stability and enhancement was as much a requisite for the survival of the economy and the Government as was assuaging land hunger.

On May 11, 1964, J.H. Angaine, Minister for Settlement, announced the Government decision to reserve the former European houses along with 100 acres for a single settlement plot.[89] The 'Z' plots as they were known were used not only to prevent the destruction of the houses and to reward high level party faithful, but also as a means of providing leadership in the settlement schemes and tying the community closer to the government and the schemes. Quite consciously the plots were reserved for the political leadership. The Department of Settlement remarked in its Annual Report:

By direction of the Cabinet a new policy was started toward the end of the year [N.B. fiscal year] whereby the better class houses on large-scale farms had a 100 acre holding planned around them, regardless of the size of the plots in the remainder of the scheme. This was done so that the house and 100 acre holdings could be sold to a leader of the community such as a member of the Central Assembly or a Senator, etc.[90]

Besides the clear 'political gravy' involved in distributing the land, planners hoped the 'Z' plots would secure a commitment by influential people to the settlement schemes. As a Settlement official later wrote, the 'Z' plots 'had the advantage of committing the leaders including many minor leaders, to

155

the scheme, since any free distribution or seizure of land would also involve their holdings.'[91]

Others involved in the transfer program were less sure of the advantages derived from the 'Z' plots. The World Bank opposed the 'Z' plots at the time. One I.B.R.D. official described them as 'absolutely scandalous.' Settlement planners also had grave misgivings about the plots. In terms of loan repayments and productivity these misgivings appeared to have been well placed.

The Van Arkadie Mission (named after its Chairman, Brian Van Arkadie, an English economist) appointed in July 1966 to more fully evaluate Kenya's experience in settlement schemes found the 'Z' plots very discouraging. The secret Report is known to have complained that there had been no competitive price in their sale. Many were owned by Ministers, Members of Parliament, Ambassadors, Permanent Secretaries and Provincial Commissioners, and these owners were not living on them or developing them in a significant way. Understandably, the owners had also not become integrated with the other farmers on the schemes. The 118 'Z' plots incorporated no fewer than 505 normal settlement size farms keeping large numbers of families out.[92] Loan repayments on these plots were worse than any other type of settlement with some of the most prominent of all 'Z' plot owners also the most serious defaulters.[93]

Ministry of Settlement files brought out the difficulty in collecting loan repayments from 'Z' plot defaulters. Although by mid-1969 the small scale holders were paying only fifty per cent of repayments, the 'Z' plot holders' rate was considerably less (exact figures not available). The Investigations Office of the Ministry, set up to boost the lagging repayment rate, offered a number of reasons for this. The 'Z' plotholders were given inadequate supervision; 100 acres was not a viable proposition vis a vis charges on the land; absentee landholders left the plots to inexperienced staff; and 'Z' plot owners felt that the foreign lenders would revise the terms if they didn't pay. A Ministry memo on the subject concluded with a final reason: 'It has been observed from experience that it is very embarrassing to resort to various remedies against the 'Z' plotholders since the sizeable section of them are public figures, persons in authority or high ranking civil servants or politicians.'[94] By mid-1969 no cases of chronic loan defaulters from 'Z' plotholders had yet been referred to the Attorney General, although by the end of 1969, 158 recommendations for eviction of other settlers had gone to the Sifting Committee in Parliament with 84 evictions resulting.[95]

The Land Bank through loans to large African farmers for the purchase of European farms played a central part in the private transfer of farms between the races. The Bank was originally expanded under European pressure in conjunction with the Million-Acre scheme. It served chiefly to aid farmers bought out under the scheme to repurchase farms in other parts of Kenya. The farmers could buy another property without risking the capital realized from the sale of their first farm. (The money was usually kept in a London bank.) However by independence the Bank has become a vehicle of increasing African ownership of mixed farms through financing of private exchanges. The move away from primarily European use of the Land Bank was illustrated by the Chart below:

Land Bank aided transfers of land
(Acreage)

	To Africans	To Europeans	To Asians	Total
1963	50,590	394,031	25,233	469,854
1964	155,714	146,693	4,063	306,470
1965 (first six months)	115,291	5,620	43	120,954
Total	321,595	546,344	29,339	897,278

Source: 'Report of the Mission Appointed to Advise on Proposals for a Further Transfer of European Farms in Kenya,' October 1965, p. 206.

International financial involvement

From the beginning of the 1960 transfer schemes the World Bank and the Commonwealth Development Corporation had been involved.[96] The British government sought this involvement, especially of the World Bank, not only to ease the financial burden on HMG, but also to help make the schemes less political, and to tie the World Bank into Kenya's future economic policies. Frequently Settlement planners spoke of the high standards of World Bank schemes and the 'loan discipline' imposed on the new government.

This 'socialization' aspect of World Bank involvement (political and economic learning through supervision and ties) was often considered more important than the actual funds by the planners. British government officials held a similar view. In March 1961 a farmer leader reported on his talks with an Assistant Under Secretary of State in the Colonial Office.

In my preliminary discussions with . . . it soon became apparent that in his mind the negotiations with the World Bank influenced much of his thinking. He explained that there is no Government in the world which has yet dared to offend this institution and, therefore, it is most important that, with Independence on the way, the Bank should be linked with Kenya's development. It would constitute a most potent stabilising factor.[97]

International finance was considered an important taskmaster in educating the nationalist regime in proper development behavior. The merits of the various choices in development strategy facing the new government need not concern us. Indeed, the purpose of the exercise was to limit this

157

choice as much as possible. However, international financing did hinder settlement schemes going in directions (relief of landless and cooperatives) for which some Kenya officials pushed.[98]

At the conclusion of the First Lancaster House Conference, in February 1960, Secretary of State Iain Macleod stated that the World Bank would be approached for financing of the projected settlement schemes.[99] By the time the Kenya representatives began discussion with the Bank, support had in fact already been garnered by British officials based in Washington. As one Kenya participant wrote, 'by the time the Kenyan people began their negotiations the World Bank was already mentally committed to the schemes. Throughout they continued to have this commitment, no doubt on political grounds.'[100]

Besides British government pressure, the World Bank may also have been responding to less formal links with Kenya. Eugene Black, the President of the I.B.R.D., paid a 'private' visit to Kenya on May 13, 1960. He stayed part of the time with Peter Marrian, President of the KNFU, and a family friend.[101] Bruce McKenzie was described as a close friend of George Woods, Black's successor at the World Bank, by an official of the organization. Funding by the Bank for not strictly 'development' projects in Kenya had a precedent in the aid given to land consolidation under the Swynnerton Plan. As former Governor Baring (later Lord Howick) wrote in *The Times*: 'Because of the statesmanlike action of Mr Eugene Black, *the World Bank has departed from its normal rules* [italics added] and lent £1 million to provide capital for the 120,000 farmers of new compact holdings.'[102]

Although a Bank official in Kenya admitted that the I.B.R.D. was financing transfers rather than development, the Bank's subsequent concern was to satisfy the organization's internal criteria for loans by assuming that the settlement schemes were developmental.[103] These conditions included that the land to be transferred be high-potential underdeveloped land and that settlement would result in substantial increase of production; that settlers be agriculturally qualified and chosen on a non-racial basis with some working capital. The plots selected had to have the capacity for more intensive settlement and be large enough to satisfy the donors that the costs of loans, services and interest (around 6½ per cent) could be borne by the farmer.[104] The I.B.R.D. also required assurances on the organization and staffing of settlement with the heads of the relevant bureaucracies subject to World Bank concurrence. I.B.R.D. and C.D.C. money did not cover land purchase which was supplied by British loans and grants. (The HMG grant varied from 25 per cent to 33 per cent of the purchase price, designed to cover the difference between an acceptable price to the seller and a bearable cost for the settler.)

The I.B.R.D./C.D.C. loans provided money for two types of schemes in 1960.[105] The Assisted-Owner and Yeoman schemes provided settlement for some 1,800 families covering 90,000 acres of high-potential land on holdings of about fifty acres for qualified settlers with a target income of £250 plus subsistence. The Yeoman scheme (as in 'sturdy English yeoman') in which the L.D.S.B. was to buy land, subdivide and sell it, never went anywhere because of African reluctance at the beginning of settlement to acquire ready-made plots not chosen by themselves, and tribal antipathies which hindered settling qualified settlers outside tribal spheres of influence. The Assisted Owner scheme, by which European farmers found their own purchasers and drew up a plan of subdivision approved by the Settlement Board, similarly failed to meet expectations. Used by European farmers as a loophole to transfer assets, many of the Assisted Owners' did not match the I.B.R.D./C.D.C. development criteria or qualify for loans under the scheme.[106]

The second I.B.R.D./C.D.C. scheme, the low-density smallholder, covering 6,000 families on 90,000 acres with a target income of £100 plus subsistence was only a bit more successful. By mid-1962, 25,481 acres had been bought at a cost of £280,671 to settle 731 families. The poor results of both schemes as well as the change in priorities to massive high-density settlement led Kenya government planners to alter the I.B.R.D./C.D.C. schemes. High Kenyan officials had for some time felt that the stipulations on finance hindered their meeting the political goals of the transfer. The then Minister for Agriculture, Michael Blundell, wrote a friendly British M.P. in mid-1961 criticizing the terms of the existing schemes:

These are schemes incorporating mainly IBRD and CDC money, which, because of the terms and conditions of the loans, necessitate the use of highest potential land in the Highlands and a large degree of selection of settler[s] – in other words they pick out the economic eyes of the European farming enterprise in Kenya and limit the impact on the landless because the selected persons have to have fairly reasonable qualifications.[107]

The planners proposed that the schemes continue, but at a slower rate, and that the smallholder project be extended to correspond to the life of the Million-Acre scheme. The Assisted Owner scheme was discontinued in June 1962. Its equivalent was handled under Land Bank financing, allowing 'Africans with money and ability' to find farms unrelated to settlement schemes.[108]

In altering the priorities and the administration of settlement, Government planners met resistance from the World Bank. The change from the L.D.S.B. supervising settlement to that of the C.L.B. had apparently gone off without incurring much opposition from the lenders. However the Ministry of Settlement's move to undercut the C.L.B. did receive their attention. In September 1962 the Ministry showed I.B.R.D. and C.D.C. representatives plans for keeping the schemes out of C.L.B. control. The planners wished to do this without getting formal amendments to Loan KE 303 which specified the terms of the funding. The lenders objected. A rather testy letter from the Ministry on December 19, 1962 thought it would not be possible to change the C.L.B. if it did not meet the Bank's wishes, but complained that the Ministry did not know what they were. The Bank was criticized for emphasizing settlement and development with adequate safeguards against political interference. 'You will, I am sure, appreciate that land settlement is at the very center of the Kenya political stage and is, in itself, a political measure.'[109]

In mid-March 1963, the C.D.C. and World Bank were still described as 'extremely perturbed' about the arrangements for settlement in the future. Until new amendments to the loan agreements were negotiated, they had declined to issue funds for schemes already in operation.[110] Apparently the lenders were upset to find settlement diverging from the original proposals. The administrative alterations designed to reflect the changing political winds worried the lenders that economic criteria would be ignored.

One of the objectives in the original program was the maintenance of the Highland's economy. To this end European farmers were to be retained and settlement was to be supportive. Settlement covering a wide area with 'uneconomic' high-density plots met immediate political needs but seemed to endanger the preservative goal. A Ministry memo underlined this change:

One of the understandings reached with the IBRD and CDC was that settlement schemes should not be a device to encourage European farmers to leave since the continuance of large numbers of them was considered essential to the economy. Policy has now changed to some extent on this since the need to maintain stability in the country takes precedence over the maintenance of the economy, or is at least a pre-requisite to it and to ensure this larger numbers of Africans must be settled.[111]

Problems arose in other areas of settlement. HMG had to subsidize part of the I.B.R.D./C.D.C.'s settlers' loan repayments as their financial burden was greater than on other schemes and was felt to be too heavy to allow the schemes to function.[112] The non-discrimination clause in the I.B.R.D./C.D.C. schemes was in fact administratively circumvented and never seriously intended by any of the parties. Asians and Europeans did not get settlement plots, and allocation of the plots was influenced by tribal considerations.

Settlement planners argued it was not possible for them to buy land for the I.B.R.D./C.D.C. schemes simply on the grounds that it was the most economically suitable. They had to buy land within tribal spheres of influence and then set aside the most suitable land therein for the schemes. This was in fact not necessarily the best land. Rather, the land selected was 'a more or less balance between the interests of various tribes in settlement and of various European farmers.'[113] At one point, the Ministry's Permanent Secretary complained to the Colonial Office that he could not find enough quality land in the Scheme to meet the acreage allotted to I.B.R.D./C.D.C. plots and still satisfy their lenders' economic criteria.[114]

However these conflicts were successfully ironed out in discussions on the revision of Loan 303-KE in the fall of 1963. I.B.R.D. representatives visited Kenya in spring 1964 and left 'very impressed' by the schemes on the ground. They said they were the best of various schemes they had seen in different parts of the world.[115]

Other influences of the World Bank were more subtle, for example in the question of cooperatives. Minor Nationalist politicians had been fairly adamant in calling for farming cooperatives in the settled areas. These were seen as incorporating economies of scale, absorbing more people, and being more appropriate to the precepts of African socialism. Planners objected to them as unrealistic, requiring trained managers, and difficult to implement across ethnic lines in the face of tribal hostility. Perhaps most centrally, the co-ops conflicted with the priority of stifling land hunger and giving the settlers a tangible stake in the system. But the lenders too had an influence in neglecting cooperatives, as a Settlement official wrote later: 'It was almost impossible to satisfy the financial sponsors on technical grounds that collectives of this kind would work and that they would get any of their money back.'[116]

The question of cooperatives arose forcefully in Nyanza, western Kenya, where a sugar scheme was planned at Muhoroni. Here the problem of people flooded out of their homes by Lake Victoria added to the unemployed, landless, and the too-few with sufficient capital for economic sugar plots. Planners knew that sugar cane required high capitalization, and regular planning and removal of cane to the factory, and this led them to favor organizing some sort of cooperative.[117]

Objections to a cooperative in Nyanza lay in management difficulties and in satisfying Luo land hunger. But a major inhibition to carrying out such a project was perceived by Ministry officials as the international lenders' objections to state farming or cooperatives.

Although we have always considered the possibilities of state farming, it would be unacceptable to IBRD and CDC, and there is not enough finance under the H.D. [High Density] scheme. It *might* be possible to get the IBRD and CDC to accept a co-operative scheme, but in their present mood it is not really advisable, except as a last resort to try anything as novel as this on them.[113]

With independence and the increased Africanization of settlement positions, the World Bank sought to retain European experts within its own organization. As told by a World Bank representative, Bruce McKenzie had urged the Bank to keep well-trained expatriates in Kenya on its own staff, or in the Agricultural Development Corporation, whose appointments were approved by the World Bank. The effort was to maintain both the effectiveness, continuity and personal contacts, in settlement as well as in Kenya's overall economic policies. The impression in the Settlement Ministry was that many Europeans had switched to working for the I.B.R.D. Others, such as N. S. Carey Jones, were offered jobs but declined them. Among those hired by the World Bank were the following: A Storrar, Director of Settlement; G. R. Henderson, Deputy Director; R. D. B. Kirkwood and W. J. England, Administrative Officers; C. P. R. Nottidge, Area Settlement Controller; V E. M. Burke, Assistant Area Settlement Controller; T. L. Martin and A. M. Mercer, Senior Settlement Officers; J. Kana, Settlement Officer.[119]

CONCLUSIONS

The initial land transfer schemes in 1960 and 1961 under the direction of the Ministry of Agriculture and the L.D.S.B. had limited economic and political goals which did not encompass the massive settlement which Government planners came to see as necessary to stabilize the Kenyan political scene. The first goal of these early schemes, besides insuring market support for European sellers, was to unscramble the Highlands; a public relations effort to show the world that 'the White Highlands weren't white anymore' one official put it. Experienced African farmers were to be given sizeable plots and integrated into the system and standards of the Highlands.

To do this, a second objective, that of strict economic criteria, had to be maintained. Not only were these important for keeping the standards of the Highlands, both in agriculture and life-style, intact and gaining European political support, but also for the flow of international finance. The British desire for international funding, both parastatal and commercial, enhanced the local European hope of preserving the large farm system. The World Bank emphasis on 'development' in the transferred areas necessitated the use of high-potential land and experienced settlers. Both criteria limited the scope of the schemes and the increasing importance of satisfying a third objective.

'Taking the steam out of the land kettle' came into conflict with the two other objectives as the rural masses became more aware of their growing political influence. In the initial years of settlement satisfying land hunger had been interpreted as buying out areas of long-standing dispute and hopefully winning away moderate, predominantly non-Kikuyu, tribes from nationalist leadership.[120] However even as these 'sore-thumb' schemes were being initiated along with Assisted-Owner and Yeoman programs, the planners saw them as inadequate. At the same time the stipulations on finance for 'development' inhibited their meeting the rising threat of insurgency. Moving to massive settlement to satisfy this last requirement then meant limiting the economic criteria placed on the transfers and accommodating to ethnic feelings which pushed for a preservation of tribal spheres of influence.

With the easing of the threat of rural insurgency, settlement planners could by 1964 more flexibly insure the continued vitality of the Highlands farming system. Although political arguments were used to induce continued British funding for the schemes, stifling land hunger took a back seat to preserving capital agriculture in Kenya. The 'Z' plots, the Land Bank financing for private transfers, and the activities of the A.D.C. in maintaining large-farm agricultural production, illustrated this redirection of emphasis. While these programs had a number of motives ranging from 'land greed' to preventing the peasantization of the Highlands, they in fact created conditions by which a middle class of Africans could obtain rights and interests in the large-farm sector to politically and economically insure its continued functioning.

Perhaps the key word which underlay the whole land transfer program was 'continuity.' Taking its cue from the process of decolonization itself, settlement sought to transfer and preserve the Kenyan political economy as intact as possible. At first this meant a minimal alteration in European ownership in the Highlands, hence settlement was to provide market support, scatter a small number of Africans throughout the Highlands, and assuage limited traditional claims to land. Later, as the threat of land seizures grew, and European confidence sagged, settlement of some million acres was needed to preserve both the economic system and a cordial political regime. Finally, with insurgency stifled, the benefits of large farms and large farmers to the economy and polity could be emphasized in the schemes. Organized settlement, while reduced to meet other economic needs, has never quite been phased out so that the sense of a gradual Africanization of the Highlands would not be lost on Kenyans.

Throughout, the thrust of settlement was to integrate and socialize segments of the African population into an on-going system. The Kenyan political economy was altered only so as to facilitate its transition. Questions of transforming the colonial system were neither answered nor posed: the value of continued dependence on large-scale private agriculture; the merits of state-owned cooperatives buying up the Highlands; the alternatives to an external development strategy; the question of simply doing nothing in the Highlands, allowing the Europeans who wished to leave to do so and rebuilding from there – these basic choices were simply outside the policy perspectives of the settlement planners and, one might add, the European and African politicians.

But one should not fault a program for failing to accomplish a transformation it was set up to prevent. In terms of economic preservation and counter-insurgency, settlement deserved high marks. Whether a political legerdemain, by which a fraction of the population received land on terms a majority of them have had difficulty paying off, has effectively stifled rural unrest and further demands for land, remains an open question. Settlement succeeded by presenting the nationalist regime with a functioning agricultural system, the structural and financial leverage to maintain it, and political tasks not essentially different from those of its predecessor.

CHAPTER 7

CONCLUSION: EUROPEANS, LAND AND DECOLONIZATION

What is a Nation?
. . . to get one's history wrong.

Ernest Renan

Africa,
don't let them
steal
your face or
take your circles
and make them squares.

Don L. Lee

This final chapter will attempt to summarize the study and integrate it into the overall process of decolonization in Kenya. European adaptation – the goals and composition of the groups, their alignments and divisions, their bargaining strategies and tactics – is discussed as an important feature of Kenyan decolonization. The land question was the key issue of the process. Its bargaining and resolution both paralleled and supported the larger process. One can argue that the explication of a major feature and critical issue of decolonization largely explains the direction the process took in Kenya.

EUROPEAN ADAPTATION

Groups, goals and strategies

As previously discussed, there was a dualistic division in the resident elite over the community's adaptive policies toward decolonization and the political ascendency of the nationalist elite.

The conservatives (or farmers) basically sought to reinforce the core group through a reaffirmation of traditional values. Their stance was reflected in a conservative view of a political grouping as quasi-organic, based on traditional ties. Opposition between colonial interests and the nationalists was seen as inevitable. From this perspective their immediate problem was internal: the division within the once-dominant group and the decay in their rectitude of rule. Alteration in the political hierarchy was considered deviant, and likely deriving from factors external to the colony (i.e., American and Communist pressure).

The conservatives appeared to derive their support from those in the colonial elite least able to adapt to the forseeable threatening changes. These included relatively small landowners unable to resume their high-status position in another setting, recent immigrants, those with absolutist tenden-

164

cies in religion and race (e.g., Afrikaners), and rural residents somewhat cut off from the flow of new ideas. Willingness and ability to survive the projected changes were the key. As a study of small European communities in Tanganyika concluded:

Those Europeans prepared 'to move with the times' were generally those who expected little difficulty in finding employment outside Tanganyika, if necessary; those opposed to non-European membership were those whose status and standard of living were most threatened by the advent of competitors for their jobs.[1]

At a later stage in Kenyan decolonization, when the choice of leaving the country was faced, the division of 'stayers' and 'goers' may have paralleled the political division. The Secretary of the conservative Convention of Associations wrote to an English friend in late 1962:

More and more do I feel that the stayers are those who can afford to stay because they have money to get themselves out of the country if they have to. The goers are those smaller farmers who have put every penny they possess back into their land, may have debts to the Land Bank for development, etc., and even if they sell, many of them will not have enough capital to start again elsewhere.[2]

In line with this perception of self, the major strategy of the conservative group became one of racial re-entrenchment. The community was to regain its ebbing power by uniting behind its own standards and traditions, thus becoming a powerful lobby group in the new setting. Alliances outside the group (other than with those of a like kind, hence the use of the Old Boy network to reach the British ruling class) were both subordinate to the core and peripheral to the problems and policies of the group.[3] Michael Blundell, leader of the liberal Kenya Europeans, wrote in his memoirs of the division in the community occurring on whether the basis of the European political role should center on their racial identity:

The difference developed and centered around whether that [European] leadership was a racial concept imposed on the Africans and one to which they could not aspire; or whether it was the projection of standards and a way of life in which all, regardless of race, could share and many would be content to follow.[4]

The liberal (or commercial) group, presented themselves as 'realists.' While not welcoming either decolonization or nationalist ascendancy, they viewed them as inevitable and attempted an accommodation on the best possible terms. The major problem the liberals faced was gaining support for the values they represented outside of their racial community. In 1960 this meant sharing positions and parties under the mantle of multi-racialism with like-minded members of other races. By 1962 public positions were eschewed for the more submerged leverages of advice and financial support. The important political divisions for the liberals were found less in personalities than in policies. Support was not in a racial unity but in an ideological one.

165

Conclusion

From this flowed the major long-term liberal strategy of restructuring the society from one split on racial lines to one divided on a class basis. The aim was to support and promote, economically, socially and politically, Africans with interests similar to those of the European community. The thrust of their policy became the building up of, and alignment with, a moderate African middle class. This class, given political authority, property rights, admission to the European economic system, and an expectation of prosperity, was to be a bulwark in the preservation of the colonial-established system and of the European interests within it.

This long-range social/political goal oriented the liberal policies toward African economic development. Blundell viewed the Swynnerton Plan of the 1950s for development of the African areas as eventually having '. . . a stabilizing even conservative influence on the political arena.[5] In a meeting of the liberal New Kenya Group Executive with Iain Macleod in late 1959, the Minutes recorded Humphrey Slade as remarking to the Colonial Secretary, 'There was a great need for economic development, so that the standards of living of the people could be raised and that we might get away from the seeming coincidence of class with race . . .'[6] The Kenya National Farmers Union used the liberal argument to push for expanded land settlement in early 1962, arguing that 'the creation of an African middle class with individual property rights will do much to create stability and to promote an expanding economy.'[7]

The liberals generally found their support from the European community in the urban areas, among relatively well-off long-term residents, in the European (and Asian) commercial and bureaucratic groups, and among influential members of the Colonial and British governments. These were groups who felt they could weather the 'winds of change.' Either because of experience with previous decolonizations, general liberal attitudes, greater liquidity of holdings or wealth held outside the colony, these groups felt more secure in the changing conditions.[8]

Each of the two groups considered the other's strategy a threat. The liberals viewed racial unity as outmoded and an obstacle to broader alignments. They worried that focusing on community interests (i.e., schools, underwriting of titles in the Highlands, etc.) would harm their attempts to submerge racial identity in the African-dominated polity.[9] For the conservatives, multi-racial politics was unrealistic and hindered the formation of a powerful European lobby. They saw the liberals as having been established by the Colonial government to split and weaken the Europeans much as the Government wished to split the Africans.

The goals of the two groups in broadly seeking to preserve various European interests (economic, social, political) were similar, although their priorities differed. The goals could be summed up as the safeguarding of (a) the colonial system and (b) European agricultural assets. The liberals stressed the overriding importance of the first goal: the preservation of colo-

166

nial-established economic, social and political ties, patterns of behavior and expectations. For the liberals, as for the metropole, the importance of decolonization was in ensuring the continuity of the system.[10] This included the preservation of the open colonial economy, the administrative and political structure, the cultural and educational orientation of the society, the external development strategy with the consequent importance of foreign investment, the sanctity of private enterprise and property, and the metropole's legal and social norms of behavior.

The conservatives, perhaps because of their largely farmer-backing and the immediate threat to those holdings, emphasized the preservation of their agricultural holdings in the Highlands. While not disagreeing with the value of preserving the colonial system, they were willing to place the continuity of that system on a lower scale of priorities. Hence they pushed for a buy-out scheme for European farmers which might have been destructive to the economy as a whole. Urging British protection and responsibility for their holdings rather than African nationalists' guarantees, they implicitly stressed the discontinuity between the colonial system and the coming independent state, and in this respect their views coincided with the initial position of the nationalists. For the conservatives, it was their economic assets which justified the retention of colonial institutions and patterns. For the liberals, the goal of ensuring the continuity of the system led to the secondary objective of preserving the assets of the European large farmers, and, at a later point, supporting their removal.

These two goals were, of course, not basically contradictory. They did, however, lead to varied policy positions. The liberals were the activists in the colonial society; they financially and politically backed moderate nationalist elements; they attempted to secure a regional constitution to support their allies; they advocated societal issues rather than community ones. The conservatives were less interested in the composition of the nationalist elite than in that elite's attitude toward European land. Hence the farmers opposed a regional constitution which would have given the liberal-backed African party increased power because of the fear that it would complicate land transfers. The liberals, for their part, retained an ambiguity toward land transfer as emphasizing racial issues and hurting the economy. This difference in priorities was sharply illustrated by Michael Blundell's request at the First Lancaster House Conference for only a limited amount of money for land transfers allegedly in order to make it as *difficult* as possible for European farmers to leave.[11]

Tactics

The tactics of the conservatives and liberals overlapped in the multipartite bargaining of decolonization. However most of the actual bargaining with the new elite fell to the liberals, largely by default. The conservatives' emphasis on traditional channels (i.e., Her Majesty's Government) as well as their introspective orientation, hindered their ability to bargain directly in the new alignments. Further, their leadership's colonialist vision of Africans (untrustworthy, incompetent) led to a tendency to deal punitatively with their opponents. Increasingly as the nationalists gained political influence, the liberals appeared to be spokesmen for the entire community. There was also, due to a thrust toward duality in the multipartite bargaining process as issues were concretized, the question of 'for' or 'against.' This led to a division of all the participants on one side or another. This split, on issues such as regionalism and expanded land transfers, did not necessarily follow racial divisions.

The tactics used by the European groupings tended to be different according to their respective definitions of the strategies and the goals to be achieved. A favored liberal tactic was to try to trade constitutional advance for economic concessions, a tactic played in close conjunction with the Colonial government. At the First Lancaster House Conference when they demanded 'safeguards' on land, at the Governor's Conference in the autumn of 1961, at the Second Lancaster House Conference, and throughout the priod in informal bargaining, the attempt was made to guarantee property rights and the large farm system by threatening to push back independence as a result of the failure to reach agreement.

For example, Lord Hastings said in introducing the Government's report on the First Lancaster House Conference to the House of Lords in March 1960: 'This problem of the White Highlands must be sorted out before Kenya ever gets to self-government, let alone independence.'[12] The militant Nationalist leader, Oginga Odinga commented that '. . . the settlers demand land guarantees as a price for accepting African advance in the constitutional field.'[13] And Michael Blundell wrote to a friendly British Member of Parliament in June 1961, 'I also feel, and have made it known to the Kenya government, that we should not make a decisive move forward in regard to the Constitution – as, for instance, the appointment of a Chief Minister with Responsible Government – until this whole issue of security of title has been thrashed out.'[14]

Another tactic widely employed by the liberals was that of penetrating and dividing African opinion. A sociologist described its use in Kenya in the early 1950s and defined the tactic as seeking 'to cut out the largest or most threatening area of opposing interest and then to muster in their favor the largest and strongest area of support remaining open to them, and to give it cohesion and solidarity.'[15] This consisted of wooing away the moderate nationalists from their more militant cohorts, thus weakening the remaining opposition. The tactic was also important in gaining African support on issues crucial to the Europeans, and cementing their own claims to a multi-racial following.

This effort to isolate the most threatening of the opposition and align with the rest was seen in the formation of KADU in mid-1960 with European financial and administrative assistance. Similarly, the early liberal backing for land settlement was not to settle areas directly threatened by militant Kikuyu land hunger. Instead, settlement was emphasized for the 'sore-thumb' areas in which there were long-standing claims to land by mostly non-Kikuyu tribes. The attempt was to buy off tribes such as the Abaluhya, the Nandi, the Kamba, among whom there was a less pressing demand for land, and thus garner support for guarantees to remaining European land holdings. Settlement schemes as they finally evolved in the mixed-farming areas also could be seen in this light.

A third tactic used was what E. E. Schattschneider called the 'privatization' of conflict. This was the effort to limit the scope of the conflict by restricting both the contested areas and the number of participants involved.[16] In the context of decolonization, 'privatization' centered on the reduction in the visibility of contentious racially-split issues. These issues were the ones useful to the nationalists for mobilizing a wider mass base with which to confront their opponents.

The liberals' efforts to emphasize development in the African areas was part of the attempt to draw nationalist attention away from the European Highlands. More intensive development as a route to a greater African share of economic wealth was clearly politically preferable for Europeans than was expansion into their own areas.[17] It was also seen as a means of promoting an African middle class. Similarly, the playing down of racial politics in terms of both organizations and actions was part of the policy of governing the political visibility of the European community, whose very existence was a matter of dispute among some sections of the nationalist party.

Privatization was also a tactic adopted by the conservative groups, but was extended by them to mean being 'non-political' – a step only taken by the liberals late in the period, due perhaps to the number of practising politicians among them. The Kenya National Farmers Union, which was carrying on most of the lobbying activities for a fund from Britain for land underwriting and transfers, consistently and publicly stressed their apoliticism. This kept them out of many inter-European fights and enabled them to stand for 'the farmers' interests. As the public relations firm handling the KNFU's 1960 lobbying mission to England put it in a memorandum to the President:

It is important in all PR activity concerned with the KNFU mission to avoid any suggestion directly or by implication that the mission is concerned with compensation for European farmers. The theme must be pursued that the mission is representative of farmers of all kinds and of all races, that the mission and indeed the KNFU is entirely non-political and that the establishment of the fund is in the national interest . . .[18]

Even the Kenya Coalition began as a non-political organization, was perhaps pushed into the political field by liberal opposition, and emphasized economic interests and goals in its approach.

The move toward submerging European participation meant that only informal political methods could be used. The effect of this was to have the European community look both 'above' and 'below' Kenya governmental institutions for influence. 'Above,' they sought influence in the British government and international financial sources, particularly the World Bank. Throughout the period there were efforts to involve the British in both formal and informal roles as guarantor of European property. Similarly, international financial aid was seen by the Europeans and Her Majesty's Government as an important post-independence constraint on Kenya government actions. In a 1960 memorandum to the British government, the Kenya National Farmers Union remarked that stabilizing post-independence land values was possible:

. . . so long as international finance is involved pre-independence, both in the source of supply and amongst the trustees. The flow of money will not only be stabilizing land values: it will also be of vital use in the development of African agriculture. No government is likely to forego such a source of supply, in order to reduce land values by arbitrary removal of price support.[19]

Channeling political influence through relatively less visible economic organizations became increasingly favored by the European community and was a major point of contention between the farmer groups and the more politically active liberals. Farmer leaders close to his position wrote to Blundell warning him of the danger of maintaining a European political presence. Peter Marrian, the President of the KNFU, wrote him in the latter part of 1960 as follows:

A European political front is not the correct method of ensuring European strength and influence. This should come through economic organizations (with if possible participation by other races where there is an identity of interest), i.e., Chambers of Commerce, Farmers' Union, Civil Servant Association, etc. Obtain the strength of unity at this level and project it through your political representatives. A European political front as such will get us nowhere.[20]

Parallel to the rise in importance of economic organizations, was the use of economic arguments. As a justification for retaining both the large farming system (i.e., plantations, marketing boards, farmers' groups) and the European farmers, the dependence of the economy on the European agricultural system was pointed to as well as the advantages of integrating African farmers into it. Stressed was the rise in African unemployment and the drop in foreign investment, both of which would (it was alleged) flow from any change in the agricultural system. The economic arguments inevitably favored the preservation of the economic and political status quo, and were biased to as slow and as limited a change as possible.

Another traditional settler tactic was the use of administrative positions to control political initiatives which might run counter to European farmer

170

interests. This tactic had been employed throughout Kenya colonial history in order to emasculate potentially threatening political moves. With the opening of the formerly European-reserved Highlands, the farmers made sure that farmer-dominated local boards would pass judgment on prospective African farmers and that these boards had wide grounds for refusal. Similarly the Land Development and Settlement Board, set up to oversee settlement in 1961, was heavily weighted to favor European farmers and ensured that the European seller would be dealing with this board on land valuation and subdivision.[21]

A final tactic favored by all the European groups was the use of traditional channels for exercising influence in Kenya affairs. Social pressures on the British government (the 'kith and kin' argument and Old Boy network), mobilizing back-bench Conservative support, garnering important financial interests in the City of London, were all important leverages in European politics. The application of this culminated in the attempt by several farmer groups to get a post-independence guarantee of European-held property in Kenya by the British government. This attempt at 'segmental colonization,' guaranteeing property by traditional colonial means in the midst of a formally independent state, was successful only to the extent that successive British governments did accept an obligation to keep a watchful eye over the European farmers' interest after independence.

The most severe threats of the liberal and farmer groups also varied. The liberals stressed the possibility of civil war if moderate Africans were excluded from the post-independence government. The farmers also emphasized the probability of violence but (probably more realistically) saw it coming from Kikuyu peasants excluded from European land they considered their own. The farmers threatened economic blackmail by running down their farms in order to make a quick profit, if their demands were not met. They warned of the chaos that would result from this: mass unemployment, widespread 'squatting,' and the possible need for a Congo-type rescue operation – and of the consequent expense to the British taxpayer.

THE LAND ISSUE

The Kenya land transfer program was supportive of both decolonization and European adaptation. The fate of the 7.5 million acres of European-owned land was the crucial issue of the period of colonial transition. As the economic issue on which African leaders had based their opposition, the 'lost lands' had stirred resentment and agitation by Africans throughout the colonial period. For the European farmer, his land encapsulated his future. If his holdings could not be insured then his position in Kenya was tenuous. To the liberals and colonial bureaucrats the land issue was both an obstacle to a smooth transition to independence, and the test of the success of turning over political authority to colonialism's nationalist heirs. Resolving the land question would not only guarantee the continuity of the economy but also stand as a mark of the 'maturity' of Kenya's new leaders in managing the inherited colonial system.

For the process of decolonization the land question was both the major bargaining issue and the major test of socialization. The nationalists began the period of colonial transition by holding to a position of not guaranteeing land rights in the Highlands until gaining control of the government. The Europeans and colonial officials maintained that steps toward independence would be dependent on resolving the Highlands question. Both sides recognized their mutual interest in not allowing rural antagonism toward European land alienation to grow beyond their control. Their concurrence on organized land transfer schemes to dissipate mass agitation, to allow the bulk of the European community to remain, to ensure some nationalist participation in the large farm sector, and to enhance the continuity of the economy, was a mutually congenial outcome of the bargaining process.

On the level of socialization the land issue enabled the nationalists to demonstrate their 'maturity.' By accepting the colonialists' economic-functionalist arguments and implicitly rejecting the historical-traditionalist claims of their followers, they pursued the route of protecting the Kenya economy. Due not only to the acceptance of the arguments but also to the terms of the foreign loans, the post-independence Kenya leaders acknowledged the continuity of the state they governed and their role over it. Working through transnational channels, the nationalist leaders proved they could control their own followers, conciliate opponents and ensure the continued functioning of the economy and interests of colonial Kenya.

The land transfers of the 1960s were supportive of European adaptive measures in a number of ways. Primarily the transfers reduced the major threat of racial conflict in Kenya. Integrating middle-level African farmers into the Highlands and establishing settlement schemes in contested areas for landless Africans pre-empted both the central issue and the supporters for any radical movement in Kenya. Buying out Europeans in these areas diminished the visibility of the community and gave those not reconciled to the political changes an opportunity to leave. Finally, the transfers helped ensure the continued functioning of the expatriate commercial interests that found an independent Kenya both pleasant and profitable.

Four themes illustrated these lobbying goals in the implementation of the land transfer programs. The first was the maintenance by European farmers of administrative control of the land transfer schemes. In the bills opening the Highlands to all races, strict control of transfers overseen by local committees composed of European farmers was written into the laws. The initial overseer of organized settlement, the Land Development and Settlement Board, was the renamed European Agricultural Settlement Board, chaired and dominated by Highland farmers.

As African political influence grew, the channels of farmer influence became more subtle. An 'independent' Central Land Board, composed largely of regional representatives, was given authority, under farmer pressure, over the terms of purchase. The attempt here was to prevent the government from reducing the prices offered to European settlers. Throughout the life of the schemes, local European farmers, largely because of their technical competence, filled nearly all the lower level administrative positions of the schemes.

The second theme was the defusing of rural unrest. This supported the pre-emptive strategy of decolonization. Reducing the pressure from land hunger on the European holdings was the major thrust behind the Million-Acre scheme. The later acceleration of the scheme in the Kikuyu areas derived directly from the fears of the nationalist leaders, Europeans, and colonial bureaucrats, that the failure to take some steps toward resolving landlessness would result in another Mau Mau-type insurgency.

In Kenya, land is the opium of the masses. The land schemes offered the new nationalist leaders an externally financed means of dealing with internal conflict. Land transfers were used as a temporary method of inhibiting insurgency in order to stabilize the nationalist regime during the period of colonial transition – and beyond.

The promotion of a landed African middle class in the Highlands both preceded and followed the second theme. The initial schemes (Yeoman and Assisted-Owner) were designed to scatter large African farmers throughout the Highlands. This aimed both to reduce the racial visibility of the area and to integrate Africans into the large-farm economy. After assuaging the rural masses appeared less pressing, large plots were transferred under the Stamp Program, the 'Z' plots and Land Bank financing. Here again the goals were to garner support for the transfer schemes among well-placed Africans, to Africanize the on-going European farming system, and to provide an indigenous breakwater against future waves of mass agitation.

In class terms, the transfers created conditions by which the African middle classes could gain control over what they perceived (incorrectly) as the dominant means of production in their economy – capital agriculture.[22] The schemes provided a method of not only creating an African landed class, but also a way of integrating the nascent class into the political-economic system at the same time. The new settlers, through land titles, loan repayments, and some felt gratitude to the new government, were expected to acquire a vested interest against any radical transformation of the society.

The orientation and ties generated by international financial backing of the land schemes was the final theme. These ties, chiefly to the World Bank (I.B.R.D.) and the Commonwealth Development Corporation (C.D.C.) referred not only to the commitment to repay loans, but also to the conditioning process in the lending procedure. The acceptance of the development criteria involved in I.B.R.D. and C.D.C. monies, and the 'discipline' of loan repayments were central in the cooptation and socialization of the nationalist regime. The involvement of these sources of funds also reflected the European and colonial hopes of using foreign investment to bolster a moderate nationalist state and to preserve European economic (and political) interests.

The solution of Kenya's first major post-colonial conflict through external financial and technical assistance may also have set a precedent. The external orientation of Kenyan development strategy towards policies closely tied to international finance and assistance probably became consolidated in the decision-makers' minds in this relatively fluid period. International funding emphasized a network of contacts, experiences and inclinations, by offering a readily-available solution to a serious domestic conflict. It also tied the nationalists into several inter-related commitments only dimly perceived at the time. For starters, there was the obligation to repay the loans, hence to make the plots 'profitable;' to maintain an open economy favorable to private investment, hence to limit nationalizations; to maintain the chief export earner, European-dominated capital agriculture (and an economic structure congenial to it), hence to refuse to expropriate Europeans or place limits on land holdings.

CONTINUITY AND DECOLONIZATION

Decolonization in Africa involved two apparently contradictory tendencies. The most visible one was the withdrawal of direct colonial authority by the metropole. Phrases such as 'emerging nations' and 'the twilight of European colonialism'[23] illustrate the emphasis which has been placed on this disjunctive aspect of decolonization. Certainly the colonial divestment involved changes in behavior and expectations for the colonized people and the indigenous elites, as well as for the metropole and the colonial elites: local rulers now held authority over a nation-state; new channels of influence were needed by colonial interests; more indigenous participation could be expected in the government and in parts of the economy.

But these disjunctive effects for the most part reinforced the underlying continuity the process of decolonization ensured. The decolonization process aimed to preserve the colonial political economy and, beyond that, to integrate an indigenous elite into positions of authority where they could protect the important interests in the system. The themes of adaptation, cooptation and pre-emption illustrated this preservative and integrative thrust. Decolonization, while breaking certain authoritative linkages, reaffirmed and enhanced others in the form of economic dependency, development assistance, foreign investment, and the political, social and economic compatibility of objectives among the involved elites.

The question of the continuity of the colonial political economy was central to the conflict among the Kenya Europeans over the land issue. The

174

farmers by calling for a British guarantee of their land holdings were attempting to hold the British responsible for their policies in Kenya Colony. Much like the militant nationalists, the farmers initially stressed the distinction between the colonial legacy and African independence. (The farmers emphasized discontinuity because they feared decolonization wouldn't work – for them. The militants' position derived from their fear that decolonization would work – against them.) By stressing the discontinuity of independence the farmers and militants directly opposed the major thrust of decolonization. Both faced isolation from the process and the subsequent political demise of both reflected the strength of the interests they unsuccessfully challenged.

The representatives of these adaptive interests, the European liberals and the British government, recognized the importance of internalizing colonial obligations into the fabric of the new state. For the political economy, which they wished to see continue, was also an extension of colonial policies. The farmers' position differed only in its greater visibility and contentiousness. The argument for the farmers' protection could be extended to other economic concerns. But more important was the precedent of the new government choosing which parts of the colonial legacy it would admit as valid. The nationalists' acceptance of responsibility for European land titles meant acquiescence to the most hated part of colonialism, and one whose reversal was a major impetus behind their movement. Consenting to the validity of land titles and to land transfers was the linchpin to the nationalists' acceptance of the continuity of the colonial system and their own role in maintaining that continuity.

The acceptance by all the participants of the 'logic' of the colonial patterns was sufficient to largely ensure the outcome of the bargaining surrounding decolonization. The almost premised irrationality of overturning a functioning political and economic system led to the viability of the decolonization process. The question of whether independence was to effect a transformation of the colonial system went unstated. Indeed, decolonization answered that question by never posing it.

NOTES

1 'Colonial transition' refers here to the period prior to independence in which the major actors accept independence as the immediate outcome of their bargaining.

2 Robert A. LeVine, 'Anti-European Violence in Africa: A Comparative Analysis,' *Journal of Conflict Resolution*, Vol. III, No. 4, December 1959, pp. 420–9. LeVine sees anti-European violence deriving from 'conflicting expectations' of the African population, and cites a 'half-century of ambivalence' prior to Mau Mau with the government aiding the settlers while granting concessions to moderate Kikuyu leaders (p. 423).

3 See Gwendolen M. Carter and Wililam O. Brown, eds., *Transition in Africa: Studies in Political Adaptation* (Boston: Boston University Press, 1958), pp. 9–16. The two editors of this early study somewhat ambiguously accept the identity of the transfer of authority leading towards social control (p. 9).

4 Without getting into an extended debate on the use of 'system,' one can argue that the pre- and post-independence political economy is composed of inter-related persisting parts conceived of as closed for heuristic purposes. A system has been characterized as having distinguishable boundaries setting it off from its environment, a tendency toward equilibrium (maintaining itself through various processes whenever it is disturbed), and various subsystems (groups and institutions developed to handle problems, select goals, mobilize resources, and make decisions). Decolonization, it will be argued (though not in systemic terms), is such a process of correcting a disturbed equilibrium by mobilizing various groups and resources to ensure the continuity of the colonial system. (William C. Mitchell, 'Political Systems,' *International Encyclopedia*, Vol. 15, pp. 473–8.)

5 From a systems analysis perspective a structure (the colonial one, in this case) can be seen as a slower, more rhythmic set of events, while the process (decolonization) is a more rapid and irregular pattern.

The definitions used here are adapted from Bertram M. Gross, 'Political Process,' in *The International Encyclopedia of the Social Sciences* (The Macmillan Company and The Free Press, 1968), Vol. 12, pp. 265–73.

6 Thomas Schelling, *A Strategy of Conflict* (Cambridge: Harvard University Press, 1961), p. 5 and Chapter 2.

7 For an example of African states involved in an unequal bargaining situation, as well as a critique of the applicability of game theory to negotiations, see William Zartman, *The Politics of Trade Negotiations between Africa and the European Economic Community* (Princeton: Princeton University Press, 1971), pp. 200–6.

8 See *A Dictionary of the Social Sciences* (New York: The Free Press, 1964), p. 8.

9 Philip Selznick, *TVA and the Grass Roots* (Berkeley: University of California, 1949), pp. 13–14, 259.

10 See Fred I. Greenstein, 'Political Socialization,' *The International Encyclopedia of the Social Sciences*, Vol. 14, pp. 551–5.

11 F.G. Bailey defines an ideal authority as being both neutral and deserving of obedience. See his *Strategems and Spoils* (London: Oxford University Press, 1970), p. 32.

12 The period of colonial transition was seldom as clearly demarcated in other parts of Africa as it was in Kenya. In Zambia the transition period proceeded by half-steps. Iain Macleod's announcement on September 28, 1960, of a constitutional conference was inferred to mean Northern Rhodesia was headed for a transfer of colonial authority. Yet complications surrounding the Central African Federation, threats of settler violence, and constitutional difficulties caused British back-pedalling. It was not perhaps until December 1962, with the formation of an African majority government, that the period of colonial transition began, ending in independence on October 24, 1964. Colonial transition in Tanganyika began in the late-1959 decision to hold elections in 1960, which the Tanganyika African National Union was expected to dominate. Independence followed on December 9, 1960.

In francophone Africa the vote of the Parti du Regroupement (PRA) on July 25, 1958, at Cotonou to press for immediate independence may be cited as the beginning of the end of the French colonies. However not until December 11–12, 1959, did France and the conservative African leaders such as Felix Houphouet-Boigny of the Ivory Coast and Philibert Tsirinana of the Malagasy Republic accept the goal of independence at the sixth meeting of the Executive Council of the Franco-African Community. The independence of all the states of French West Africa by the end of 1960 made the period of colonial transition a fairly brief one. In the case of the Entente states (Ivory Coast, Upper Volta, Niger and Togo) the formal negotiations surrounding post-independence relations with France actually occurred *after* independence. This reflected not only a desire to humiliate the Maliens, who had pressured France into an early independence date, but also French confidence in their leverage over the leaders of the Entente states. (See Michael Crowder, 'Independence as a Goal in French West African Politics: 1944–60,' in William H. Lewis (ed.), *French-Speaking Africa* (New York: Walker, 1965), pp. 15–44.)

13 David Goldsworthy, *Colonial Issues in British Politics, 1945–61* (Oxford: Oxford University Press, 1971), p. 1.

14 Dan Horowitz, 'Attitudes of British Conservatives Toward Decolonization in Africa During the Period of the Macmillan Government, 1957–1963' (Ph.D. dissertation, Oxford University, 1967), pp. 72–3. Horowitz sees the speech as nothing novel in Her Majesty's Government's policies of the time.

15 Sir Andrew Cohen, *British Policy in Changing Africa* (Evanston: Northwestern University Press, 1959), p. 61.

16 Horowitz, p. 358.

17 Peter Worsley, *The Third World*, 2nd edition (Chicago: The University of Chicago Press, 1967), p. 21.

18 For an excellent discussion of the concept of 'maturity' see Trevor G. Munroe, 'Political Change and Constitutional Development in Jamaica, 1944–1962' (Ph.D. dissertation, Oxford University, 1969), p. 306.

19 One student of decolonization discussed Secretary of State Reginald Maudling's role in Kenya in 1962 in these terms: 'Maudling's role in helping the Africans to resolve their own conflicts was a consequence of the policy of disengagement and of the supposition that in order to avoid a Congo-like situation unity among the Africans should be a precondition for independence.' Horowitz, 'Attitudes of British Conservatives,' p. 177.

20 E.E. Schattschneider, *The Semisovereign People* (New York: Holt, Rinehart and Winston, 1960), p. 129.
21 Iain Macleod, 'Trouble in Africa,' *Spectator*, January 31, 1964, p. 127.
22 Munroe, 'Political Change,' pp. 317–18.
23 E.E. Schattschneider points out that the exclusion of Black people from southern politics in the United States was brought about only at the price of establishing a one-party system. (*The Semisovereign People*, p. 15.)
24 Even in a state with progressive leadership, the insignificance for the population of modern political activities has received comment. See Henry Bienen, 'The Ruling Party in the African One Party State: T.A.N.U. in Tanzania,' *Journal of Commonwealth Political Studies*, Vol. V, No. 3, November 1967, p. 15.
25 Richard T.A.R. Rathbone, 'The Transfer of Power in Ghana, 1945–57' (Ph.D. dissertation, University of London, 1968), p. 195 and Chapter 10.
26 Munroe, 'Political Change,' pp. 49–52.
27 I. Wallerstein, 'The Colonial Era in Africa,' in Vol. 2 of *Colonialism in Africa,* ed. by Gann and Duignan (London: Cambridge University, 1970), pp. 399–421.
28 John Fletcher-Cooke, 'Parliament, The Executive and the Civil Service,' in Sir Alan Burns (ed.), *Parliament as an Export* (London: Allen and Unwin, 1966), pp. 142–65. He also remarks that Africans clamored for 'the Westminster Model, the whole Model and nothing but the Model' (p. 159). The 'Westminster Model' referred to representative democracy as practiced in England, including a ministerial system of administration, parliamentary selection of the executive, an impartial civil service, and a strongly centralized governmental structure.
29 Rathbone, 'The Transfer of Power in Ghana,' Chapter 10.
30 An example of this assertion can be found in the land transfers supporting decolonization in Kenya. Promoting the economic viability of either the schemes or the economy was a less important consideration for the bureaucrats involved than was preserving certain economic interests and political relationships through the transfers. See below, Chapter 6.
31 For example, not until President DeGaulle was securely in power was the French government strong enough to embark on a policy of decolonization in Algeria.
32 Ronald H. Chilcote, *Portuguese Africa* (New Jersey: Prentice-Hall, 1967), pp. 124–6.
33 James Duffy, *Portugal in Africa* (Cambridge: Harvard University, 1962), pp. 191–203.
34 A. Cabral, 'Speech at Central Hall Westminster, Tuesday, October 25, 1971,' in *GUERRILHEIRO*, Bulletin of the Committee for Freedom in Mozambique, Angola and Guinea, No. 7, November–December, 1971. How the recent decolonizations in Mozambique and Guinea-Bissau and the contested one in Angola affect the analysis is uncertain at this time. The author is not familiar with any evaluation of the role played in the decolonization process by the multinational or agricultural interests within the former territories or the metropole, or that of foreign powers such as South Africa and the United States. Nonetheless the thrust of this analysis would project regimes more conservative than was expected by John Saul in his article on the internal politics of Frelimo. (See John S. Saul, 'FRELIMO and the Mozambique Revolution,' in Giovanni Arrighi and John S. Saul, *Essays on the Political Economy of Africa* (New York: Modern Reader, 1973), pp. 378–405.)

35 Rathbone, 'The Transfer of Power in Ghana,' p. 378.
36 R.E. Robinson and J. Gallagher, 'The Imperialism of Free Trade,' *The Economic History Review*, Vol. 6, No. 1, 1953, pp. 1–15.
37 *Ibid.*, p. 13. Egypt is cited as an example of the failure of informal rule due to the undermining of the satellite state by investments and pseudo-nationalist reaction to foreign influence.
38 J.M. Lee, *Colonial Development*, pp. 248–9.
39 Rathbone remarks that Ghanaian decolonization showed that 'Britain could, if the results of the Ghana experiment were considered, groom its political successors, and by tinkering with franchises might have a real hand in determining who these might be in the rest of Africa.' Rathbone, 'The Transfer of Power in Ghana,' p. 379.
40 Munroe, 'Political Change,' pp. 242–3. Munroe argues that the only alternative for the nationalists was complete rejection of the existing order – its institutions and values. This was unlikely because of the logic of anti-colonialism, the illogicality of revolution, and the attractiveness of continuity.
41 An example of the use of this political socialization occurred in Kenya in early 1963. A meeting was called by the Deputy Governor on January 18, 1963, to discuss breaches of the conventional code of behavior by Parliamentary Secretaries. Specifically at issue were statements by J. G. Kiano, Parliamentary Secretary for Constitutional Affairs and Economic Planning, and a KANU leader. Kiano, in public statements and a letter to the *East African Standard* on January 9, 1963, had said that nationalization would be inevitable with self-government, no matter what was said by the present interim coalition government. The Deputy Governor warned the Parliamentary Secretaries that during their participation in the government they must avoid critical statements of the government and stick to collective responsibility. 'Record of a Meeting of Parliamentary Secretaries Held in Government house at 11 A.M. on Friday 18 January 1963,' 10 pp., Governor's Office, January 22, 1963, The Papers of P.D. Marrian, private collection.
42 Besides the works cited elsewhere in the text, there is a fairly extensive bibliography generally available on the continuity of colonial structures and patterns into the independence period in Africa. In the field of administration A. L. Adu's *The Civil Service in Commonwealth Africa* (London, 1969) and James Nti (ed.) *The Task of the Administration: Report of the Sixth Inter-African Public Administration Seminar* (Ghana, 1968) stress the emphasis on security rather than development goals as an inheritance of colonialism. The continuity of economic patterns and institutions in Africa has been dealt with by Rene Dumont, *False Start in Africa* (New York: Praeger, 1966) and R.H. Green and Ann Seidman, *Unity or Poverty? The Economics of Pan Africanism* (London: Penguin, 1968).

The psychological burden of colonialism on the colonized is described in Albert Memmi's *The Colonizer and the Colonized* (Boston: Beacon, 1965), especially Part 2; O. Mannoni, *Prospero and Caliban: The Psychology of Colonization* (New York: Praeger, 1956); and Frantz Fanon, *Black Skin, White Masks* (New York: Grove Press, 1967 – all centering on the French experience.

Specific case studies of colonial continuity can be garnered from William J. Foltz, *From French West Africa to the Mali Federation* (New Haven: Yale, 1965); Aristide Zolberg, *One Party Government in the Ivory Coast* (Princeton: Princeton University Press, 1969); C.S. Whitaker, 'A Dysrhythmic Process of Political Change,' in *World Politics*, 19 (2), January 1967, pp. 190–217, centering on northern Nigeria; Guy de Lusignan,

French-Speaking Africa Since Independence (New York: Praeger, 1969); and Bob Fitch and Mary Oppenheimer, *Ghana: End of an Illusion* (New York: Monthly Review Press, 1966).

General approaches to the problem are found in Stanislaw Andreski, *The African Predicament* (London: Michael Joseph Ltd., 1968); Pierre Jalée, *The Pillage of the Third World* (New York: Modern Reader, 1968); and Kofi Ankomah, 'The Colonial Legacy and African Unrest,' in *Science and Society* (Summer 1970, Vol. XXXIV, No. 2, pp. 129–45).

[43] David Apter, *Ghana in Transition* (New York: Atheneum, 1968), p. 282.

[44] The President of Senegal, Leopold Senghor, living in the former Governor's palace with his French wife, spending summers in France, surrounded by avenues honoring Frenchmen, guarded by a French garrison, and writing French poetry glorifying *negritude*, may be a model of sorts for this. See Irving L. Markovitz, *Leopold Sedar Senghor and the Politics of Negritude* (New York: Atheneum, 1969).

[45] 'Conservative' is useful in encapsulating this grouping's view of a political group as quasi-organic, based on traditional ties, hence seeing opposition between Europeans and Africans as inevitable. 'Liberal' is used to emphasize this grouping's flexibility of tactics and alliances, their stress on competition based on ideas and interest, and their efforts to minimize conflict.

[46] Explication and evidence for these themes can be found in Chapter 7.

CHAPTER 2

[1] Readily available general approaches to Kenyan colonial history include George Bennett, *Kenya: A Political History* (London: Oxford University Press, 1963); Vincent Harlow *et al.* (ed.), *History of East Africa*, Vol. II (Oxford: Clarendon Press, 1965); Y.P. Ghai and J.P.W.B. McAuslan, *Public Law and Political Change in Kenya* (Nairobi: Oxford University Press, 1970); E. A. Brett, *Colonialism and Underdevelopment in East Africa* (New York: NOK, 1973).

Studies on the history of the nationalist movement can be found in Carl G. Rosberg and John Nottingham, *The Myth of 'Mau Mau': Nationalism in Kenya* (New York: Praeger, 1966); M.P.K. Sorrenson, *Land Reform in the Kikuyu Country* (Oxford: Clarendon Press, 1967); and the autobiographies of Oginga Odinga, *Not Yet Uhuru* (London: Heinemann, 1967) and Tom Mboya, *Freedom and After* (London: André Deutsch, 1963).

Critical studies of European settlement can be found in M.P.K. Sorrenson, *Origins of European Settlement in Kenya* (Nairobi: Oxford University Press, 1968) and Norman M. Leys, *Kenya* (London: Hogarth Press, 1924).

More favorable accounts would include Elspeth Huxley, *White Man's Country: Lord Delamere and the Making of Kenya*, 2 vols. (London: Chatto and Windus, 1935), Michael Blundell, *So Rough a Wind* (London: Weidenfeld and Nicolson, 1964), and J.F. Lipscomb, *White Africans* (London: Faber and Faber, 1956).

[2] Rosberg and Nottingham, *The Myth of 'Mau Mau,'* pp. 198–200.

[3] One scholar of white settlers in Africa has characterized them as 'basically anti-imperialist,' claiming that throughout the colonial period they were in conflict with their parent countries' ambivalent attitude toward colonialism. See Arghiri Emmanuel, 'Colonialism and Imperialism,' *New Left Review*, 73 (May–June, 1972), 35–57.

4 The Organskis point out that those regions sparsely populated, with a temperate climate, were the most likely to become colonies settled by Europeans and later independent under the settlers' rule (i.e., the United States, Australia). Tropical, sparsely populated regions were most prone to be colonized the longest without European settlement. Kenyan colonial history may be seen as embodying both conflicting trends. (K. and A.F.K. Organski, *Population and World Power* [New York: Knopf, 1961], pp. 53 – 60.)

5 See R.S. Odingo, 'Observations on Land Use and Settlement in the Kenya Highlands,' *Ostafrikanische Studien* (Nurnberg: 1968), pp. 254–77.

6 For an example of a more successful colonization in Africa in which intermarriage was an integral feature, see 'Settler and Native in the Urban Centres of Roman Africa,' in L. Thompson and J. Ferguson, *Africa in Classical Antiquity* (Ibadan: Ibadan University Press, 1969), pp. 132–82.

7 Republic of Kenya, Ministry of Economic Planning and Development, *Statistical Abstract, 1969*, p. 13. In Rhodesia, Europeans were about 8 per cent of the population; in South Africa, 20 per cent. Lord Hailey, *An African Survey* (London: Oxford University Press, 1957), Chapter 2.

8 Rosberg and Nottingham, *The Myth of 'Mau Mau,'* p. 292.

9 The Mau Mau uprising itself seems to have been 'blown up' during and after the conflict, both by Europeans and nationalists. A number of points can be made. The 15,000 people (not fighters) in the forest at the height of the conflict for sundry reasons is not a lot. The massacre at Lari which initiated the most violent phase of the Emergency appears in retrospect to have been unconnected with Mau Mau, and was instead 'a gruesome conclusion to a long-standing land feud.' (Sorrenson, *Land Reform in the Kikuyu Country*, p. 100.)

Rosberg and Nottingham refer to one of the most 'intense battles,' where sixteen attackers were killed, and stress the panic leading to the Declaration of a State of Emergency (*The Myth of 'Mau Mau,'* pp. 298–9). The economy does not seem to have been harmed by the conflict. The official casualty figures, with ten times as many guerillas killed as captured–wounded, seem to indicate both inflation and indiscriminate killings. (*Ibid.*, p. 303.)

The connection of many of these statistics to Mau Mau origins has been questioned by Sorrenson. The same author emphasizes the class nature of the conflict within the Kikuyu, pointing out that 'the active loyalists were, on the whole, from the landed and wealthy classes.' (p. 107).

The point being that Mau Mau was important chiefly in terms of the overreaction to it and its effects on colonial thinking toward Kenya, e.g., 'We can't afford another one.'

10 C.C. Wrigley, 'Kenya: The Patterns of Economic Life, 1902–1945,' in Harlow *et al., History of East Africa*, Vol. II, p. 215, and E.A. Brett, (Chap. 6) 'Kenya—Settlers Predominant,' *Colonialism and Underdevelopment in East Africa*, pp. 165–216.

11 See Wrigley, in Harlow, *et al.*, pp. 225–42. Wrigley points out that the demand for restricting the reserves came not from a desire for more land (the settlers already had more land than they could use) but from the need to force the Africans to earn their subsistence by paid labor (p. 230).

12 See L.D. Smith, 'Resource Allocation, Income Redistribution and Agricultural Pricing Policies' (unpublished paper, University Social Sciences Council Conference, Nairobi, 1969), 16 pp.

13 Wrigley, in Harlow *et al.*, p. 236. He points out that in the period before 1945 imports were rarely less than double exports, and that much of European farming was rather amateurish (p. 247).

181

14 E.A. Brett, *Colonialism and Underdevelopment*, p. 212.
15 Colin Leys, 'The Limits of African Capitalism: The Formation of the Monopolistic Petit-Bourgeoisie in Kenya' (unpublished manuscript, April 1972).
16 Lal Patel, 'History and Growth of Labour in East Africa' (unpublished paper, University Social Sciences Council Conference, Nairobi, December 1969), 30 pp.
17 Sorrenson, *Land Reform in the Kikuyu Country*, pp. 41–2. Coffee was allowed for the Meru, Embu and Kisii in the 1930s, their areas being some distance from European planters.
18 Great Britain, East Africa Royal Commission, 1953–1955, *Report* (London: Her Majesty's Stationery Office, June 1955), pp. 182, 303–6.
19 Sorrenson, *Land Reform*, pp. 229–30, 250–1.
20 Wrigley, in Harlow *et al.*, pp. 260–1.
21 *East African Standard*, March 17, 1956.
22 Kenya Government, *Economic Survey, 1968*, pp. 5, 105ff., in *Who Controls Industry in Kenya?* (National Christian Council of Kenya, Nairobi, 1968), p. 215.
   The business sector was also rather sharply limited. In 1963 only thirteen industries out of thirty-eight categories produced about 70 per cent of the total value added by manufacture – £28.6 million. The three leading banks (Barclays, D.CO; Standard Bank; and National and Grindlays) held over 80 per cent of the total banking assets of East Africa in 1966. (Ann Seidman, 'The Dual Economies of East Africa,' *East Africa Journal*, VII, No. 5 (May 1970), pp. 11 and 15.)
23 L.H. Brown, 'Agricultural Change in Kenya, 1945–1960,' *Food Research Institute Studies in Agricultural Economics, Trade and Development*, Vol. VIII, No. 1 (Stanford, 1968), p. 74.
24 Seidman, p. 7.
25 Great Britain, *Report of the Mission Appointed to Advise on Proposals for a Further Transfer of European Farms in Kenya* (unpublished report, October 1965), pp. 56–7.
26 Bennett, *Kenya: A Political History*, p. 100.
27 Sir Geoffrey de Freitas, quoted in Richard West, *The White Tribes of Africa* (New York: Macmillan, 1965), pp. 19–20.
28 As early as the 1920s 'the talk of increased cotton growing caused alarm that Manchester and peasant agriculture might dominate at the expense of settler farming.' (Bennett, p. 56.)
29 Bennett, pp. 32, 42–3.
30 E.S. Atieno-Odhiambo, 'The Economic Basis of Kenya Settler Politics in the 1930s,' (paper, Universities of East Africa Social Science Conference, Dar es Salaam, December 27–31, 1970).
31 Bennett, pp. 78–9, 94.
32 Lord Francis Scott papers, quoted by Atieno-Odhiambo, 'The Economic Basis.'
33 Rosberg and Nottingham, *The Myth of 'Mau Mau,'* p. 196.
34 Blundell, *So Rough a Wind*, p. 155.
35 Constitution and Rules of the Convention of Associations, Nairobi, January 1962, File 8. Oxford University, Rhodes House, The Files of the Convention of Associations.
36 Bennett and Rosberg, *The Kenyatta Elections* (London: Oxford, 1961), pp. 25–6.
37 *Ibid.*, pp. 92–6.

38 Kenya National Farmers Union, *Annual Report 1952–53*, 'History of the KNFU,' pp. 7–9. The office files of the Kenya National Farmers Union, Nakuru, Kenya.

39 The President's Committee consisted of the President, the two Vice Presidents, a delegate from an area branch and the Vice Chairman of the Stockowners' Association. The Stockowners had, in 1949, voted itself part of the Kenya National Farmers Union while keeping its subscriptions and financial administration separate.

40 During most of the years over half of the income of the Union derived from the individual members' subscriptions. The part of income coming from the cess went from about one-fourth of the 1954 income, to one-third in 1962, to over half in 1969. It would appear that the wealthier members were increasingly supporting the Union. (KNFU *Annual Reports*, 1953–4, 1961–2, 1968–9.)

41 Kenya National Farmers Union, *Annual Report 1952–1953*, p. 12.

42 With the heightened activities of the early 1960's, leadership was centralized even further. A President's Committee consisting of the President and three Vice Presidents met weekly to discuss urgent matters – mainly the bargaining over the land issue. The Executive Committee continued to meet once a month. (KNFU, *Annual Report 1960–1961*, p. 2.)

43 KNFU, *Annual Reports 1951–1957*.

44 KNFU, *Annual Report 1948–1949*, p. 12. There was also pressure on the Union from the International to include African members. (First Conference of the KNFU, 'Minutes,' November 11, 1947, KNFU files.)

45 *KNFU Fact Sheet*, March 1960, KNFU files. Among the African members was Harry Thuku, an early nationalist leader, and by 1960 a wealthy coffee farmer well known for his anti-Mau Mau views.

46 KNFU, *Annual Reports*, 1959–60, 1962–4, 1966–9.

47 As Minister of Agriculture, Cavendish-Bentinck had asked R. S. Swynnerton to prepare a comprehensive plan for African agrarian development in October 1953. (John Harbeson, 'Nationalism and Nation-Building in Kenya: The Role of Land Reform,' unpublished Ph.D. dissertation, University of Wisconsin, 1970, p. 69.)

48 Lord Francis Scott papers, quoted by Atiendo-Odhiambo, 'The Economic Basis.'

49 Blundell, *So Rough a Wind*, p. 178. Blundell attributes Cavendish-Bentinck's influence in the settler community to his being heir-presumptive to a dukedom and 'the trust and confidence which the farming community had in his ability to look after their interests' (p. 62).

50 *Who's Who in East Africa 1965–1966* (Nairobi: Marco Publishers, 1966), p. 78. Also P. Marrian, letter to The Acting Governor, April 30, 1962, Marrian papers.

51 *Ibid.*, p. 27; also Lord Delamere, interview, September 28, 1970.

52 *East African Standard*, May 26, 1961.

53 Convention of Associations, Executive Committee, 'Minutes,' November 25, 1961, Convention of Associations files.

54 C.O. Oates, letter to H.B.W. MacAllan, September 15, 1961, Convention of Associations papers.

55 *East African Standard*, May 26, 1961.

56 Convention of Associations, 'Minutes of a Joint Meeting of the Executive and Council Held in the Town Hall, Nakuru, Wednesday, April 18, at 2:30 P.M.,' May 1, 1962, 7 pp., Convention of Associations files.

57 An example of these fund raising appeals was one in April, 1962, to pay

for expenses incurred at Second Lancaster House. Circular 'Appeal for Funds,' April 1962, Convention of Associations files.

[58] Major B.P. Roberts, letter to R. (Ronnie) Mann of Eastern Produce, April 6, 1961. R. Mann, letter to C.O. Oates, April 27, 1961, Convention of Associations files.

[59] Throughout the bargaining period, the farmers' missions to England involved not only talks with Her Majesty's Government officials but fairly extensive discussions with City firms. In the visits in the summer of 1960 and 1961, Cavendish-Bentinck, Oates and Delamere spoke with City interests concerned with East Africa.

[60] This is not to argue that access can be equated to influence. The argument is less ambitious. It is simply that the access and social standings of the European leadership were perceived by them as mobilizable resources in lobbying government decision-makers.

[61] *Who's Who*, 1963–4, 1965–6.

[62] Goldsworthy, *Colonial Issues in British Politics*, pp. 361–72. A number of these men had substantial economic interests in Rhodesia, notably Lord Salisbury and Patrick Wall.

[63] F.T. Thompson, Memorandum, February 3, 1960, Convention of Associations papers.

[64] Lord Delamere, interview, September 28, 1970. Happy Valley, usually referring to Subukia Valley near Nakuru, was alleged to have been the center of a life-style more akin to late-Roman than twentieth-century English. Most Kenya Europeans felt, somewhat regretfully, that the rumors were exaggerated.

[65] Sir Ferdinand Cavendish-Bentinck, interview, August 28, 1970.

[66] Blundell, *So Rough a Wind*, p. 266.

[67] Wilfred Havelock referred to the United Country Party as 'the germ of the idea' behind the New Kenya Group. (Sir Wilfred Havelock, interview, December 9, 1970.)

[68] United Country Party, *Kenya – A Nation* (Nairobi: United Country Party, March 21, 1956), p. 9.

[69] Michael Blundell later termed the United Country Party 'probably a mistake.' (Blundell, *So Rough a Wind*, p. 180.)

[70] The United Country Party's policy statement argued that since the Party's policies coincided more closely with government positions than those of their opponents 'the probability is that Ministers will be appointed from among successful United Country candidates.' (United Country Party, *Kenya – A Nation*, p. 3.)

[71] Blundell, *So Rough a Wind*, pp. 246–7.

[72] Mboya, *Freedom and After*, p. 124.

[73] Blundell, *So Rough a Wind*, pp. 147–8. In an interview Blundell remarked that the New Kenya Group had probably made it easier for the British to leave. (Blundell, interview, October 28, 1970.)

[74] In his letter to the Secretary of State, Blundell stated that the major aim of the group was to rally and steady European opinion in order to preserve European influence. (Blundell, *So Rough a Wind*, p. 247.)

[75] New Kenya Party, Articles of Association, n.d., 5 pages; also 'Press Statement by the New Kenya Group,' Fall 1959, 5 pages; also A. B. Goord, 'Preliminary Appreciation of the Situation – August 1959,' 7 pages; also New Kenya Group, 'The Challenge of New Kenya' (draft re September 1959); also unsigned Press Release, June 30, 1959. The papers of Mrs Dorothy Hughes, Office, Nairobi, Kenya.

The separation of the Group from the Party was due to the members from the Government side of the Legislative Council feeling it improper for them to join a political party.

76 In an interview, Blundell described his political position as that of a 'radical conservative.' Blundell, interview, October 28, 1970.

77 *Who's Who, 1963–4.*

78 Jack Lipscomb, letter to Michael Blundell, April 27, 1959, Oxford University, Rhodes House Archives, the papers of Sir Michael Blundell.

79 Michael Blundell, interview, December 17, 1970; also, W. Havelock, interview, December 9, 1970.

80 National Christian Council of Kenya, *Who Controls Industry in Kenya?* (Nairobi: East African Publishing House, 1968), pp. 133, 146.

81 *Ibid.*, pp. 105, 115, 145.

82 Ind Coope was, in turn, associated with Allied Breweries Ltd, which ranked 24th in '*The Times* 300'. (*Ibid.*, pp. 102–3.)

83 *Ibid.*, pp. 103, 167.

84 Harold Travis, an English financier who in 1968 held forty-three directorships in Kenya (the largest number held by any individual), replaced Blundell and agreed to relinquish the chairmanship when Blundell was available again.

85 National Christian Council, *Who Controls Industry in Kenya?*, p. 102. Former New Kenya Group members Slade, Ghersie, Rubia and C.W. Muchura were directors of East African Breweries Ltd, while two other leaders of the Group (M.S. Amalemba and F.W.G. Bompas) in 1967 were directors of the City Brewery Ltd. City is associated with the English brewers Whitbread and Company, Ltd.

86 Blundell, letter to Michael Watson, June 2, 1961, Blundell papers. In the letter Blundell urged his hesitant employer, Michael Watson of Ind Coope, to give the donation to KADU which Lord Howick had requested.

87 Leaflet of The Progress Foundations for Economic Development in Eastern Africa (n.d.) includes letter from Iain Macleod to Lord Portsmouth, June 30, 1961. New Kenya Group, 'Minutes,' October 25, 1960.

88 British Standard Portland Cement Company Ltd, letter to Dorothy Hughes, September 25, 1960, Hughes papers.

89 M. Blundell, letter to W. Havelock, May 4, 1960, and Roy Welensky, letter to Blundell, December 28, 1961, Blundell papers.

90 J.M. Lee, *Colonial Development*, p. 10, quoting Blundell, *So Rough a Wind*, p. 185.

91 Lennox-Boyd, letter to M. Blundell, September 4, 1959, Blundell papers.

92 Governor Baring, letter to M. Blundell, October 23, 1959, Blundell papers.

93 I. Macleod, letter to M. Blundell, March 6, 1961, Blundell papers. Macleod in a meeting with the New Kenya Group in Kenya shortly before First Lancaster House kept the Group uninformed of his plans for the Conference. While praising the Group's activities and urging them to create a 'first-class political machine,' Macleod gave them little information of his proposals. The Group's leaders apparently were as surprised at the Conference's results as the other delegates. (New Kenya Parliamentary Group, 'Minutes of the Meeting of the Executive Committee,' December 14, 1959, 5 pp.)

94 Lord Boyd, letter to M. Blundell, November 17, 1961, Blundell papers.

95 Apparently both the British and American governments were concerned about Mboya's activities in the States with American blacks.

96 Bennett, p. 148.

97 The Colonial Secretary did offer £5 million in loans for settlement schemes.

See Great Britain, Kenya Constitutional Conference, 1960, *Report of the Conference*, Cmnd 960 (London: Her Majesty's Stationery Office, 1960), p. 10.
98 Tom Mboya, *Freedom and After*, p. 128.
99 *East African Standard*, February 22, 1960, p. 1.

CHAPTER 3

1 Convention of Associations, 'Minutes,' May 25, 1960.
2 *East African Standard*, February 12, 1960.
3 *KNFU Annual Report* 1960–1, p. 7.
4 KNFU Executive Committee Meeting, 'Minutes,' March 10, 1960.
5 KNFU, 'The Defence of Kenya's Economy,' memo 87/60 revised as 93/60. Press statement issued March 14, 1960.
6 *East African Standard*, April 29, 1960.
7 J. H. Feingold, interview, June 16, 1970.
8 KNFU press statement, March 14, 1960.
9 *Ibid.*
10 P. Marrian, letter to W. L. Gorrell-Barnes, The Colonial Office, March 8, 1960, KNFU files.
11 *East African Standard*, April 29, 1960.
12 KNFU Executive Committee, 'Minutes,' April 14, 1960.
13 *Ibid.*
14 *East African Standard*, April 15, 1960, p. 8.
15 'Minutes,' April 14, 1960.
16 Great Britain, Kenya Constitutional Conference 1960, *Report of the Conference* (London: February 22, 1960), p. 10.
17 'Minutes,' April 14, 1960.
18 Lord Delamere, interview, September 28, 1970.
19 Viscount Kilmuir, speech at East African Dinner Club, June 28, 1960, Blundell papers.
20 *East African Standard*, January 10, 1961, p. 1.
21 P. D. Marrian, memorandum, 'Kenya Economy: Finance for Land Development and the Stabilisation of Land Values,' April 4, 1960, KNFU files.
22 P. Marrian, letter to A. Ward, March 29, 1960, KNFU files.
23 A. Ward, letter to P. Marrian, March 30, 1960, KNFU files.
24 A. Ward, letter to P. Marrian, April 7, 1960, KNFU files. Three meetings were called: for Nakuru and Kitale on April 19, for Nairobi on April 21.
25 Dunford, 'PR Notes,' March 14, 1960, KNFU files.
26 G. Kramer, president of Nakuru and District Chamber of Commerce, Industry and Agriculture, letter to President KNFU, March 9, 1960, KNFU files.
27 P. Marrian, letter to I. Macleod, March 8, 1960, KNFU files.
28 Dunford, 'Public Relations Notes.' It did not work out quite this well as a cable from Dunford indicated a week later that Reuter's stories were implying that the mission was designed to protect Europeans. (Dunford cable, March 22, 1960, KNFU files.)
29 Members of KNFU Agricultural Support Mission, 'Press Statement,' March 14, 1960, KNFU files.
30 Lord Delamere, circular, n.d., KNFU files.
31 J. Pollard, letter to M. Blundell, November 7, 1960; M. Robinson (vice-president), letter to M. Blundell, December 15, 1960, Blundell papers.
32 P. Marrian, letter to M. Blundell, November 26, 1960, Blundell papers.

[33] *Ibid.*
[34] J. Pollard, letter to M. Blundell, November 7, 1960, Blundell papers.
[35] Convention of Associations, meeting of district chairmen, Circular 47, March 11, 1960, KNFU files.
[36] Convention of Associations, 'Minutes,' March 11, 1960, KNFU files.
[37] P. Marrian, letter to United Party, April 21, 1960, KNFU files.
[38] Fifth meeting Coalition Land Committee, 'Minutes,' June 8, 1960, KNFU files.
[39] P. Marrian, letter to Capt. L.R. Briggs, April 22, 1960, KNFU files.
[40] Sir Ferdinand Cavendish-Bentinck, interview, August 28, 1971.
[41] D. Whetham, letter to P. Marrian, April 13, 1960, KNFU files.
[42] This 'disturbance allowance,' though never clearly defined, meant some amount above the valuation of the farmer's property to compensate him for the hardship of being displaced. Though a bone of contention between the European groups it was not included in the actual buy-out schemes, and seemed to have been used as a bargaining ploy by the farmers in negotiations.
[43] A. Ward, letter to D.K. Knight, June 20, 1960, KNFU files.
[44] Minutes of a special plenary meeting of the NKG, February 27, 1960, Hughes papers.
[45] Blundell thought the Colonial Office proposal was a watered down version of his paper. Sir Michael Blundell, interview, December 17, 1970.
[46] 'Statement by the "New Kenya Group,"' May 5, 1960, Hughes papers.
[47] New Kenya Group, 'Land' (re June 1960), Hughes papers. This referred to the 'sore thumb' areas sought predominantly by the NKG-allied KADU tribes.
[48] NKG, 'Land,' draft as amended at meeting of November 23, 1960.
[49] NKG, 'Approach to Party Politics,' memorandum, May 23, 1960, 3 pp.
[50] In interviews with ex-Colonial officials and European leaders, Governor Renison was variously described as 'a complete disaster' and 'a typical colonial bureaucrat.' The consensus was that the Governor neither understood nor knew how to cope with the nationalist parties.
[51] KNFU Executive Committee, 'Minutes,' June 9, 1960, KNFU files.
[52] *East African Standard*, April 29, 1960, p. 8.
[53] M.W. Dunford, 'PR Notes,' March 14, 1960, KNFU.
[54] Bruce McKenzie, 'Highland Produce is Life Blood of Kenya,' *East African Standard*, June 10, 1960; and 'Extracts of Minister of Agriculture Speech; May 11, 1960, KNFU files.
[55] *East African Standard*, June 10, 1960, p. 3.
[56] For further discussion of the use of this tactic in the implementation of the land schemes, see Chapter 6.
[57] Extracts from Minister's speech, Legislative Council, May 11, 1960, KNFU files.
[58] President's speech to Council on mission to London, May 12, 1960, KNFU files.
[59] *East African Standard*, May 13 and 20, 1960.
[60] A. Ward, letter to the Private Secretary of the Governor, May 14, 1960, KNFU files.
[61] A. Ward, letter to Lord Delamere, May 19, 1960, KNFU files.
[62] A. Ward, letter to Lord Delamere, May 26, 1960, KNFU files.
[63] Michael Robinson, 'Report of a Meeting of the Board of Agriculture attended by Ministers for Agriculture and Lands on African Attitudes to S.P.10 and Land Question in General,' June 16, 1960, KNFU files.

[64] Bennett and Rosberg, p. 36.
[65] Bennett and Rosberg, pp. 39–40.
[66] Susanne Dorothy Mueller, *Political Parties in Kenya: Patterns of Opposition and Dissent 1919–1969*, Unpublished PhD Dissertation, Princeton University, March 1972.
[67] *East African Standard*, February 19, 1960.
[68] R. Ngala, Leader, 'African Elected Members' Stand on Land Policy,' n.d. (re. February 1960).
[69] *Ibid.*
[70] *Ibid.*
[71] At a rally in Mombasa Ngala said: 'If a farm in the Highlands is oversized, it is going to be cut down and taken over.' *East African Standard*, February 29, 1960, p. 1. Marrian described Ngala's statement as 'a political gimmick,' *Ibid.*, March 3, 1960.
[72] Michael Robinson, June 16, 1960, KNFU files.
[73] P. Marrian, letter to R. H. R. Hayne, Subukia, June 23, 1960, KNFU files. Insight into the African tactics, whether inadvertent or not, can be found in Thomas Schelling's remark, 'The protection against extortion depends on refusal, unavailability, or inability, to negotiate.' Schelling, *The Strategy of Conflict*, p. 30.
[74] Cherry Gertzel, *The Politics of Independent Kenya* (Nairobi: East African Publishing House, 1970), p. 10.
[75] G. Bennett and C. Rosberg, pp. 27, 42.
[76] See Y.P. Ghai and J.P.W.B. McAuslan, pp. 182–3, and John Harbeson, *Nation-Building in Kenya: The Role of Land Reform* (Evanston: Northwestern, 1973), p. 46.
[77] Among the reasons for this lack of pressure on European land from these tribes were: They were located far from the Highlands; they were not suffering as much from overpopulation; they were pastoral with less need for more lands; or they were fearful of Kikuyu expansion.
[78] R. Slaughter, interview, November 3, 1970.
[79] L. Melville, interview, November 3, 1970.
[80] W. Havelock, interview, December 9, 1970.
[81] Reginald Alexander, interview, December 9, 1970.
[82] Further details on the sources and channels for this funding can be found in Chapter 2.
[83] Kenya Legislative Council, *Debates*, Vol. 86, pp. 63, 80.
[84] *The KANU Manifesto for Independence, Social Democracy and Stability*, Nairobi, 1960, pp. 15–17.
[85] KNFU Executive Committee Meeting, 'Minutes,' June 9, 1960.
[86] Lord Delamere, letter to A. Ward, May 30, 1960, KNFU files.
[87] This was the famous/notorious 'leader unto death and darkness' reference to Kenyatta by the Governor which led to such bitter feelings. Apparently former Colonial Secretary Lennox-Boyd was applying pressure on this point.
[88] M. Blundell, letter to I. Macleod, April 28, 1960, Blundell papers.
[89] M. Blundell, letter to Havelock, April 28, 1960, Blundell papers. The 'sore thumb' schemes of 1961 were another attempt by the New Kenya Group to gain political mileage from the land schemes. In that case the effort was to assuage African allies so as to maintain their moderate position on land.
[90] NKP, 'Press Handout,' June 16, 1960. Garnering liberal support might be considered another justification for KNFU's non-party approach and formal detachment from the Cavendish-Bentinck Delegation.

91 KNFU, Executive Committee Meeting, 'Minutes,' June 9, 1960.
92 NKG, unsigned draft, n.d. (apparently written by Blundell).
93 *East African Standard*, August 12, 1960.
94 Conference of the Convention of Associations, 'Minutes,' October 7, 1960, 15 pages, Convention of Associations files.
95 *East African Standard*, July 29, 1960.
96 Iain Macleod, letter to P. Marrian, November 4, 1960, KNFU files.
97 *Ibid.*
98 As quoted by Bennett and Rosberg, p. 91.
99 'Minutes,' October 7, 1960.
100 *Ibid.*
101 Convention of Associations, 'Minutes,' May 25, 1960, KNFU files.
102 'Minutes,' October 7, 1960. In an interview Cavendish-Bentinck insisted that from the beginning he was trying to ease the farmers out. (He denied there was any trouble gaining European agreement on the land question.) Later this was probably true, but in 1960, though there was some ambivalence, the emphasis was on 'stay' schemes. Cavendish-Bentinck, interview, August 28, 1970.
103 'Minutes,' May 25, 1960.
104 Havelock, interview, December 9, 1970.
105 'Minutes,' October 7, 1960.
106 Letter, September 2, 1960, KNFU files.
107 *East African Standard*, December 2, 1960.
108 Great Britain, Colonial Office, *Report on Colony of Kenya 1960*, 1963, p. 37.
109 *East African Standard*, September 9, 1960, p. 8.
110 The East African Pioneering Society, 'Plan for the Formation of a Public Company,' pamphlet, December 19, 1960, 2 pp.
111 *East African Standard*, January 2, 1961.

CHAPTER 4

1 See George Bennett and Carl Rosberg, *The Kenyatta Elections* (London: Oxford University Press, 1961). Blundell himself squeaked through the primaries with 26.7 per cent of the European vote.
The following table summarizes the 1961 Common Roll Election results:

53 seats (44 contested)

Party	Votes	Percentage	Seats
Kenya African National Union (Official and Party-independent)	590,661	67.4	19
Kenya African Democratic Union (Official and Party-independent)	143,079	16.4	11
Baluhya Political Union	28,817	3.3	1
New Kenya Party	28,284	3.2	4
Kenya Indian Congress	10,488	1.2	3
Kenya Coalition	8,891	1.1	3
Minor parties	15,964	1.8	3
Independents	48,925	5.6	9
Totals	875,109	100.0	53

Adapted from Bennett and Rosberg, p. 204.

2 A. Ward, letter to J. H. Auret, Kitale, April 4, 1961, KNFU files.
3 KNFU, 'Land Titles,' Public Circular 91/61, February 16, 1961, KNFU files.
4 'Memo for Mr Seys on Visit to UK in February and March 1961,' n.d., KNFU files.
5 A. Ward, letter to J. A. Seys, March 21, 1961, KNFU files.
6 *East African Standard*, April 7, 1961, June 1, 1961.
7 A. Ward, letter to H. Oduor, February 23, 1961, KNFU files.
8 H. Oduor, letter to A. Ward, March 1, 1961, KNFU files.
    The GAWU was essentially a sweetheart union of the KNFU. The farmers union was heavily involved in starting the workers' union, financing it, and influencing the composition of its leadership and the policies it followed.
9 J.'A. Seys, letter to Delamere, March 3, 1961, 128/61, KNFU files.
10 KNFU, Memorandum for the Secretary of State, 'The Defence of Kenya's Economy,' by Executive Officer, February 27, 1961.
11 *Ibid.*
12 An illustration of this feeling in early 1961 was the concluding part of a curt letter Ward sent to a Rhodesian real estate agent who had asked that his offer of land be circularized. The reply: 'My President, Lord Delamere, feels that it is not the role of the Kenya National Farmers Union to assist in its own demise.' (A. Ward, letter to Southern Rhodesian Real Estate Agent, February 25, 1961, KNFU files.)
13 Seys, letter to Delamere, March 3, 1961, KNFU files.
14 *Ibid.*
15 The Study Group appointed by the Minister for Agriculture, 'Proposals for Land Reform in the Scheduled Areas Designed to Preserve the Economy of the Country,' 255/61, May 12, 1961, KNFU files.
    The Study Group was composed of Lord Delamere and Seys from KNFU; Messrs. Gunson and Mills from the Board of Agriculture; Messrs. K. Hill, L. Welwood and J. Lipscomb for Agricultural Settlement Trust; and many officials.' Proposals were unanimous. (A. Ward, letter to O. R. Arnell, November 9, 1961, KNFU files.)
16 *East African Standard*, June 1, 1961, p. 5.
17 The Study Group, 'Proposals.'
18 L. Welwood, letter to F. Cavendish-Bentinck, June 2, 1961, Convention of Association files.
19 F. Cavendish-Bentinck, letter to L. Welwood, June 8, 1961, C. of A. files.
20 B.P. Roberts, letter to R. Mann of Eastern Produce, April 6, 1961, C. of A. files.
21 B.P. Roberts, letter to C.O. Oates, June 16, 1961, C. of A. files.
22 Cavendish-Bentinck, letter to C.O. Oates, June 8, 1961.
23 Cavendish-Bentinck, letter to Welwood, June 8, 1961, C. of A. files.
24 C. Salter (?), letter to Major B.P. Roberts, June 21, 1961, C. of A. files. Unsigned, but writer thanks Roberts for sending him a copy of his June 16 letter, on which is written 'Copy to Clive.'
25 Cavendish-Bentinck, letter to L. Welwood, June 8, 1961.
26 C.O. Oates, 'Letter to Editor,' *Manchester Guardian*, May 6, 1961.
27 Welwood, letter to Cavendish-Bentinck, June 2, 1961, C. of A. files.
28 Convention of Associations Executive, 'European Representation and Policy at the Coming Constitutional Talks,' Draft, August 22, 1961.
29 *East African Standard*, June 2, 1961, p. 1.
30 Convention of Associations, 'Press Release,' n.d.; also Ward, letter to O.G. Allanson-Winn, November 2, 1961, KNFU files. (The meeting had been

agreed to earlier by the KANU delegation meeting with the Secretary of State in London on June 27. Their statement made clear their agreement to discuss constitutional advance and matters relating to the land problem with all interested parties under the chairmanship of H. E. the Governor.)

31 *East African Standard*, April 21, 1961, p. 8.
32 The policy of settling outstanding tribal claims was also seen by the liberals as a means of keeping KADU to its position of not confiscating land.
33 In reply to the warning of permanent dependence one African member of KADU predicted that UK aid would taper off to virtually nothing in five years.
34 Seys to Lord Delamere, March 3, 1961, KNFU files. This reaction may have been due to Macleod's thoughts that Mboya might join the government hence splitting KANU. (Macleod, letter to Blundell, March 6, 1961, Blundell papers.)
35 *East African Standard*, April 22; May 5 and 6, 1961 (all page 1).
36 Cavendish-Bentinck's presentation to the Secretary of State on July 13, 1961, was forwarded to the Kenya government on July 17, and by July 24 European members of KADU had it.
37 M. Blundell, letter to I. Macleod, June 20, 1961, Blundell papers.
38 *Ibid.* In his reply Macleod said he would tell the delegation that the matter was under discussion with the Kenya government and himself. (I. Macleod, letter to M. Blundell, July 6, 1961, Blundell papers.)
39 Blundell, letter to Philip Goodhart, MP, June 2, 1961, Blundell papers.
40 *Ibid.*
41 M. Blundell, letter to F.M. Bennett, MP, June 22, 1961, Blundell papers.
42 *Ibid.*
43 *Ibid.*
44 P. Broadbent, 'Notes on Michael Blundell's Address to Joint East and Central African Board,' November 14, 1961, Blundell papers.
45 F.M. Bennett, letter to M. Blundell, May 29, 1961; and P. Goodhart, letter to M. Blundell, April 5, 1961, Blundell papers.
46 Hansard, 'Kenya (Land),' March 30, 1961, pp. 1603–6, Blundell papers.
47 A. Ward, letter to Col. J.F. Lance, Elburgen, March 27, 1961, KNFU files.
48 Blundell to Bennett, June 22, 1961.
49 *East African Standard*, May 25 and 26, 1961.
50 *Ibid.*, June 1, 1961, p. 5; May 26, 1961, p. 8.
51 *Ibid.*, May 26, 1961, p. 8.
52 'Memorandum by the Executive of the Convention of Associations for the Rt. Hon. Hugh Fraser,' n.d. [May 1961], KNFU files. Similarly in a memo to the Governor the former members of the European Agricultural Settlement Board referred to settlers as 'financial prisoners.' ('Memo to Governor from all the Former Members of the European Agricultural Settlement Board,' March 28, 1961, KNFU files.)
53 *East African Standard*, May 26, 1961, pp. 4, 6.
54 M. Blundell, letter to Philip Scott, Njoro, June 20, 1961, Blundell papers.
55 M. Blundell, letter to Edward Thompson, Ind Coope Ltd, July 5, 1961, Blundell papers.
56 'Series of Joint Committee Meetings of KADU and KANU from 10th August 1961 to 24th August,' Blundell papers.
57 'Memorandum for Talks Under the Chairmanship of H. E. the Governor of Kenya,' n.d., Blundell papers.

58 KADU/KANU Joint Committee, 'Minutes,' tenth day of meeting, Wednesday, August 23, 1961.
59 'Memorandum for Talks Under the Chairmanship of H.E. Governor of Kenya,' n.d., Blundell papers.
60 *Ibid.*
61 From Blundell's papers, it appears that neither the Governor nor Blundell were very favorable towards Convention of Associations representation: the former worried about the door being opened to more requests, while Blundell likely stood against racial representation of his European opponents. It would seem that the Secretary of State's previous invitation overrode their objections. (Blundell, Memorandum 'On Continuing Study Group,' July 18, 1961, Blundell papers.)
62 The Coastal Strip was the ten-mile wide territory along the coast of Kenya owned by the Sultan of Zanzibar which the British had administered and leased since the establishment of the Protectorate in 1895. The Arabs said they would consider devolution to a successor African government as a breach of faith, while the nationalists asserted they did not recognize the 1895 Agreement. By independence in 1963 a financial settlement resolved the issue with the full integration of the territory into Kenya.
     The Northern Frontier problem was that of the Somali people of the region who were demanding political unity with Somalia. This was to eventually lead to sporadic clashes with Somalia and Kenyan Somalis after independence.
     Civil Service rights concerned the questions of pensioners, retirement, or continued service of colonial officials in Kenya.
63 In a speech on October 2, he referred to the nationalists as 'immature and unrealistic' but said he was eager to help the country forward to independence 'if it is the right kind of independence. Some of you have grown into such habits of oppositionism that you are not easy to help.' (Speech by Governor, October 2, 1961, in 'Minutes of Constitutional Talks, September 1961,' Blundell papers.)
64 Speech by H.E. the Governor at the Opening of the Constitutional Talks at Government House Beginning 4 September 1961,' Blundell papers.
65 'Minutes,' Fourth meeting, September 7, 1961.
66 'Minutes,' Thirteenth meeting, September 26, 1961.
67 'Memo for Talks Under the Governor.'
68 Ngei, recently released from detention, addressing a rally of sixty thousand people in Nairobi apparently got a bit carried away. He said in reference to the Highlands, 'I will not admit that all this land does not belong to the Africans.' He then condemned those who gave assurances to the Europeans that the land they held was theirs. He warned there would be no peace in the country until the Africans had their land back. (*East African Standard*, September 11, 1961, p. 3.)
     A few days later he remarked that although he wanted African land returned he did not mean to advocate robbing European property such as farms, houses and cattle. (*East African Standard*, September 14, 1961, p. 5.)
69 'Minutes,' Sixth meeting, September 11, 1961.
70 'Minutes,' Tenth meeting, September 20, 1961.
71 'Minutes,' Fifteenth meeting, October 6, 1961.
72 'Minutes,' Seventeenth meeting, November 3, 1961.
73 Blundell, letter to M.W. Boynton, Ol Pejeta, Laikepia, July 7, 1961, Blundell papers.
74 M. Blundell, letter to Duncan Sandys, October 25, 1962, Blundell papers.

[75] P. Broadbent, Director, 'Some Points from Mr. Michael Blundell's Address to the Council and Members of the Joint East and Central African Board on Tuesday November 14, 1961 at 11:15 am,' Blundell papers.

[76] Blundell to Bennett, June 22, 1961, Blundell papers.

[77] M. Blundell, letter to W. Havelock, June 19, 1961, Blundell papers.

[78] M. Blundell, letter to I. Macleod, September 13, 1961, Blundell papers.

[79] P. D. Marrian, letter to M. Blundell, July 19, 1961, Blundell papers.

[80] M. Blundell, letter to P.D. Marrian, July 20, 1961, Blundell papers.

[81] M. Blundell, letter to Edward Thompson, December 14, 1960, Blundell papers.

[82] Blundell to Macleod, September 13, 1961, Blundell papers.

[83] 'Brief for Michael Blundell,' n.d. [end of 1961], Blundell papers.

[84] Lord Howick, letter to M. Blundell, January 13, 1961, Blundell papers.

[85] 'Article written for *The Times* by M. Blundell,' January 15, 1962, Blundell papers.

[86] M. Blundell, letter to M.P. Hill, March 8, 1962, Blundell papers. Note the reference to 'Africans who oppose these two' rather than 'KADU.'

[87] M. Blundell, letter to F.M. Bennett, MP, June 15, 1962, Blundell papers.

[88] P. Broadbent, 'Blundell's Address,' November 14, 1961.

[89] M. Blundell, letter to W. Havelock, February 1, 1962, Blundell papers.

[90] George Bennett, *Kenya: A Political History* (London: Oxford University Press, 1963), pp. 137 and 156.

[91] The idea of devolving formal powers to 'higher' as well as 'lower' levels was suggested by Leslie Melville, in a memo on the Coastal Strip. He advocated moving the High Commission to Mombasa and having the port become the concern of all three East African territories through a semi-independent body. (J. D. L. Melville, 'Coastal Strip and High Commission,' May 11, 1960.)

[92] P.J.H. Okondo, 'Proposals for Regional Governments and A Federal Constitution for Kenya,' London, October 1961.

[93] KADU, 'Initial Submission to Sir Ralph Hone,' December 11, 1961, Blundell papers.

[94] KADU Circular, 'KADU's Plan for National Unity,' October 24, 1961, Blundell papers.

[95] *East African Standard*, March 29, 1962.

[96] M. Blundell, 'Memorandum to Rt. Hon. Baron Colyton,' May 1, 1962, Blundell papers.

[97] *East African Standard*, March 30, 1962.

[98] Lord Delamere, letter to M. Blundell, March 20, 1962, Blundell papers.

[99] M. Blundell, letter to Lord Delamere, March 30, 1962, Blundell papers.

[100] R.E. Wainwright, Office of the Chief Secretary, letter to M. Blundell, July 22, 1961, Blundell papers.

[101] K.W.S. Mackenzie, 'Memorandum,' October 5, 1961, Blundell papers.

[102] Lord Howick, letter to Blundell, January 13, 1962, Blundell papers.

[103] KNFU, 'Land Policy: Proposed Talks Under the Chairmanship of the Governor,' Aide Memoire, 416/61, August 14, 1961. The *Aide Memoire* was sent to all the agricultural industries for comments – all of which were favorable or had no comment.

[104] Convention of Associations, 'Draft for Talks with African Leaders,' August 8, 1961, KNFU files.

[105] KNFU, Confidential Memorandum to the Secretary of State for the Colonies, 488/61, November 1961, KNFU files.

[106] *Ibid.*

107 *Ibid.*
108 President of KNFU, letter to Mr Ronald Ngala and Mr James Gichuru, October 12, 1961, KNFU files.
109 KNFU Executive Committee, 'Minutes,' October 18, 1961, KNFU files.
110 A. Ward, letter to W. F. B. McLellan, August 8, 1961, KNFU files. One should note that the original suggestion came from a Coalition member as a tactical step 'to counter the revolutionary land plans which Kenyatta will probably spring on us.' And on the question of Africans in the organization, McLellan had commented: '. . . it is immaterial whether or not Africans on the Council have the majority, as it is submitted that a small core of hand-picked European members would be competent to guide the new administration on sound lines.' (W.F.B. McLellan, 'KNFU Administration and Land Settlement,' August 1, 1961, KNFU files.)
111 'Resolutions Passed at the 14th Annual Conference,' November 23 and 24, 1961, 494/61, November 27, 1961, KNFU files.
112 M. Blundell, letter to L. R. Maconochie Welwood, January 19, 1962, Blundell papers.
113 D. Whetham, letter to Superintendent of Police, Eldoret, January 25, 1961, KNFU files.
114 R.E. Livingstone-Bussell, Chairman Sotik Settlers' Association to Governor's Private Secretary, April 6, 1961; and R. E. Bastard, letter to Lord Delamere, April 6, 1961, KNFU files.
115 Memorandum by the Executive of the Convention of Associations for the Rt. Hon. Hugh Fraser, n.d. [spring 1961], KNFU files.
116 'Details of 1961 Sales' (up to February 20, 1961), May 26, 1961; and 'Details of Sales from February 20, 1961,' June 1, 1961. Also, Acting Commissioner of Land's covering confidential letter to Executive Officer KNFU, May 26, 1961, KNFU files.

CHAPTER 5

1 Blundell, *So Rough a Wind*, pp. 300–5. However this contradicted his letter in the fall to Havelock stating that HMG was willing to back regionalism. (See below, p. 116.)
2 C.O. Oates, letter to N.M.S. Irwin, February 28, 1962, and Conference Report No. 2, March 2, 1962, Convention of Associations files.
3 Conference Report No. 2.
4 Oates, letter to Lorna Hill, March 15, 1962, Convention of Associations files.
5 *East African Standard*, March 28, 29 and 30, 1962.
6 KNFU, 'Report from the President on the Kenya Constitutional Conference – Lancaster House 1962,' n.d., 3 pp. (presented at April 18, 1962, Executive Committee Meeting), KNFU files.
7 *East African Standard*, April 2, 1962.
8 N.S. Carey Jones, letter to G. Wasserman, November 17, 1971. Carey Jones, former Permanent Secretary of the Ministry of Lands and Settlement, also referred to the C.L.B. as having been 'a rather hurried decision by people who had been engaged in complicated discussions on many matters for several weeks.'
    In the next chapter it will be shown how the Ministry of Settlement managed to emasculate the C.L.B. and make the Conference's decision a non-starter.
9 KNFU, 'Press Release,' November 25, 1961, 489/61, KNFU files.

10 Lord Delamere, Circular, January 3, 1962, KNFU files. In the same circular Delamere said that he still wanted to enlist the support of all European Elected Members and not limit himself to the Coalition.
11 KNFU Executive Committee, 'Minutes,' December 20, 1961, 521/61, 6 pp., KNFU files.
12 Seys, letter to Lord Delamere, December 21, 1961, KNFU files.
13 KNFU Executive Committee, 'Minutes,' January 24, 1962, 29/62, 4 pp., KNFU files.
14 KNFU Executive Committee, 'Minutes,' February 21, 1962, 5 pp., KNFU files.
15 'Resolutions Passed at the 14th KNFU Annual Conference,' November 23 and 24, 1961, 494/61, November 27, 1961, 3 pp., KNFU files.
16 J. H. Auret, Kitale, letter to the Department of Lands, November 3, 1961, KNFU files.
17 'Minutes,' January 24, 1962.
18 'Minutes,' February 21, 1962.
19 J. Pollard, Acting President, confidential letter to President Lord Delamere, February 28, 1962, 87/62, KNFU files.
  What the farmers feared was aptly phrased by L. R. M. Welwood, the leader of the Coalition delegation at Second Lancaster House. 'If nothing is done to move more land into African ownership, the mixed farmer will find himself defending a title which he wishes to dispose of against those who wish to acquire it but have not the financial means of doing so.' (*East African Standard*, March 9, 1962, p. 8.)
20 *Ibid.*, March 12, 1962, p. 1.
21 KNFU, 'Draft Suggestions for KNFU Memoranda to be Presented to the Coalition Members of the Legislature and Mr Blundell in his Position as Minister of Agriculture,' 27/62, January 23, 1962, 6 pp.
22 C. O. Oates, letter to General N. M. S. Irwin, February 28, 1962, Convention of Associations files.
23 'Situation Report from the President of the KNFU and the Chairman of Convention,' 2 pp. (n.d.) (re March 10, 1962), KNFU files.
24 The Kenya Coalition, Parliamentary Group, 'Memorandum on the Kenya Land Problem,' 7 pp., March 7, 1962, KNFU files.
25 *Ibid*. It should be noted that neither of the plan's formulators was primarily a mixed farmer: Oates worked for Brooke-Bond, while Delamere owned/owns some fair-sized ranches.
26 *Ibid.*, p. 6
27 Conference Report No. 2, March 2, 1962.
28 'Situation Report.' Oates and Delamere viewed any suggestion that HMG buy out plantations as doomed to failure.
29 Harry MacAllan, letter to Lorna Hills, March 10, 1962, Convention of Associations files.
30 Convention of Associations, 'Minutes of a Joint Meeting of the Executive and Council Held in the Town Hall, Nakuru on Wednesday, April 18, 1962, at 2:30 P.M.,' May 1, 1962, 7 pp.
31 Oates, letter to L. Hill, March 15, 1962, Convention of Associations files. Earlier Blundell had told Welwood he would not approach the Secretary of State for the underwriting of land. (*Executive Committee Minute Books,* January 19, 1962, Convention of Associations files.)
32 'Resolution No. 3, Passed at Convention's Annual General Meeting on December 14, 1961,' Convention of Associations files.

33 Irwin, letters to Oates, March 1 and March 6, 1962, Convention of Associations files.
34 Irwin, letter to L.R. Maconochie Welwood, March 30, 1962, Convention of Associations files.
35 L. Hill, letter to C.O. Oates, March 12, 1962, Convention of Association files.
36 The plan read: 'The effect of a reduction in the number of European mixed farms cannot fail to be to the advantage of the remainder, who decide to continue farming in Kenya. This is due to the fact that Kenya is unable, like most other countries, to subsidise farm produce, and the exportable surplus is sold on the World Market at a low figure, thus depressing the average price of the product. A limited number of European mixed farms producing sufficient for the local demands of wheat, milk, meat, etc., *without* any considerable export surplus are economically in a sounder position.' ('Memorandum,' March 7, 1962.)
37 Convention of Associations, 'An Account of a Meeting Between Convention/Kenya Coalition and the KNFU President's Committee, Nakuru, March 10, 1962,' March 13, 1962, 3 pp., KNFU files.
38 J. Pollard, letter to Lord Delamere, 'Re Plan,' n.d. [early March], KNFU files.
39 Oates, letter to Irwin, March 13, 1962, Convention of Associations files.
40 MacAllan, letter to Hill, March 9, 1962, Convention of Associations files.
41 Oates, letter to Hill, March 19, 1962, Convention of Associations files.
42 'Minutes of a Joint Meeting . . .,' May 1, 1962.
43 H. MacAllan, letter to L. Hills, March 10, 1962, Convention of Associations files.
44 Conference Liaison Committee, 'A Suggested Operation,' n.d., 2 pp., Convention of Associations files. Some KNFU members were considering chartering two ships for a mass exodus from Kenya to Parliament Square. (Irwin, letter to Oates, March 1, 1962, Convention of Association files.)
45 KNFU, 'Report from the President on the Kenya Constitutional Conference – Lancaster House, 1962,' 125/62, nd., 3 pp. (presented at 18th April 1962 Executive Committee Meeting).
46 *Ibid.*
47 C.O. Oates, letter to All Members of Executive Committee, April 3, 1962, Convention of Associations files.
48 H.B.W. MacAllan, 'London Talks and Land Problems,' *East African Standard*, April 13, 1962, p. 8.
49 Convention of Associations, 'Minutes of Joint Meeting,' April 18, 1962. The leadership also alleged that disputes between the two African parties had set independence back.
50 M. Blundell, letter to Havelock, November 8, 1961, Blundell papers.
51 *Ibid.*
52 A. Ward, letter to B. Darvill, Area Branch Chairman, Kipkabus, November 4, 1961, KNFU files.
53 M. Blundell, letter to the Earl of Perth, Minister of State for Colonial Affairs, October 24, 1961, Blundell papers.
54 Ward, letter to Darvill.
55 M. Blundell, Memorandum for the Secretary of State, October 12, 1961, 2 pp., Blundell papers.
56 See above, Chapter 4.
57 Blundell was referring here to the ex-forest fighters whom the Europeans

saw as a large part of the radical wing of KANU. However, the leader of this 'Ginger Group' was a Luo, Oginga Odinga. Odinga was to eventually split with KANU to form the ill-fated Kenya Peoples Union (KPU). Other leaders of the KANU militants at this time included Bildad Kaggia and Achieng Oneko.

58 P.B. Broadbent, 'Blundell's Address,' Blundell papers.

59 M. Blundell, 'Article,' January 15, 1962, Blundell papers.

60 Blundell, letter to Rt. Hon. Baron Colyton, May 1, 1962, Blundell papers.

61 Blundell, interview, October 28, 1970; Havelock, interview, December 9, 1970.

62 M. Blundell, letter to Lord Alport, October 17, 1961, Blundell papers.

63 M. Blundell, letter to Viscount Boyd of Merton, May 2, 1962, Blundell papers. In July Secretary of State Maudling remarked to a group of young European farmers that there was little future for the European mixed farmer and none for his children in Kenya. (*East African Standard*, July 11, 1962.)

64 M. Blundell, letter to C.F. Sayers, Conservative Research Department, London, July 10, 1962, Blundell papers.

65 James Gichuru, Kenya Minister of Defence, interview, October 13, 1970.

66 J.M. Kariuki, Kenyatta's private secretary, interview, November 5, 1970. Thomas Okelo-Odongo, former MP, interview, November 17, 1970.

67 A member of the Kenya Information Service complained four months after the Conference that he had not received any requests from KANU for copies of the Summary of the Lancaster House Decisions. (Ian McCulloch, letter to P. Marrian, July 13, 1962, Marrian papers.)

68 See Waruhiu Itote, *'Mau Mau' General* (Nairobi: East African Publishing House, 1967), pp. 249–60, 272.

69 *East African Standard*, February 9, 1962, p. 12.

70 *East African Standard*, February 14, 1962, p. 3.

71 *East African Standard*, March 23, 1962, p. 1.

72 M. Blundell, letter to R. Ngala, April 2, 1962, Blundell papers.

73 Oates described Mboya at Second Lancaster House as 'the Secretary of State's pet.' (Oates, letter to Hill, March 15, 1962, Convention of Associations files.)

74 Blundell, memo to Colyton, May 1, 1962. Blundell now viewed independence as two or three years away at most.

75 KADU's Plan, 'Land Tenure and Agricultural and Pastoral Development for Independent Kenya,' July 5, 1962, 11 pp.

76 *Ibid.*

77 Kenya Coalition Parliamentary Group, 'Memorandum on Land for the Secretary of State,' March 29, 1962, KNFU files.

78 Convention of Associations, 'Report on Delegation's Interview with Mr Reginald Maudling, July 9, 1962,' 2 pp., KNFU files.

Maudling was running into a number of obstacles. Suggested names proved unacceptable to one side or the other. Arthur Gaitskell, former Chairman of the Sudan Gezira Board and a member of the East African Royal Commission, 1955, was rejected by KADU because of his advisory role in co-heading an agricultural and educational survey for KANU. Sir Robert Jackson, a development adviser to the Governments of Ghana and India, had liberal support but not apparently KANU's.

Besides party jockeying, Bruce McKenzie, Minister of Settlement, was intent on whittling down the authority of the C.L.B. and sought to delay the Chairman's appointment to ensure that the person appointed would not threaten Ministry control of settlement. See Chapter 6. (M. Blundell, letter to R. Maudling, May 18, 1962, Blundell papers.)

79 The delegation consisted of Chairman Oates, Vice-Chairman MacAllan and General N.M.S. Irwin from the Convention, Lord Delamere, KNFU, and Laurence Maconochie Welwood, Leader of the Kenya Coalition Parliamentary Group.

80 'Report,' July 9, 1962.

81 *East African Standard*, July 11, 1962.

82 KNFU, Minutes, Settlement Sub-Committee, July 11, 1962, 3 pp.

83 Convention of Associations, 'Special Conference,' July 21, 1962, KNFU files.

84 Report of Council Meeting, August 30, 1962, 4 pp., Convention of Associations files. In an open letter to the Governor the Convention wrote that having settlement schemes 'in the hands of a Minister in whom, – at any rate the sellers, – have no confidence lends them to think that the over-riding principle is political expediency.' (Convention of Associations, Open Letter to Sir Patrick Renison, November 1, 1962, Convention of Associations files.)

85 Interviews with Cavendish-Bentinck, August 28, 1970; Peter Marrian, September 2, 1971; and Humphrey Slade, May 28, 1970.

86 KNFU Executive Committee, 'Minutes,' October 24, 1962, 5 pp., KNFU files.

87 Meeting of Chairmen of Area Branches, Executive Committee and Settlement Sub-Committee, 'Minutes,' Nairobi, October 5, 1962, KNFU files.

88 KNFU 'Press Release,' 310/62, October 5, 1962.

89 Settlement Sub-Committee, 'Minutes,' July 11, 1962, 209/62, KNFU files.

90 Meeting, 'Minutes,' October 5, 1962.

91 'Minutes,' October 24, 1962.

92 Memorandum to Secretary of State, 'Finance for Land and Agricultural Bank of Kenya,' February 15, 1963, 53/63, KNFU files.

93 Report of Council, August 30, 1962.

94 Council Meeting, 'Minutes,' June 8, 1962, 5 pp., Convention of Associations files.

95 Convention of Associations, Circular Appeal for Funds, April 1962, Convention of Associations files.

96 Executive Committee Minutes Books, November 5, 1962, Convention of Associations files. In an August speech Kenyatta spoke of Europeans and Asians who 'have sucked the blood of Africans and should be told the blood of Africans should no longer be sucked.' (*East African Standard*, August 21, 1962.)

97 'Minutes of Meeting of the Council, November 2, 1962,' November 5, 1962, Convention of Associations files.

98 Crime rates for 1962 did not show any drastic rise in reported offenses. The total number of cases reported to the police rose 4.7 per cent in 1962 over 1961 with a greater proportional rise in crimes against persons (7,028 to 7,655) than against property (33,610 to 34,155).

Only the year 1960, with its growth in cases reported of 22.9 per cent over 1959, seemed to justify the European farmers' fears. Crimes against property rose drastically, largely in the Settled and Urban Areas and, one would presume, against European property. The figures for crimes against property over the four years were:

Offenses against property	1959	1960	1961	1962
Nairobi City	6,340	8,303	8,419	9,102
Mombasa Urban	3,635	3,703	3,587	2,516
Remainder of Settled and Urban Areas	8,533	11,434	11,922	12,388
African Areas	8,399	9,704	9,682	10,149
Total	26,907	33,144	33,610	34,155

Crimes against persons in the Settled Areas showed a slight rise from 1,896 cases in 1959 to 1,955 in 1962. *Sources:* Colonial Office, *Report on the Colony and Protectorate of Kenya for the Year 1960* (London, 1963), 188 pp.; for the year *1961*, 210 pp.; for the year *1962*, 203 pp.

99 Convention of Associations, *The Kenya Prospect*, October 3, 1962, 3 pp., Convention of Associations files.
100 *Ibid.*
101 H.B.W. MacAllen, 'Situation in Kenya,' October 1, 1962, 2 pp. In March 1963, the *East African Standard* reported that one police team in Nakuru had arrested 1,708 people, found 368 home-made guns, 53 partly-made weapons and 767 rounds of ammunition. (Issue of March 15.)
102 *East African Standard*, November 17, 1962.
103 Convention of Associations, C.O. Oates, 'To All Affiliated Associations,' June 12, 1962, Convention of Associations files.
104 'Minutes of Council Meeting, June 8, 1962,' June 15, 1962, 5 pp., Convention of Associations files.
105 Annual General Meeting, 'The Future Role of Convention,' December 7, 1962, Convention of Associations files.
106 Executive Committee, 'Minutes,' May 14, 1963, Convention of Associations files. An indication of why the new organization was a non-starter is brought out by the reply of a Mr Henderson who headed the Nairobi Chamber of Commerce. When asked to join he said his organization had always been multi-racial, proud of the fact, and hence would not consider membership in the new group. (L. Hill, letter to H. MacAllan, January 4, 1963, Convention of Associations files.)
107 John Harbeson, 'Land Reforms and Politics in Kenya, 1954–70,' *The Journal of Modern African Studies*, 9, 2 (1971), pp. 231–51. A more lengthy argument is found in Harbeson's book, *Nation-Building in Kenya*, Evanston: Northwestern University Press, 1973.
108 *Ibid.*, pp. 241–2.
109 *Ibid.*, p. 250.
110 A similar question in a welfare program would be whether it can be assumed to aid poor people without examining the political system in/for which it operates.
111 See Richard Sandbrook, 'Patrons, Clients, and Unions: The Labour Movement and Political Conflict in Kenya,' *Journal of Commonwealth Political Studies*, X, 1 (March 1972), pp. 3–27.

¹¹² Clearly within the Kenya government the bureaucratic-expatriate and the political-nationalist structures are somewhat distinct. If one had to choose one would emphasize the bureaucratic-expatriate structure as dominating the Kenya government's 'issue-area' of land at this time. But within the bureaucratic structure there were different perspectives on decolonization between the provincial administration and the technical departments. The former leaned toward the settlers position because of their vested interest in colonial power relations threatened by African political advance, while the latter tended toward the liberal position as a result of their vested interest in the continuity of the colonial pattern of economic development.

¹¹³ Ministry of Land Settlement and Water Development, 'A Project to Settle 50,000 to 70,000 African Farmers in the Scheduled Areas,' July 21, 1962, 29 pp.

¹¹⁴ 'Loan 303-KE-Revision,' Fall 1963. In the papers of N.S. Carey Jones, former Permanent Secretary of the Ministry of Settlement.

¹¹⁵ N.S. Carey Jones, letter to W.H. Howell, September 5, 1962, Carey Jones papers. McKenzie spoke of the 'prime purpose' of the schemes as African resettlement. (*East African Standard*, August 1, 1962.)

¹¹⁶ Carey Jones, letter to M. Webster, Colonial Office, June 29, 1962, Carey Jones papers.

¹¹⁷ See also N.S. Carey Jones, 'The Decolonization of the White Highlands of Kenya,' ·*The Geographical Journal*, Vol. 131, Part 2. (June 1965, pp. 186–201; and Goldsack and Nottidge, *The Million-Acre Settlement Scheme 1962–66, passim.*)

¹¹⁸ Council of Ministers, 'Expanded Land Settlement Scheme in Scheduled Areas,' Memorandum by Ministry for Land Settlement and Water Development, CM(62)363, 2 pp., December 15, 1962.

¹¹⁹ P.D. Marrian, interview, September 2, 1971.

CHAPTER 6

¹ *Who Controls Industry in Kenya?* (1968), p. 212; and the Republic of Kenya, *Development Plan, 1970–74*, p. 200. The three-fourths figure comes from the former source, quoting the *Economic Survey* (1968); the two-thirds figure is from the *Development Plan*.

² Convention of Associations, 'Situation Report,' March 10, 1962.

³ See Bruce McKenzie's speech to the Kenya National Farmers' Union recommending this step. *East African Standard*, November 11, 1960.

⁴ Great Britain, East Africa Royal Commission, 1953–1955, *Report, 1955*, Sir Hugh Dow, Chairman (London: Her Majesty's Stationery Office, 1955).

⁵ Colony and Protectorate of Kenya, *Sessional Paper No. 6 of 1959/60*, 'Land Tenure and Control Outside the Native Lands,' (1960), p. 6.

⁶ *East African Standard*, February 16, 1960.

⁷ *Ibid.*, October 17, 1960. Both the Chambers of Commerce and Mboya are referring to S.P. 10 of 1958/59 rather than the final S.P. 6 of 1959/60. However, the later bill, by removing a Land Trust Corporation and some government control over inter-racial transfers, restricting the governor's power to appropriate land for public purposes, and easing conversion from leasehold to freehold, went far to assuage European farmers' reservations rather than African objections. As the KNFU said about the effects of its Memorandum on S.P. 10, 'It is no idle boast to say that this memorandum

formed the basis of the revision of Sessional Paper No. 10 in its sister paper, No. 6, issued this year.' *Ibid.*, 'Royal Show Supplement,' September 23, 1960, p. ix.

8 N.S. Carey Jones, 'Land Settlement Schemes in Kenya,' n.d. (re early 1964), 9 pp., The Papers of N.S. Carey Jones, Office, The University of Leeds.

9 *East African Standard*, June 10, 1960, p. 3.

10 *Ibid.*, May 13, 1960.

11 The L.D.S.B. apparently derived from a committee headed by Lipscomb in June 1960. L. Winston Cone and J.F. Lipscomb, *The History of Kenya Agriculture* (Nairobi: University Press of Africa, 1972), p. 122.

12 T.A. Watts, interview, August 21, 1970.

13 I.B.R.D. Application, 'Particulars of A Project for the Development and Settlement of Land in the Scheduled Areas of Kenya, (re late 1960), 21 pp.

14 T.A. Watts, *A Review of the Activities of the Land Development and Settlement Board, January 1st, 1961–July 31st, 1962*, p. 1.

15 L.D.S.B., 'Minutes,' Friday, July 28, 1961, 6 pp., KNFU files. The Ministry had agreed to the sellers' demands, fearing that 'unless the terms of the installment system are sufficiently attractive to the vendor, there is a grave danger that insufficient land for the scheme will be offered for sale.' (Council of Ministers, 'Settlement Schemes,' draft, September 5, 1961, 2 pp.)

16 T.A. Watts, *A Review*, p. 2.

17 N.S. Carey Jones, letter to F.N. Brockett, June 27, 1962, Carey Jones papers.

18 C.P.R. Nottidge and J.R. Goldsack, *The Million-Acre Scheme, 1962–1966* (Nairobi: Department of Settlement, 1966), p. 4.

19 The duties of the old L.D.S.B. were not carried on directly by the C.L.B. under the Constitution. Two other bodies were to have influence over parts of the transfer. The Settlement Fund Trustees, consisting of the Ministers for Finance, Settlement, and Agriculture were to handle the funding and the administering of the schemes through the executive authority of the Kenya government. The Presidents of the Regions concerned with the area to be transferred were to nominate the people to be settled. The C.L.B. was supposed to implement the settlement schemes, and this was the crux of the later dispute with the Ministry. Nottidge and Goldsack, p. 4.

20 N.S. Carey Jones, letter to G. Wasserman, February 14, 1972.

21 Council of Ministers, 'Memorandum by the Minister of Land Settlement and Water Development, Central Land Board, May 26, 1962, C.M.M. (62), 141, 4 pp.

22 *Ibid.*

23 The Secretary of State, letter to L.R.M. Welwood, April 7, 1962, KNFU files. Interviews with Ministry officials emphasized their feelings that the C.L.B. solution arrived at by the Second Lancaster House Conference was not carefully thought out and was administratively impractical.

24 Council of Ministers, May 26, 1962.

25 N.S. Carey Jones, letter to J.W. Howard, May 23, 1962, 2 pp., Carey Jones papers.

26 N.S. Carey Jones, interview, October 12, 1971. These discussions included African leaders of both parties.

27 N.S. Carey Jones, letter to H.F. Wainwright, Office of the Minister of State, May 23, 1962, Carey Jones papers.

28 'Draft Letter for Renison to Reply to Monson,' August 31, 1962, 6 pp., Carey Jones papers.
29 N.S. Carey Jones to J.P.D. Nobriga, September 18, 1962, Carey Jones papers.
30 Brief for the Minister for Settlement, 'Reasons Why the Department of Settlement should be retained by the Government,' January 17, 1963, 2 pp.
31 Carey Jones, letter to W.A.T. Stewart, March 16, 1963, Carey Jones papers.
32 Permanent Secretary, 'Brief for Minister of LS and WD,' March 18, 1962.
33 Carey Jones, letter to W.A.T. Stewart, March 16, 1963, Carey Jones papers.
34 Carey Jones, 'Draft,' November 8, 1963, Carey Jones papers.
35 In July 1962 the Chairman of the L.D.S.B. complained about the lack of involvement by the Board in the replacement of its Chief Executive and the appointment of the Director of Settlement acting in this position. 'In this and other matters the Minister appears to ignore the existence of the Board.' J.W. Howard, letter to N.S. Carey Jones, July 3, 1962, Carey Jones papers.
36 Central Land Board, 'A Report on the First Year's Working of the Central Land Board, 1963–64,' 16 pp.
37 'Report of the Officer Administering the Settlement Fund,' May 26, 1964, 5 pp., Carey Jones papers.
38 C.P.R. Nottidge, interview, July 14, 1970.
J.R. Goldsack, interview, July 6, 1970.
Some of the potential settlers were also not well-disposed to the settlement officials. Nottidge remembered having to replace his windshield a half dozen times in the period of his work in the Kinangop.
39 'Extract from letter from P.C. Nyeri, in N.S. Carey Jones letter to M. Webster, Colonial Office, June 29, 1962, Carey Jones papers.
40 Central Land Board, *Final Report, 1964–1965*, p. 7.
41 See N.S. Carey Jones, *The Anatomy of Uhuru* (Manchester: Manchester University Press) 1966, pp. 140, 151, 158–9, 168–9.
42 Ministry of Settlement, Carey Jones, 'Draft,' n.d. [re December, 1962], Carey Jones papers.
43 Permanent Secretary, *Memorandum: Of Kalou Farmers*, MSW/SETT/A/ 218, June 22, 1963, 4 pp.
44 *Ibid.*, p. 3. A letter from the Ministry to the Colonial Office on May 16, 1963, hoped for agreement to the accelerated Kikuyu program 'before the Central Land Board begins . . . since the Central Land Board with its seven regional representatives will be unlikely to recognize the need for accelerated Kikuyu settlement.' N.S. Carey Jones, letter to F.D. Webber, Colonial Office, May 16, 1963.
45 Earlier it had been thought that Kikuyu, at least on the higher-level assisted-owner schemes, could be settled anywhere in the Highlands. But a 1962 Ministry memo reported that due to the deterioration in the tribal situation Kikuyu could not be settled in the Mau Narok area. N.S. Carey Jones, letter to the Executive Officer, L.D.S.B., September 1, 1962, Carey Jones papers.
46 *East African Standard*, January 26, 1962, p. 13.
47 Permanent Secretary, 'Memo South Kinangop,' Ministry of Land Settlement, March 31, 1962, 3 pp.
48 Great Britain, *Kenya: Report of the Regional Boundaries Commission*, Cmnd. 1899, London, December 1962, pp. 6–7.
49 *Ibid.*, p. 11. The actual decision to buy in the Kinangop was made in April or May 1962 by Bruce McKenzie on political grounds against the plan-

ners' advice. The Regional Boundaries Commission followed the outlines of the settlement plans in arriving at boundaries except for the inclusion of Ol Kalou which, combined with the abandonment of farms there, meant the area had to be settled. N.S. Carey Jones, letter to G. Wasserman, June 16, 1972.

50 Governor, letter to Secretary of State (Griffith-Jones to Webber), 'Draft,' re end of May 1963.

51 Memorandum, 'The Second Million-Acre Scheme,' Ministry of Settlement, August 27, 1963, 16 pp.

52 The Cabinet, *Nyandarua*, Paper B, Memorandum by the Ministers of Lands and Settlement, Agriculture, and Finance (re November 1, 1963).

53 Republic of Kenya, Department of Settlement, *Annual Report, 1963/64*, p. 5.

54 Acting Minister for Land Settlement and Water Development, 'Memorandum,' March 22, 1963.

55 Minister for Lands and Settlement (J.H. Angaine), memorandum, 'Selection of Settlers on High Density Schemes,' June 1963, 4 pp.

56 *Ibid.*

57 Carey Jones, telegram to Webber, September 1962, Carey Jones papers.

58 Draft Savingram to the Secretary of State, 'Ol Kalou Farmers, MSW/SETT/A/219, June 22, 1963, 3 pp.

59 N.S. Carey Jones, 'Draft' (re December 5, 1962). Earlier the Permanent Secretary had described squatters as being 'magnetized' to land not kept in operation. Carey Jones, letter to Permanent Secretary, Governor's office, September 17, 1962, Carey Jones papers.

60 In some cases European's who because of their activities during the Emergency were felt to be 'a security danger,' were bought out under the Compassionate Case Scheme. In a 1962 meeting MacKenzie had assured European farmers that Compassionate cases would include those involved in security and anti-Mau Mau activities, depending on recommendations of the Special Branch (the Kenya F.B.I.). KNFU, Executive Committee meeting, 'Notes Taken when B.R. McKenzie was present,' May 25, 1962, KNFU files.

61 John Harbeson, 'Land Reforms and Politics in Kenya, 1954–70,' *Journal of Modern African Studies*, 4, 2 (1971), p. 242.

62 Ministry of Land Settlement, 'A Project to Settle 50,000 to 70,000 African Farmers in the Scheduled Areas,' July 21, 1962, p. 7.

63 Carey Jones, draft letter to Charles Castle, March 19, 1963. However, two months later the Ministry decided to lease compassionate farms instead of selling them at prices which depressed the market. (Carey Jones, letter to Chairman, Board of Agriculture, May 22, 1963, Carey Jones papers.)

64 Carey Jones telegram (reply to telegram 517), May 10, 1963. In a recent letter the former Permanent Secretary wrote: 'The real fear with compassionate cases was that their land would be squatted on, and the squatters would not only set an example of seizure of land but cause trouble to neighboring farmers. They could also become Land Freedom Army bases. I had considerable doubts myself about the benefits to the individuals themselves – they had little means, and would eke out a pretty miserable existence in England.' (N.S. Carey Jones, letter to G. Wasserman, January 4, 1972.)

65 The original Kenya government proposal for a Million-Acre scheme had hoped 'that after an initial attack on the problems through very high density

schemes the tension will have relaxed sufficiently to proceed with more productive schemes.' In the latter stages of the Million-Acre scheme planners deliberately increased the acreages to obtain a better standard of farming. Ministry of Land Settlement, 'A Project to Settle 50,000 to 70,000 African Farmers . . .,' p. 6.

66 In comments on an earlier draft of this chapter, N.S. Carey Jones wrote, 'The creation of a middle class of Africans in the Highlands was, I think, quite conscious. If you refer back to the Swynnerton Plan, there was a similar sort of objective in that.' N.S. Carey Jones, letter to G. Wasserman, June 16, 1972.)

67 Deputy Secretary for Agriculture, 'Memorandum,' October 24, 1960.

68 J.W. Maina, Director of Settlement, *Settlement Patterns and Prospects* (Ministry of Lands and Settlement, April 4, 1966), 9 pp.

69 Ministry of Lands and Settlement, 'Memorandum: The Second Million-Acre Scheme,' August 27, 1963, 16 pp. The 'political implications' referred to the pressure wealthy influential Africans could bring to bear on the government.

70 Letter, April 17, 1964, KNFU files.

71 Nairobi Chamber of Commerce, 'Address by Honorable Bruce McKenzie Minister for Agriculture and Animal Husbandry,' Annexure A to Minutes of Governing Council, August 24, 1964, 10 pp.

72 A. Ward, letter to J. Feingold, September 2, 1964, KNFU files. McKenzie was Ward's source of the information.

73 Members of the Mission 'Appointed to Advise on Proposals for a Further Transfer of European Farms in Kenya' were: Honorable A. Maxwell Stamp, Chairman, Mr G.J. Caren (partner in a firm of Chartered Surveyors), Dr A.M.M. McFarquhar (School of Agriculture, University of Cambridge), and Mr R.J.M. Swynnerton (Agriculture Advisor to the Commonwealth Development Corporation).

74 Specifically the lack of mention of the priority for land consolidation in the African areas, or development outside the Mixed Areas, or the dangers of concentrating resources on land purchase.

Sessional Paper No. 10 of 1965 on African Socialism apparently started life as a Treasury document in pre-independence days. It was written by an expatriate. (N.S. Carey Jones, interview, November 13, 1971.)

75 The Mission's conclusions and recommendations were released in a Statement by The Right Honorable Barbara Castle, M.P., Minister of Overseas Development, *British Assistance to Kenya*, Ministry of Overseas Development, November 18, 1965.

76 Castle's Statement.

77 'Notes of the Overseas Development Ministry Meeting at 10:00 a.m. on Monday, 25 October 1965 with KNFU,' 3 pp.

78 *The Financial Times*, November 11, 1965.

79 *East African Standard*, November 17, 24 and 25, 1965, the *Daily Telegraph*, November 11, 1965. Also, 'Summary of Terms and Conditions for British Financial Assistance for Kenya 1966–70 Land Transfer Programme' (re November 1965), 2 pp.

80 John Pollard, interview, September 17, 1970.

81 The economy's continuing dependence on the large farm sector was brought out by a chart in the Report, showing gross farm revenue by commodity in 1964, in thousands of pounds.

	Large-scale farming areas	Small-scale areas
	Laikipia, Nyandarua, Nakuru Kitale, Uasin Gishu, Thika	Central Nyanza, Nandi, Kericho, Machakos, Kiambu, Nyeri, and Coast
Wheat	3,454	190
Maize	1,107	40
Barley	344	33
Cattle and calves	2,087	455
Sheep and lambs	233	13
Whole milk	1,937	637

Source: Agricultural Census, 1964, in A.W. Peers, *Land Purchase Programme Proposals 1966–69*, Ministry of Agriculture and Animal Husbandry, April 12, 1966, p. 7.

82 This didn't signify that the Ministry was resistant to political pressure in defining *which* areas would be considered vital to the economy. The Molo area was scheduled for direct block purchase because of the high concentration of British nationals who wished to leave, and, secondarily, because of its concentration of breeding sheep. (Peer's *Report*, p. 4.)

83 *Ibid.* Other Ministry officials put the price per acre at around £11 for land purchased under the Million-Acre scheme.

84 Republic of Kenya, *Development Plan 1970–1974*, 1969, p. 209; and Agricultural Development Corporation, *A Summary of Its Activities* (Nairobi Show, 1970), p. 5. The average acreage of the farms handled by the A.D.C. was 1,538 acres.

85 *Development Plan 1970–1974*, p. 207.

86 *Ibid.*, pp. 192, 200.

87 *Ibid.*, p. 209.

88 Capital Aid Department, British High Commission, Nairobi, *U.K./Kenya Loan No. 3, 1966*, July 10, 1970, 5 pp.

89 J.H. Angaine, 'Circular Letter', Ministry of Settlement, May 11, 1964.

90 Department of Settlement, *Annual Report, 1963–64*, p. 5.

91 N.S. Carey Jones, *The Anatomy of Uhuru*, 1966, pp. 164–5. He went on to say: 'In spite of a growing resentment amongst the people at the new large-scale African farmer, the new Kulak, the new rich African, sometimes a natural envy, sometimes prompted by a diet of Marxism, it was remarkable the number of African leaders who sought these larger holdings. As they have to be paid for, however, some hostages have been given, as far as general recovery of debts under the scheme is concerned.'

92 By mid-1968 a total of 258 'Z' plots had been planned. Purchase requirements were a down payment of ten per cent of the valuation plus £500 working capital. Department of Settlement, *Five-Year Review and Annual Report 1967/68*, p. 3.

93 Republic of Kenya, Report of the Mission on Land Settlement in Kenya, December 1966, pp. 58, 184–6. B. Van Arkadie, Chairman. The Mission's general impression was that the Stamp Report had been 'a very gloomy view' of settlement. They were more sanguine about settlement's contribution to stability, social relief and development.

205

94 Senior Investigations Office, Ministry of Lands and Settlement, memo, 'Loan Repayments – 'Z' plotholders,' June 23, 1969, 3 pp.

95 Ministry of Lands and Settlement, 'Report on Visit by Messrs R.J.M. Swynnerton and W.J.R. Cox on 20th, 25th and 26th March 1970,' Kenya Land Development and Settlement Scheme (KLDS), 9 pp.

96 The discussion which follows deals mainly with relations with the World Bank. That institution gave most of the money coming from international institutions and inspired most of the correspondence from Kenya officials over varying interpretations of the goals and methods of settlement. The C.D.C. was a less vocal contributor to the settlement process, perhaps because agreement with HMG could be expected to bring with it concurrence from the C.D.C. Unfortunately the author was not allowed to use the World Bank library in Nairobi.

97 J.A. Seys, letter to Lord Delamere, March 3, 1961, 128/61, 4 pp., KNFU files.

98 In her book on World Bank financing in Latin America, Teresa Hayter remarked that aid was not available to countries which nationalized foreign-owned assets without compensation, and in which there were claims by foreign investors the Bank considered should be settled: 'Aid is, in general available to countries whose internal political arrangements, foreign policy alignments, treatment of foreign private investment, debt-servicing record, export policies, and so on, are considered desirable, potentially desirable, or at least acceptable, by the countries or institutions providing aid, and which do not appear to threaten their interests.' (Teresa Hayter, *Aid as Imperialism* [London: Penguin, 1971], pp. 15–16.)

99 Great Britain, Kenya Constitutional Conference, 1960, *Report of the Conference*, Cmnd. 1700, February 22, 1960, p. 10.

100 N.S. Carey Jones, letter to G. Wasserman, November 17, 1971.

101 *East African Standard*, April 29, 1960.

102 Lord Howick, 'Land of Dangers and Hope,' *The Times*, August 10, 1960. It should be noted that the former Kenya Governor was in the early 1960s head of the Commonwealth Development Corporation.

103 Hayter remarks that for the World Bank the question of agriculture 'is seldom discussed in relation to the general improvement of conditions in rural areas. The desirability of land reform, for example, is in practice evaluated in terms of its effect on agricultural production and on public finances.' (Hayter, p. 159.)

104 See *East African Standard*, September 8, 1961, p. 7.

105 The ratio of development loans was two-thirds from I.B.R.D., one-third from C.D.C. Nottidge and Goldsack, *The Million Acre Scheme*, pp. 9–10.

106 'A Project to Settle 50,000 to 70,000 . . .,' p. 1. Five per cent of the target for families and 50 per cent of the acreage target had been achieved by the end of June 1962.

107 M. Blundell, letter to F.M. Bennett, June 22, 1961, Blundell papers.

108 'A Project to Settle . . .,' pp. 2–4.

109 N.S. Carey Jones, letter to S. Noel McIvor, I.B.R.D., December 19, 1962, Carey Jones papers.

110 Ministry for Settlement, 'Brief for Minister of LS and WD,' March 18, 1963. By March 31, 1963, 45,941 acres of I.B.R.D./C.D.C. schemes had been purchased at a cost of £481,397.

111 Ministry of Settlement, 'Memo: Assisted Owner Schemes (I.B.R.D./C.D.C.)' [re July 1962], 3 pp.

112 'Handing-Over Notes,' Mr P.M. Gordon, letter to Mr N.S. Carey Jones, September 26, 1961, Carey Jones papers.

113 N.S. Carey Jones, letter to P.V. Dixon, Colonial Office, May 10, 1963, Carey Jones papers.

114 N.S. Carey Jones, letter to D.J. Derx, Colonial Office, February 2, 1963, Carey Jones papers.

115 Officer Administering the Settlement Fund, 'Final IBRD Meeting on May 27, 1964,' May 28, 1964.

116 Carey Jones, *The Anatomy of Uhuru*, p. 170. The opposition of the planners also had an ideological element. Carey Jones thought co-ops went against the Kenyans 'natural impulses' (p. 193) and, he maintained, a peasant's ambition was to own his own land. A recurring phrase in discussions with expatriates involved in settlement was that 'Africans are by nature capitalists.'

117 N.S. Carey Jones, 'Memo: Muhoroni Sugar Scheme, May 20, 1963,' Carey Jones papers.

118 *Ibid.*, p. 2. The Ol Kalou Salient, largely deserted by the Afrikaner farmers there, was settled with 19 large-scale farms under central management by the Department of Settlement in 1964 and 1965. Because of the land's unsuitability for subdivision the 141,000 acres were settled by 2,000 families as a cooperative. The funds for the Ol Kalou Scheme came from the British government. *Development Plan*, p. 208.

119 Department of Settlement, *Annual Report 1962/63*, pp. 30–2. The World Bank also seemed to favor Kenya in their financing in East Africa. As of October 15, 1970, of $53.7 million to the three countries individually $40.1 million went to Kenya. IDA Credits were more evenly disbursed, $48.7 million out of $139.1, while IFC investments showed $17.7 million going to Kenya out of a total of $25.9 million. Aid totals to the three countries and the East African Community since 1955 was $385.5 million. (Source: IBRD, Nairobi, *World Bank Group Financing in East Africa*, October 15, 1970.)

120 Note the acreage transferred to non-Kikuyu areas as opposed to Kikuyu in the first years of the transfer and the reversal in priorities in the following years. (See chart, pp. 144–5.)

CHAPTER 7

1 Ralph Tanner, 'Who Goes Home?,' *Transition,* Vol. 3, No. 9 (June 1963), pp. 32–6.

2 Lorna Hill, letter to Captain C.T. Todd, November 7, 1962, Convention of Associations files.

3 This racial re-entrenchment policy of a conservative colonial elite was illustrated in the more successful actions by the Rhodesian European community to strengthen its position through consolidation in a political party (the Rhodesian Front), culminating in the unilateral declaration of independence in 1965. See Larry W. Bowman, 'Organization, Power and Decision-Making Within the Rhodesian Front,' *Journal of Commonwealth Political Studies* (July 1969), pp. 145–65.

4 Blundell, *So Rough a Wind*, p. 81.

5 *Ibid.*, p. 208.

6 Minutes of a Meeting of the Executive Group of the New Kenya Parliamentary Group, December 14, 1959, 5 pages, Hughes papers.

7 'Draft suggestions for KNFU Memoranda to be Presented to the Coalition Members of the Legislature . . .' 27/62, January 1962, 6 pp., KNFU files.

8 The author of a study of the French community in Senegal remarked: 'Those Europeans in more secure business and professional positions were able to accept alterations with minimum of difficulty.' Rita Cruse O'Brien, *White Society in Black Africa: The French of Senegal* (London: Faber and Faber Ltd, 1972), p. 97.

9 Blundell wrote a critic in late 1959, 'As long as the present racial African franchise exists, there is not a hope for any moderate African to join us . . . You have always denied that the African Elected Members would split, but they did split and it was mainly the Government's bad handling of the land issue which forced them together. Contributory factors were intimidation, as I have noted above, and the power of the more extreme leaders to organize "have-nots" in each constituency and meetings organized on the present racial lines.' (Michael Blundell, letter to Roy Lewis, December 21, 1959, Blundell papers.)

10 In a speech to the English Speaking Union in Edinburgh, September 12, 1957, Blundell said, 'I think the real challenge for us is how can we give Africans enough conviction and force to carry forward our own ideas and our own civilization and not be solely dependent on us to carry it forward for them?' (Blundell, *So Rough a Wind*, pp. 242–3.)

11 'Minutes,' October 7, 1960, Convention of Associations files.

12 House of Lords. *Official Report* (Hansard) Motion – Kenya (Col. 305), Vol. 222, No. 60 (Monday, March 28, 1960), p. 315.

13 Oginga Odinga, *Not Yet Uhuru* (London: Heinemann, 1967), p. 179.

14 Michael Blundell, letter to F.M. Bennett, June 22, 1961, Blundell papers.

15 Mary Parker, 'Race Relations and Political Development in Kenya,' *African Affairs*, Vol. 50, No. 198 (January 1951), pp. 41–2.

16 Schattschneider, *Semisovereign People*, Chapter 1, 'The Contagiousness of Conflict,' pp. 1–19.

17 This was an old problem which the colonial government had dealt with in a similar way. A 1946 meeting of Provincial Commissioners emphasized the 'necessity to avoid any suggestion that the provision of more land could permanently solve the inherent difficulties of the present land congestion problems.' (Quoted by Bruce Berman, 'Organizational Factors in the Formulation and Implementation of Development Policy in Colonial Kenya, 1945–52,' paper presented at the Canadian Political Science Association Conference, Montreal, June 2–5, 1972, p. 16.)

18 M.W. Dunford, 'Preliminary Notes on Public Relations,' March 14, 1960, KNFU files.

19 Memorandum, Kenya Economy: Finance for Land Development and the Stabilization of Land Values, April 4, 1960, KNFU files.

20 Peter Marrian, letter to Michael Blundell, November 26, 1960, Blundell papers.

21 See L. Winston Cone and J.F. Lipscomb, *The History of Kenya Agriculture* (Nairobi: University Press of Africa, 1972), p. 122. Lipscomb, former Chairman of the European Agriculture Settlement Board (1951–9), served as Chairman of the L.D.S.B. 1960–1.

22 See above, Chapter 2, for why this perception was incorrect.

23 This phrase is taken from the title of a book by Stewart C. Easton (New York: Holt, Rinehart and Winston, 1960), in which the author concludes that colonialism '. . . will soon be a phase of history to be studied only by historians, and its passing governmental forms . . . will no longer be of anything but historical interest to students of government.' (p. 542)

SELECTED BIBLIOGRAPHY

BOOKS

Apter, David. *Ghana in Transition*. New York: Atheneum, 1968.

Attlee, Lord. *Empire into Commonwealth*. New York: Oxford University Press, 1961.

Bailey, F. G., *Stratagems and Spoils: A Social Anthropology of Politics*. Oxford: Basil Blackwell, 1970.

Bennett, George, and Rosberg, Carl G. *The Kenyatta Election: Kenya 1960–1961*. London: Oxford University Press, 1961.

Bennett, George. *Kenya: A Political History, The Colonial Period*. London: Oxford University Press, 1963.

Bienen, Henry. *Kenya: The Politics of Participation and Control*. Princeton: Princeton University Press, 1974.

Blixen, Karen. *Out of Africa*. London: Putnam, 1937.

Blundell, Michael. *So Rough a Wind*. London: Weidenfeld and Nicholson, 1964.

Brett, E. A. *Colonialism and Underdevelopment in East Africa*. New York: NOK, 1973.

Burns, Sir Alan Cuthbert, ed. *Parliament as an Export*. London: Allen and Unwin, 1966.

Buttner, Karl. *Theories on Africa and Neo-Colonialism*. Leipzig: Karl Marx University, 1971.

Carey Jones, N. S. *The Anatomy of Uhuru: An Essay on Kenya's Independence*. Manchester: Manchester University Press, 1966.

Carter, Gwendolen M., and Brown, William O., eds. *Transition in Africa: Studies in Political Adaptation*. Boston: Boston University Press, 1958.

Chilcote, Ronald H. *Portuguese Africa*. New Jersey: Prentice-Hall, 1967.

Cohen, Sir Andrew. *British Policy in Changing Africa*. London: Routledge and Kegan Paul, 1959.

Cone, L. Winston, and Lipscomb, J. F. *The History of Kenya Agriculture*. Nairobi: University Press of Africa, 1972.

Cruse O'Brien, Rita. *White Society in Black Africa: The French of Senegal*. London: Faber and Faber Ltd, 1972.

Delf, George. *Jomo Kenyatta: Towards Truth about 'The Light of Kenya'*. London: Victor Gollancz, 1961.

Diamond, Stanley, and Burke, Fred, eds. *The Transformation of East Africa: Political Anthropology*. New York: Basic Books, 1966.

Duffy, James. *Portugal in Africa*. Cambridge, Mass.: Harvard University Press, 1962

Easton, Stewart C. *The Twilight of European Colonialism*. New York: Holt, Rinehart and Winston, 1960.

Emerson, Rupert. *From Empire to Nation*. Boston: Beacon Press, 1960.

Fanon, Frantz. *The Wretched of the Earth*. Harmondsworth: Penguin Books, 1967.

First, Ruth. *Power in Africa*. New York: Pantheon Books, 1970.

Gann, L. H. and Duignan, Peter. *White Settlers in Tropical Africa*. Harmonds-worth: Penguin Books, 1962.
  Colonialism in Africa, 1870–1960; Volume II: *The History and Politics of Colonialism, 1914–1960*. London: Cambridge University Press, 1970.
Gertzel, Cherry. *The Politics of Independent Kenya 1963–8*. Nairobi: East African Publishing House, 1970.
Ghai, Dharam P. *Portrait of a Minority: Asians in East Africa*. London: Oxford University Press, 1965.
Ghai, Y. P., and McAuslan, J.P.W.B. *Public Law and Political Change in Kenya*. Nairobi: Oxford University Press, 1970.
Goldsworthy, David. *Colonial Issues in British Politics 1945–1961*. Oxford: Clarendon Press, 1971.
Harbeson, John W. *Nation-Building in Kenya: The Role of Land Reform*. Evanston, Ill.: Northwestern University Press, 1973.
Harlow, Vincent, Chilver, E. M., and Smith, Allison. *History of East Africa*, Vol. II. Oxford: Clarendon Press, 1965.
Hayter, Teresa. *Aid as Imperialism*. Harmondsworth: Penguin Books, 1971.
Huxley, Elspeth. *No Easy Way: A History of the Kenya Farmers' Association and the UNGA Limited*. Nairobi: East Africa Standard, n.d.
  White Man's Country, Lord Delamere and the Making of Kenya. 2 Vols. London: Macmillan and Company, 1935.
  With Forks and Hope. New York: William Morrow, 1964.
Itote, Waruhiu. *'Mau Mau' General*. Nairobi: East African Publishing House, 1967.
Key, V. O., Jr. *Politics, Parties and Pressure Groups*. 5th ed. New York: Thomas Y. Crowell, 1964.
Kirkman, W. P. *Unscrambling an Empire, A Critique of British Colonial Policy 1956–1966*. London: Chatto and Windus, 1966.
Kuper, Leo and Smith, M. G. *Pluralism in Africa*. Berkeley: University of California Press, 1971.
Lee, J. M. *Colonial Development and Good Government*. London: Oxford University Press, 1967.
Leys, Colin. *Underdevelopment in Kenya: The Political Economy of Neo-Colonialism*. Berkeley: University of California Press, 1974.
Lipscomb, J. F. *White Africans*. London: Faber and Faber Ltd., 1955.
Mannoni, O. *Prospero and Caliban, The Psychology of Colonization*. London: Methuen, 1956.
Marco Surveys. *Who's Who in East Africa, 1963–64, 1965–66*. Nairobi: Marco Surveys, 1964, 1966.
Marx, Karl and Engels, Frederick. *On Colonialism*. Moscow: Progress Publishers, 1965.
Mboya, Tom. *Freedom and After*. London: Andre Deutsch, 1963.
Memmi, Albert. *The Colonizer and the Colonized*. Boston: Beacon Press, 1967.
Mulford, David C. *Zambia: The Politics of Independence. 1957–64*. New York: Oxford University Press, 1967.
National Christian Council of Kenya, A Working Party. *Who Controls Industry in Kenya?* Nairobi: East African Publishing House, 1968.
Nottidge, C.P.R., and Goldsack, J. R. *The Million-Acre Scheme, 1962–1966*. Nairobi: Department of Settlement, Republic of Kenya, 1966.
Odinga, Oginga. *Not Yet Uhuru*. London: Heinemann, 1967.
Ominde, S. H. *Land and Population Movements in Kenya*. London: Heinemann, 1968.

Select bibliography

Perham, Margery. *The Colonial Reckoning.* New York: Alfred Knopf, 1962.
Plamenatz, John. *On Alien Rule and Self-Government.* London: Longman's, 1960.
Richmond, Anthony H. *The Colour Problem.* Harmondsworth: Penguin Books, 1961.
Rosberg, Carl G. and Nottingham, John. *The Myth of 'Mau Mau': Nationalism in Kenya.* Nairobi: East African Publishing House, 1966.
Ross, W. McGregor. *Kenya from Within.* London: George Allen and Unwin Ltd, 1927.
Rothchild, Donald S. *Racial Bargaining in Independent Kenya: a study of minorities and decolonization.* London: Oxford University Press, 1973.
Ruthenburg, Hans. *African Agricultural Production Development Policy in Kenya, 1952–1965.* Berlin: Springer-Verlag, 1966.
Schattschneider, E. E. *The Semisovereign People.* New York: Holt, Rinehart and Winston, 1960.
Schelling, Thomas C. *The Strategy of Conflict.* Cambridge, Mass.: Harvard University Press, 1963.
Sorrenson, M. P. K. *Land Reform in Kikuyu Country.* Nairobi: Oxford University Press, 1967.
   Origins of European Settlement in Kenya. Nairobi: Oxford University Press, 1968.
Ward, Kendall. *The Kenya Land Question: The History of African and European Land Settlement.* London: Voice of Kenya, 1952.
West, Richard. *The White Tribes of Africa.* London: Macmillan, 1965.
Wood, Susan. *Kenya: The Tensions of Progress.* London: Oxford University Press, 1962.

ARTICLES

Ankomah, K. 'The Colonial Legacy and African Unrest.' *Science and Society,* 2 (Summer, 1970), 129–45.
Barber, William J. 'Land Reform and Economic Changes Among African Farmers in Kenya.' *Economic Development and Cultural Change,* 19, 1 (October, 1970), 6–24.
Bienen, Henry. 'The Ruling Party in the African One-Party State: TANU in Tanzania.' *Journal of Commonwealth Political Studies,* V, 3 (November 1967), 214–30.
Blundell, Michael. 'The Present Situation in Kenya.' *African Affairs,* 54 (January, 1955), 99–108.
Brown, L. H. 'Agricultural Change in Kenya, 1945–1960.' *Food Research Institute Studies in Agricultural Economics, Trade, and Development,* VIII, 1 (1968), 33–90.
Carey Jones, N. S. 'The Decolonization of the White Highlands of Kenya.' *Geographical Journal,* 131, 2 (June, 1965), 186–201.
Emmanuel, Arghiri. 'White-Settler Colonialism and the Myth of Investment Imperialism.' *New Left Review,* 73 (May–June, 1972), 35–57.
Esseks, John D. 'Economic Dependence and Political Development in New States of Africa.' *The Journal of Politics,* 33, 4 (November, 1971), 1052–75.
Etherington, D. M. 'Land Resettlement in Kenya: Policy and Practice.' *East African Economics Review,* X, 1 (June, 1963), 22–35.
Harbeson, John. 'Land Reforms and Politics in Kenya, 1954–70.' *Journal of Modern African Studies,* 9, 2 (1971), 231–51.

211

Kilson, Martin L., Jr. 'Land and Politics in Kenya: An Analysis of African Politics in a Plural Society.' *Western Political Quarterly*, X, 3 (September, 1957), 559–81.

'Land and the Kikuyu: A Study of the Relationship Between Land and Kikuyu Political Movements.' *Journal of Negro History*, XL, 2 (April, 1955), 103–53.

LeVine, Robert A. 'Anti-European Violence in Africa: A Comparative Analysis.' *Journal of Conflict Resolution*, III, 4 (December, 1959), 420–9.

Lonsdale, J. M. 'European Attitudes and African Pressures: Missions and Government in Kenya Between the Wars.' *Race*, X, 2 (October, 1968), 141–51.

'Some Origins of Nationalism in East Africa.' *Journal of African History*, 9, 1 (1968), 119–46.

Macleod, Iain. 'Blundell's Kenya.' *Spectator*, March 20, 1964, 366.

McWilliam, Michael. 'The World Bank and the Transfer of Power in Kenya.' *Journal of Commonwealth Political Studies*, II, 2 (July, 1964), 1965–9.

'Economic Problems During the Transfer of Power in Kenya.' *The World Today*, 18, 1 (January, 1962), 164–75.

Mohiddin, Ahmed. 'An African Approach to Democracy.' *East Africa Journal*, VII, 2 (February, 1970), 4–11.

Morgan, W. T. W. 'The "White Highlands" of Kenya.' *Geographical Journal*, 129, 2 (June, 1963), 140–55.

Odingo, R. S. 'Observations on Land Use and Settlement in the Kenya Highlands.' *Ostafrikanische Studien* ('East African Studies'). Nurnberg: Wirtschafts-und Sozialgeographische Arbeiten, 1968, 254–77.

Okoth-Ogendo, H. W. O. 'The Politics of Constitutional Change in Kenya Since Independence, 1963–69.' *African Affairs*, 71, 282 (January 1972), 9–34.

Parker, Mary 'Race Relations and Political Development in Kenya.' *African Affairs*, 50, 198 (January, 1951), 41–52.

Perham, Margery. 'White Minorities in Africa.' *Foreign Affairs*, April, 1959, 637–48.

Robinson, Ronald and Gallagher, John. 'The Imperialism of Free Trade.' *The Economic History Review*, 2nd Series, 6, 1 (1953), 1–15.

Rothchild, Donald. 'African Nationalism and Racial Minorities.' *East Africa Journal*, II, 8 (December, 1965), 14–22.

Sanger, Clyde and Nottingham, John. 'The Kenya General Election of 1963.' *Journal of Modern African Studies*, II, 1 (1964). 1–40.

Seidman, Ann. 'The Dual Economics of East Africa.' (Part I) *East Africa Journal*, VII, 4 (April, 1970), 13–18.

'The Dual Economics of East Africa.' (Part II) *East Africa Journal*, VII, 5 (May, 1970), 6–19.

Storrar, A. 'A Guide to the Principles and Practices of Land Settlement in Kenya.' *Journal of Local Administration Overseas*, III, 1 (January, 1964), 14–19.

Tanner, Ralph. 'Who Goes Home?' *Transition*, June, 1963, 32–6.

Theroux, Paul. 'Tarzan Is an Expatriate.' *Transition*, August/September, 1967, 13–19.

Vasey, Sir Ernest A. 'Economic and Political Trends in Kenya.' *African Affairs*, LV, 219 (April, 1956), 101–8.

Wasserman, Gary. 'The Independence Bargain: Kenya Europeans and the Land Issue, 1960–1962.' *Journal of Commonwealth Political Studies*, XI, 2 (July, 1973) 99–120.

'Continuity and Counter-Insurgency: The Role of Land Reform in Decolonizing Kenya, 1962–70.' *Canadian Journal of African Studies*, VII, 1, (1973),
133–48.

Whetham, Edith. 'Land Reform and Settlement in Kenya.' *East African Journal
of Rural Development*, 1, 1 (January, 1968), 18–30.

MANUSCRIPT COLLECTIONS

Carey Jones, N. S. The Papers of Mr N. S. Carey Jones. Office, The University
of Leeds, Leeds, England.

Hughes, Dorothy. The Papers of Mrs Dorothy Hughes. Office, Hughes Building,
Nairobi, Kenya.

Kenya National Archives. The Papers of Sir Wilfred Havelock. Nairobi, Kenya.

Kenya National Archives. The Papers of Mr Kendall Ward. Nairobi, Kenya.

Kenya National Farmers Union. Office Files of the Kenya National Farmers
Union. Kenya Farmers' Association Building, Nakuru, Kenya.

Marrian, Peter D. The Papers of Mr Peter D. Marrian. Office, 45 South Molton
Street, London, England.

Oxford University. Rhodes House Archives, The Papers of Sir Michael Blundell, MSS Afr.s.746.

Oxford University. Rhodes House Archives, The Files of the Convention of
Associations.

Raw, Joyce. The Papers of Mrs Joyce Raw, Secretary of the Capricorn Executive Committee. Home, Nairobi, Kenya.

Whetham, S. D. The Papers of Mr S. D. Whetham. Office, Kenya National
Farmers Union, Nakuru, Kenya.

THESES, PAPERS AND OTHER UNPUBLISHED WORKS

Atieno-Odhiambo, E. S. 'The Economic Basis of Kenya Settler Politics in the
1930s.' Paper presented at the 1970 Universities of East Africa Social Science Conference, Dar es Salaam, December 27–31, 1970.

Berman, Bruce. 'Organizational Factors in the Formulation and Implementation
of Development Policy in Colonial Kenya, 1945–1952.' Paper presented at
the Canadian Political Science Association Conference, Montreal, June 2–
5, 1972.

Brett, E. A. 'Economic Development in East Africa, 1919–1929: A Study of
the Evolution of British Colonial Aid. Policies.' Seminar paper, Institute of
Commonwealth Studies, University of London, October, 1963.

Charnley, F. E. (Deputy Commissioner of Lands). 'Some Aspects of Land
Administration in Kenya.' Memorandum, Nairobi, April 2, 1966.

Clough, R. H. 'Some Economic Aspects of Land Settlement in Kenya.' Unpublished paper, Egerton College, Njoro, Kenya, June 1965.

Grundy, Kenneth W., Hughes, Barry B., and Pulford, Cedric. 'East African
Business Elites: A Composite Portrait.' Paper presented at the 14th annual
meeting of the African Studies Association, Denver, Colorado, November
3–6, 1971.

Harbeson, John W. 'Land Resettlement and Development Strategy in Kenya.'
Paper No. 38, Institute for Development Studies, University College, Nairobi, January 1967.

Horowitz, Dan. 'Attitudes of British Conservatives towards Decolonization in Africa During the Period of the Macmillan Government, 1957–63.' Unpublished Ph.D. dissertation, Oxford University, May 1967.

Leys, Colin. 'Politics in Kenya: The Development of Peasant Society.' Paper No. 102, Institute for Development Studies, University of Nairobi, December 1970.

'The Limits of African Capitalism: The Formation of the Monopolistic *Petit-Bourgeoisie* in Kenya.' Unpublished manuscript, April 1972.

Munroe, Trevor G . 'Political Change and Constitutional Development in Jamaica, 1944–62.' Unpublished Ph.D. dissertation, Oxford University, 1967.

Patel, Lal. 'History and Growth of Labour in East Africa.' Paper presented at the 1969 Universities of East Africa Social Science Council Conference, Nairobi, December 1969.

Rathbone, Richard J. A. R. 'The Transfer of Power in Ghana, 1945–57.' Unpublished Ph.D. dissertation, University of London, 1968.

OFFICIAL DOCUMENTS (listed by country, and within the country listed in chronological order)

Great Britain. Land Settlement Commission. 'Report of the Commission Appointed to Inquire into and consider the practicability of a Land Settlement Scheme for Soldiers in British East Africa.' Nairobi: Government Printers, 1919.

Great Britain. East Africa Royal Commission, 1953–1955. Report, 1955. London: Her Majesty's Stationery Office, 1955.

Great Britain. Report of the Kenya Constitutional Conference Held in London. January and February, 1960. Cmnd. 960. London: Her Majesty's Stationery Office, 1960.

Great Britain. Parliament. Parliamentary Debates (House of Lords), Vol. 222, No. 60 (March 28, 1960). London: Her Majesty's Stationery Office, 1960.

Great Britain. Colonial Office. Report of the Kenya Constitutional Conference, 1962. Cmnd. 1700. London: Her Majesty's Stationery Office, 1962.

Great Britain. Kenya: Report of the Regional Boundaries Commission. Cmnd. 1899, London, 1962.

Great Britain. Statement by the Rt. Hon. Barbara Castle, M.P., Minister of Overseas Development, on 'Kenya Land Purchase and General Development.' Issued by British Information Service, Nairobi, November 19, 1965.

Colony and Protectorate of Kenya. Settlement Board. Accepted Schemes for European Settlement: Post-war Settlement in Kenya. Nairobi: Government Printer, 1945.

Colony and Protectorate of Kenya. Department of Lands. Annual Reports, 1959–63. Nairobi: Government Printer, 1960–4.

Colony and Protectorate of Kenya. Sessional Paper No. 10 of 1958/59. 'Land Tenure and Control Outside the Native Lands.' Nairobi: Government Printer, 1959.

Colony and Protectorate of Kenya. Sessional Paper No. 6 of 1959/60. 'Land Tenure and Control Outside the Native Lands.' Nairobi: Government Printer, 1960.

Colony and Protectorate of Kenya. Report of the Committee on the Organization of Agriculture. Sir Donald MacGillivray, Chairman. Nairobi: Government Printer. 1960.

Select bibliography

Colony and Protectorate of Kenya. Legislative Council. Debates. 1960–3. Nairobi: Government Printer.
Colony and Protectorate of Kenya. Land Development and Settlement Board. 'A Review of the Activities of the Land Development and Settlement Board.' January 1, 1961–July 31, 1962. Nairobi, nd.. [1962].
Colony and Protectorate of Kenya. The Ministry of Agriculture, Animal Husbandry and Water Resources. 'African Land Development in Kenya.' Nairobi, 1962.
Republic of Kenya. Department of Settlement. Annual Reports, 1962–8. Nairobi, n.d.
Republic of Kenya. Ministry for Economic Planning and Development. Development Plan, 1964–1970. Nairobi, 1964.
Republic of Kenya. Ministry for Economic Planning and Development. Agricultural Census, 1965–1968. Nairobi, n.d.
Republic of Kenya. Ministry of Lands and Settlement. The Work of the Ministry of Lands and Settlement. Nairobi, May 1966.
Republic of Kenya. Ministry for Economic Planning and Development. Development Plan 1970–1974. Nairobi, November 1969.
Republic of Kenya. Ministry for Economic Planning and Development. Statistical Abstract 1969. Nairobi, November 1969.
Republic of Kenya. Ministry for Economic Planning and Development. Economic Survey 1970. Nairobi, June 1970.
Republic of Kenya. National Assembly. Report of the Select Committee on Unemployment. Nairobi, December 8, 1970.

OTHER DOCUMENTS AND NEWSPAPERS

Agricultural Development Corporation. P. N. Sifuma, Chairman. Annual Reports, 1966–1969. Nairobi, July 18, 1968; November 30, 1969.
Agricultural Development Corporation. A Summary of its Activities. Pamphlet at Nairobi Show, 1970.
Convention on Social and Economic Development in the Emerging Kenya Nation. Report of the Convention (August 12–17, 1962). 'The Kenya We Want.' Nairobi: East African Printers, n.d. [1962].
International Bank for Reconstruction and Development. The Economic Development of Kenya: Report of a Mission Organized by the International Bank for Reconstruction and Development. Baltimore: Johns Hopkins Press, 1963.
Kenya African National Union. The KANU Manifesto for Independence, Social Democracy and Stability. Nairobi, 1960.
Kenya African National Union. 'What a KANU Government Offers You.' Nairobi, 1963.
Kenya Central Land Board. Annual Reports, 1963–1964, 1964–1965. Nairobi, n.d.
East African Standard, 1955–70.
Kenya Weekly News, 1960–5.
Daily Nation, 1960–70.

INTERVIEWS

Alexander, R. S., former NKG member. Bruce Travel Service, Nairobi. December 9, 1970.

215

Amalemba, Musa, former NKG member. Office, Kenya Farmers' Association, Nakuru, Kenya. September 4, 1970.

Blundell, Sir Michael, former NKG leader and Minister of Agriculture. Office, Tusker House, Nairobi. October 18, December 16–17, 1970.

Carey Jones, N. S., former Permanent Secretary, Ministry of Lands and Settlement. Office, The University of Leeds, Leeds, England. November 12 and 13, 1971.

Cavendish-Bentinck, Sir Ferdinand, former head of the Kenya Coalition. Office, City House Nairobi. August 28, 1970.

Charnley, F. H., Commissioner of Lands. Office, Department of Lands, Nairobi. November 17, 1970.

Delamere, Lord, former President of KNFU. Elmenteita Estates, Nakuru, Kenya. September 28, 1970.

Feingold, J. H., former KNFU President. Stag's Head Hotel, Nakuru, Kenya. June 16 and 23, October 1 and 6, 1970.

Gichuru, James, former KANU President and Minister for Defense. Office, Harambee House, Nairobi. October 13, 1970.

Goldsack, J. R., Settlement Administrator. Office, Ministry of Agriculture, Nairobi. July 16, 1970.

Gotha, Martin, European farmer. Rift Valley Sports Club, Nakuru, Kenya. September 30, 1970.

Havelock, Sir Wilfred, former Chairman NKG. New Stanley Hotel, Nairobi. December 9, 1970.

Hill, C. D., European farmer. Farm, Njoro, Kenya. September 5, 1970.

Hughes, Dorothy, former NKG member. Office, Hughes Building, Nairobi. November 10–11 and 20; December 1, 1970.

Hutton, William, General Manager ADC. Office, Development House, Nairobi. September 21, 1970.

Jackson, G. V., Assistant, Overseas Development Administration. Office, Stag's Place, London. June 23, 1971.

Kariuki, J. M., former private secretary to Jomo Kenyatta and KANU M.P. Office, Ministry of Tourism and Wildlife, Nairobi. November 5, 1970.

Kydd, Dermott, former Senior Land Valuer, C.L.B. Office, Department of Lands, Nairobi. August 20 and 25; November 17, 1970.

Marrian, Peter D., former KNFU President. Office, 45 South Molton Street, London. September 2 and 29; December 14, 1971.

Melville, L. D., former NKG Executive Officer. Office, Nairobi. November 8, 1970.

Munene, Charles, KNFU Labour Relations Officer. KNFU offices, Nakuru, Kenya. October 13, 1970.

Ngigi, Dickson, settlement farmer. New Stanley Hotel, Nairobi. October 30, 1970.

Nightingale, Jim, European farmer. Sasumua Estates, Njoro, Kenya. June 26, 1970.

Nimmo, J. N., former L.D.S.B. and C.L.B. Chairman. Naivasha, Kenya. October 6, 1970.

Nottidge, C.P.R., former Settlement Administrator. Office, Uniafric House, Nairobi. July 14, 1970.

Okelo-Odongo, Thomas, former KANU M.P. Norfolk Hotel, Nairobi. November 17, 1970.

Patel, T. K., Official of the Department of Settlement. Office, Department of Settlement, Nairobi. July 16, 1970.

Select bibliography

Pollard, John, former KNFU President. Glencairn Estate, Nakuru, Kenya. September 17; October 8, 1970.

Raw, Joyce, Editor of Hansard (Kenya). Office, Parliament Building, Nairobi. November 10, 1970.

Sifuma, Peter, KNFU President. Nairobi Show, Nairobi. September 30, 1970.

Slade, Humphrey, former NKG member. Office, Hamilton, Harrison and Matthews, Nairobi. May 28; October 13, 1970.

Slaughter, Richard, former KADU Treasurer. Office, Nairobi. November 3 and 8, 1970.

Sprott, F. H., former KNFU President. Home, Karen, Kenya. February 10, 1971.

Van Arkadie, Brian, Chairman of the Van Arkadie Commission. Home, 46 Westbourne Terrace, London. December 11, 1971.

Ward, Kendall, former Kenya Coalition member. Home, Karen, Kenya. February 24, 1970.

Watts, T. A., former L.D.S.B. Executive Officer. Office, Law Courts Building, Nairobi. August 21; November 18, 1970.

Whetham, S. D., Chairman KNFU Settlement Committee. KNFU Office, Nakuru, Kenya. September 14, 1970.

Willems, Jan, I.B.R.D. Representative. Inter-Continental Hotel, Nairobi. December 9, 1970.

Wilson, Robert, Vice-Chairman of the A.D.C. Office, Development House, Nairobi. September 1, 1970.

INDEX

Abaluhya tribe, 90, 169
Adaptation in decolonization
  as a condition, 11
  definition of, 5–6
  in land schemes, 17, 138–45
  summary of, 164–75
African labor, 22–6
African middle class
  development of, 25
  promotion of, as a political tactic, 128,
    137, 151–2, 155–7, 163, 166, 169,
    173
Agriculture
  European directed, 22–6
  government management of, 24
  land consolidation in, 25
  role of plantations in, 25
Agricultural Development Corporation,
  138, 161
Alexander, R. S., 39, 41
Amalemba, Musa, 39, 41, 88–90
Anatomy of Uhuru, The, 146
Angaine, J. H., 148
Arap Moi, Daniel, 62, 66, 107
Asians
  as immigrants, 21
  in decolonization, 3
  role in the economy, 25

Baring, Governor (Lord Howick), 38,
  43, 97, 100, 158
Bennett, Fred M., 87, 95
Bennett, George, 66
Bill of Rights, 64–5, 106
Black, Eugene, 36, 158
Block, Jack, 41
Blundell, Michael, 28, 33, 46, 67, 165,
  167, 168
  analysis of resettlement schemes, 127
  and land transfer schemes, 140, 159
  and regionalism, 99–100
  as actor, 132
  at First Lancaster House, 44–5, 56
  at Governor's Conference, 90–4
  at Joint Committee Meeting, 88–90
  at Second Lancaster House, 109, 111,
    120–1
  biography of, 39–43
  decision to resign, 118
  in London, 69

land policies of, 72, 79–81, 85–7
political tactics of 95–98, 115–17
relations with conservatives, 51–3,
  71–3, 82
relations with N.K.G., 56
Bond Scheme, 79–80
Bourne, Sir Geoffrey, 143
Boyd, Lord, 36
Braine, Bernard (M.P.), 49
Briggs, L. R., 45, 54
Britain, 23–4, *see also* British government (H.M.G.)
British colonial system, 12
  authoritative administration of, 19–22
  colonization in, 19–22
  continuity of, 14
  divided attitude of, 21–2
  economic trends in, 22
  see also British government (H.M.G.)
British government (H.M.G.), 59, 105–6
  analysis of Kenyan economic policies,
    49
  and Central Land Board, 123–5, 143
  and Delamere Oates Plan, 109–15
  and international finance, 157–62
  conditions for settlement, 131
  land proposals of, 47, 50
  relations with conservatives, 77–84,
    108–9
  relations with K.A.D.U., 84–5
  relations with liberals, 68–71, 85–8,
    115–18
  role in settlement, 129–33, 152–7
British Policy in Changing Africa, 8
Broadbent, Philip, 49
Brooke, Bond, 33
Burke, V. E. M., 162

Carey-Jones, N. S., 146, 161
Castle, Barbara (M.P.), 135, 154
Cavendish-Bentinck, Sir Ferdinand
  and demise of Convention/Coalition,
    125
  as Minister of Agriculture, 137
  as secretary of the Convention, 28
  career of, 33
  chairman of Kenya Coalition, 54
  in the formation of Kenya Coalition,
    29
  mission to England, 69

Index

Cavendish-Bentinck (*continued*)
  political bargaining ('61), 81–5
  split with liberals, 71–3
  views on British support, 37
Central Land Board, 99–100, 106, 114–
    15, 128, 131, 173
  and counter-insurgency program, 146–
    50
  and international finance, 157–62
  downgrading of, 143–5
  establishment of, 141
  opposition to, 141–3
  predecessors of, 137, 140–1
Chataway, Christopher, 36
Churchill, Winston, 75
Coffee, 23–5, 100
Cohen, Sir Andrew, 8
*Colonial Development and Good Gov-
  ernment*, 12
Colonial Development and Welfare Act,
  70
Colonial Issues in British Politics, 12
Colyton, Lord, 36, 117
Commercial interests
  in colonial period, 24–6
  relations with conservatives, 35–6, 51
  relations with liberals, 16, 40–3
  strategy of, 136, 165–7, 172–3
Commonwealth Development Corporation, 41, 48
Consensual decolonization, 5–17
  and settlement schemes, 135–8
  as a process, 13–15
  in Kenya, 15–17
  historical conditions of, 7–8
  situational conditions of, 9–13
  see also Decolonization
Conservative group
  at First Lancaster House, 43–5
  background of, 27–34
  bargaining ('61), 81–4
  bargaining ('62), 105–6
  bargaining resources of, 34–7
  composition of, 16
  goals of, 16
  relations with H.M.G., 68–73, 76–84
  relations with liberals, 68, 71–3
  strategy of, 16, 46–7, 71–3, 75–6, 103,
    105–6, 122–5, 133
  summary of strategies, 165–6
  summary of tactics, 167–8, 170–1
  see also Convention/Coalition, Kenya
    National Farmers Union, and Farm-
    ers
Convention/Coalition, 16, 124
  at Governor's Conference, 90–4
  at Second Lancaster House, 107–9

attempts to form a European front,
    53–5
  bargaining ('61), 81–4, 100–3
  demise of, 125–7
  land proposals, 54–5, 100–2
  reactions to Delamere Oates Plan, 112
  relations with liberals, 69–73
  strategy of, 71–3, 81–4
  see also Conservative group, Conven-
    tion of Associations, and Kenya Co-
    alition
Convention of Associations, 16
  bargaining resources of, 34–7
  lobbying ('60), 53–5
  origins of, 27–9
  see also Conservative group, Conven-
    tion/Coalition
Cooperatives, 161
Cooptation in decolonization, 6
  as a condition, 9–11
  as a liberal tactic, 66–8, 87
  definition of, 6
  in land schemes, 17

Decolonization, 1–3
  and land transfer schemes, 135–8
  and socialization, 13–14, 17
  as a bargaining process, 5, 7–13
  definition of, 4–5
  summary of, 164–75
  three themes of, 5–7
  transition period, 7
de Freitas, Sir Geoffrey, 16
Delamere, Lord, I, 27
Delamere, Lord, II
  and Million Acre Scheme, 109–15
  and regionalism, 99–100
  at Governor's Conference, 90–4
  at Second Lancaster House, 107–9
  career of, 34
  lobbying in England, 49, 68–70, 83–4,
    123, 125
  lobbying on land titles, 77
  views on British support, 37
Delamere Oates Plan, 109–15
Devonshire Pledge, 20
Douglas-Hume, Alex, 152

East African Breweries, 41
East African Standard, 50, 61, 70, 74, 84,
    88
England, W. T., 162
English allies, 87–8
English National Farmers Union, 36, 49
Europeans, 1–3, 22–6, 73–4, 128, 164–
    75; *see also* Settlers

220

European Agricultural Settlement Board, 40, 59, 137
Evans, Will, 30

Fanon, Frantz, 4, 135
Farmers, 2–3
  and C.L.B., 141–4
  and Governor's Conference, 90–4
  and L.D.S.B., 141
  and land transfer schemes, 138–51
  and regionalism, 99–100
  bargaining ('47–'55), 76–84, 107–9, 152–7
  colonial political role, 19–22
  organizations of, 27–37
  reactions to Delamere Oates Plan, 111–15
  rebut Stamp report, 153
  relations with H.M.G., 76–84, 108
  relations with Nationalists, 121–2
  weak economic position of, 20–7
  see also Settlers, Kenya National Farmers Union, and Conservatives
Federalist No. 10, 19
Financial Times, 153
First Lancaster House Conference, 1, 43–5, 73, 139, 168
  aftermath of, 46
  and the Nationalists, 64–5
Fraser, Hugh, 80, 87–8, 104

General Agricultural Workers Union (G.A.W.U.), 77
Gertzel, Cherry, 66
Ghai, Y. P., 66
Ghersie, Lt. Col. S. G., 48
Gichuru, James, 63, 85, 88, 89, 148
Goldsworthy, David, 12
Goldsack, J. R., 145
Goodhart, Philip, 87
Governor's Conference, 90–4
Greenbrier philosophy, 13
Griffith-Jones, E. N., 98
Grogan, Ewart, 27, 29

Haley, Sir William, 50
Harbeson, John, 66, 127–9
Harbenga, P. J., 88–90
Hare, J. (M.P.), 36
Harper, T. H., 27
Hastings, Lord, 168
Havelock, Wilfred, 38, 61, 67, 116–18, 127
Henderson, G. R., 162
Hilliard, R. J., 126
Hilton Young Commission, 28
Hodson, H. V., 46
Howick, Lord, *see* Governor Baring

Houphouet-Boigny, Felix, 14
Howard, J. W., 142
Hughes, Mrs. Dorothy, 29, 38, 40, 42–3

Ind Coope Ltd., 41, 88
I.B.R.D./C.D.C. schemes, 157–62; see *also* World Bank
International Bank for Reconstruction and Development (I.B.R.D.), *see* World Bank
International finance
  in land proposals, 47–51, 59–60, 70, 101, 110–11
  involvement in land transfer schemes, 157–62
  role in decolonization, 170
Irwin, General N. M. S., 111–13
Ivory Coast, 1, 14

Jet schemes, 137, 148–50
Joint Committee Meeting, 88–90
Joint East and Central African Board, 95, 117
Jones, E.T., 41

Kalenjin Political Alliance, 63
Kalenjin tribe, 67, 90
Kamba tribe, 169
Kana, J., 162
Kenya
  as a case study, 1–3, 15–17
  colonial history of, 19–27
Kenya African Democratic Union (K.A.D.U.), 129, 137
  and cooptation, 169
  at Governor's Conference, 90–4
  at Joint Committee Meeting, 88–90
  land policies of, 64–6, 121–2
  land proposal, 121–2
  mission to London, 84–5
  origins of, 62–4
  regional plan, 98–9
  relations with liberals, 41–2, 47, 66–8, 75–6, 96–8
  tactics at Second Lancaster House, 104–7
  see also Nationalists
Kenya African National Traders and Farmers Union (K.A.N.T.A.F.U.), 77, 100
Kenya African National Union (K.A.N.U.)
  at Governor's Conference, 90–4
  at Joint Committee Meeting, 88–90
  basic positions of, 63–4
  land policy of, 64–6, 68, 118–21
  origins and support of, 62–3
  reaction to land settlement, 123,

Index

(K.A.N.U) (*continued*)
127, 137
relations with H.M.G., 85, 115, 129
relations with K.A.D.U., 64, 75–6
relations with liberals, 65–6, 95–8, 116, 120–1
tactics at Second Lancaster House, 106–7, 120
see also Nationalists
Kenya African People's Party, 63
Kenya African Union, 63
Kenya Coalition, 16, 169, 124
and C.L.B., 122–4, 142–3
bargaining resources of, 34–7
demise of, 125–6
formation of, 29–30
see also Convention/Coalition and Conservative group
Kenya Council of Ministers, 131
Kenya Government, 26
and C.L.B., 141–5
and Kikuyu tribe, 145–50
land proposals ('64), 152–7
policies during bargaining, 58–61
rebut the Stamp Report, 153
role in settlement, 129–32
views of regionalism, 99–100
Kenya Independence Movement, 62–3
Kenya Land Company, 80
Kenya Legislative Council, 28, 44, 62
Kenya National Farmers Union (K.N.F.U.), 16, 91, 93, 166–71
apoliticism of, 51–3
at Second Lancaster House, 107–15
background of, 30–4
bargaining resources of, 34–7
differences with Coalition, 124
efforts to unify the Europeans, 51
finances of, 35
lobbying on land issue, 47–51, 69–70, 76–84, 100–3, 107–15, 122–5
mission to England ('61), 49–50
plan for land reform ('60), 48–9
Private Yeoman Farmer Scheme, 78–9
relations with H.M.G., 53–5, 108
relations with Kenya Government, 59–61, 99
relations with liberals, 69–73
Kenya National Mills, Ltd., 40
Kenya National Party, 62
Kenyatta, Jomo, 33, 91, 129, 148
relations with K.A.N.U., 62–6, 115, 118–20
relations with liberals, 82, 97–8, 120–1
Kiano, Julius, 63–4, 93
Kikuyu tribe, 97–9, 128–9
and C.L.B., 144
and counter-insurgency program,

145–50
and security situation, 103–4, 125–6, 130–1, 137, 171
relations with K.A.D.U., 62–8, 121
relations with liberals, 68
reserves of, 24–5
Kilmuir, Viscount, 50
Kinangop Scheme, 148–50; *see also* Jet schemes
Kirkwood, R. D. B., 162
Koinange, ex Senior Chief, 46

Land Bank, 59, 84, 125, 151, 155–7
chart on aided transfers of land, 157
Land Development and Settlement Board (L.D.S.B.), 57, 78, 101–2, 108, 112, 137, 140–4, 172
Land Freedom Army, 125–6, 145
Land Purchase Program, 144–5; *see also* Land Transfer Schemes
Land Transfer Schemes
and counter-insurgency program, 45–50
and International finance, 157–62
four themes of, 136–8
involvement of European farmers in, 138–45
major economic goal of, 135–6
summary of, 162–3, 171–4
transferring large scale plots, 151–7
see also Settlement Schemes and Land Purchase Program
Lee, Don L., 164
Lee, J. M., 12
Lennox-Boyd, Alan, 38, 42–3
Liberal group
and multi-racialism, 102
and regionalism, 98–100
and settlement schemes, 127–32
at First Lancaster House, 43–5
background of, 27, 37–9
bargaining ('61), 84–8
bargaining ('62), 105–6, 114–18
bargaining resources of, 40–3
goals of, 16–17
land policies of, 56–7, 79–81, 85–7
leadership of, 39–40
relations with H.M.G., 68–74, 85–8, 95–8
relations with Nationalists, 65–8, 88, 90, 95–8, 120–1
split with conservatives, 68, 71–3, 102
strategy of, 57–8, 71–3, 75–6, 103, 105–6
summary of goals and strategies, 165–7, 174–5
summary of tactics, 167–71
tactics of, 95–8

222

Liberal group (*continued*)
  see also New Kenya group and Commercial interests
Lipscomb, Jack, 40, 140
Lloyd, Selwyn, 36
Luo tribe, 62–3, 66, 68, 96, 161
Lyttleton Constitution, 29

MacAllen, H. B. W., 113, 115
MacKenzie, K. W. S., 99
Macleod, Iain, 10, 42–4, 46, 69–70, 94
  and World Bank, 158
  at First Lancaster House, 44
  relations with conservatives, 49–50, 79, 83–4
  relations with liberals, 85–7, 95–6
Macleod, Rhoderick, 43, 57, 67
Macmillan, Harold, 4, 85
Maina, J. W., 151
Mair, Lucy, 46
Maize, 23–4
Markham, Sir Charles, 29, 41
Marrian, Peter
  and apoliticism, 52–3, 170
  career of, 34, 36
  links to World Bank, 158
  lobbying in England, 47–50, 55, 70
  lobbying ('61), 77
  relations with K.A.N.U., 96
  response to Kenya Government Plan, 60–1
  visits Kenyatta, 82
Martin, T. L., 162
Marx, Karl, 105
Maudling, Reginald, 107, 110–11, 115, 122–5
Mau Mau, 2, 125
  and settlement schemes, 145
  emergency, 21–2
Mboya, Tom
  A.F.L.-C.I.O. support of, 129
  and K.A.N.U., 62–3
  at Joint Committee Meeting, 88–90, 92–3
  First Lancaster House, 44–5
  land policies, 64–5, 68, 139
  relations with liberals, 96–8, 117
  views on N.K.G., 38
McAuslan, J. P. W. B., 66
McKenzie, Bruce, 77
  and international finance, 158, 161
  and Kikuyu tribe, 146, 148–50
  and London bargaining, 69, 79
  and Ministry of Agriculture Land Scheme, 59–61
  as an actor, 132–3
  as Minister of Settlement, 124–5, 140–3

in stamp bargaining, 152–3
memo on H.M.G., 131
relations with Nationalists, 64–7, 77, 83–4, 95, 97
Melville, Leslie, 67
Mercer, A. M., 162
Million Acre Scheme, 109–15, 131, 137, 144–50; *see also* Delamere Oates Plan
Ministry of Agriculture Scheme, 59–61
  Bond scheme, 79–81
Ministry of Lands and Settlement, 139, 141–62 *passim.*
Mitchell, Sir Philip, 20
Mixed farmer, 23, 31–2
  and settlement schemes, 129, 136, 153
Mohiddin, Ahmed, 135
Muliro, Masinde, 62–3, 67, 69
Multi-racialism
  and economic organizations, 53, 102
  and liberals, 102, 165, 170
  in colonial politics, 20–2, 24–5
Murray, Gilbert, 19

Namier, L. B., 105
Nandi tribe, 169
National Members, 44
Nationalists, 3, 8, 129
  and cooperatives, 161
  and "Z" plots, 138
  at First Lancaster House, 43–5, 64–5
  background of, 62–6
  in colonial period, 20–1
  land policy of, 64–6, 89, 118–22
  opposition to farmers, 62, 115
  relations with liberals, 66–8, 96–8, 168–9
  split within, 62–4
  strategy of, 46, 133
  summary of position, 172–3
  see also K.A.D.U. and K.A.N.U.
New Kenya Group 16, 166
  at First Lancaster House, 43–5
  at Governor's Conference, 90–4
  background of, 27, 37–40
  bargaining resources of, 40–3
  financial backing of, 42
  land proposals of, 51, 57, 85–7, 98–100
  opposition to farmers, 56–8, 68–73
  relations with Nationalists, 65, 66–8, 72–4, 90, 95–8, 129
  strategy of, 46, 57–8, 102, 133
  see also Liberals
New Kenya Group Finance Committee, 38, 40, 42
New Kenya Parliamentary Group, 42, 57

Ngala, Ronald, 107
  at First Lancaster House, 44, 64
  at Governor's Conference, 92, 94
  at Joint Committee Meeting, 88–90
  relations with liberals, 44, 67
  relations with Nationalists, 62–6
Ngei, Paul, 93
Nicol, George, 29
Nottidge, C. P. R., 145, 162

Oates, C. O., 29
  and demise of Convention/Coalition, 125–6
  and Million Acre Scheme, 109–15
  as Chairman of Convention, 54
  at Governor's Conference, 90
  at Second Lancaster House, 106, 109
  career of, 33
  political bargaining ('61), 81–4
Odinga, Oginga, 91
  and Joint Committee Meeting, 88–90
  and origins of K.A.N.U., 62–3
  on land policy, 68, 168
  relations with H.M.G., 129
  relations with liberals, 95–8, 120
Old Boy System, 36, 42–3, 49, 171

Peers, A. W., 154
Peers Report, 154
Perth, Lord, 49, 111
Plantations, 22–6, 35, 70, 110, 114, 136
Pollard, John, 53, 107–8, 112
Portugese decolonization, 11–12
Powles, S. H., 116
Pre-emption in decolonization, 5, 6–7
  as a condition, 9–10, 14
  definition of, 6
  in land schemes, 17, 145–50, 173–5
Private Yeoman Farmer Scheme, 78, 86, 159, 162

Rathbone, Richard, 10
Regionalism, 105–7
  background of, 98
  farmers' opposition to, 99–100
  K.A.D.U. plan for, 98–9
Renan, Ernest, 164
Renison, Sir Patrick, 42–3, 58–9, 61, 69, 90–4, 125
Rhodesia, 3, 42
Roberts, Major B. P., 82
Robinson, Michael, 36
Rosberg, Carl, 66
  and John Nottingham, 22
Rubia, C. W., 40

Salter, Clive, 54, 82, 91, 93
Salisbury, Lord, 36

Sandys, Duncan, 95, 152
Schattschneider, E. E., 169
Scheduled Areas, 110
Scott, Lord Francis, 27
Second Lancaster House Conference, 147
  and C.L.B., 141, 168
  and Million Acre Scheme, 109–15
  origins of, 105–6
  overview of, 106–7
Second Million Acre Scheme, 148, 151–5; *see also* Stamp Program
Senghor, Leopold, 14
Sessional Paper No. 10, 139
Settlement Schemes, 78–81
  as a support of decolonization, 129–32
  chart on the progress of, 149
  threats to, 150
  transferring large scale plots, 151–7
  see also Land Transfer Schemes and Land Purchase Program
Settlers
  conflict with colonial government, 26
  environment of, 73–4, 103–4
  influence on politics, 28
  tactics of, 170–1
  see also Farmers and Europeans
Seys, J. A., 77–9, 108
Shikuku, Martin, 99
Sifuma, P. N., 33
Sisal, 13, 23, 25
Slade, Humphrey, 38–9, 40, 166
Slaughter, Richard, 67
Society of Kenya Europeans, 126
Stamp Program, 137, 153–7, 173
Stamp mission, 152–3
Storrar, A., 162
Swann, Sir Anthony, 126
Swynnerton Plan, 25, 130, 151, 166

Tea, 25, 110
Thompson, F. T., 36
Thomson, G. M., 87
Times (London), 50, 117, 158
Towett, Taita, 62, 66–7
Triangle Fertilizers Ltd., 40
Troup Report, 32
Turton, Robin (M.P.), 36

Uganda, 2
United Country Party, 37–8
United Party, 51

Van Arkadie Mission, 156
Vincent, Sir Alfred, 28

Wall, Patrick (M.P.), 36
Wallerstein, Immanuel, 10
Ward, Alec, 36, 51, 76–7, 116

Wedgewood, Lord, 36
Welensky, Roy, 42
Welwood, L.R.M., 54, 71, 80–1, 123
White Highlands, 17
  and land transfer schemes, 136–55
  passim., 171–4
  and Nationalists, 64–5
  description of, 21, 23
  importance of, 46–7
Wilson, Harold, 152
Woods, George, 158

World Bank, 36, 48–9, 170, 131
  assistance to government plan, 60, 79
  influence on cooperatives, 161
  involvement in land transfer schemes,
  138, 157–62
  role as seen by H.M.G., 47, 70, 157
  role in decolonization, 170
  see also International Finance
Worsley, Peter, 8

"Z" plots, 137–8, 151, 155–6, 163, 173